Endogenous Development

The beginning of the twenty-first century has been characterized by the expansion of economics, politics and institutional relations. Using international case studies, this book illustrates the local answer to the challenge of increasing competition.

The book introduces the idea of endogenous development, identifying the theoretical roots and defining its main features. It then goes on to indicate how this concept can be used to understand economic dynamics, and to show how the concept is relevant in economic analysis and policy implementation in times of globalization.

After an introduction discussing globalization and development, the book is organized in three parts:

* Part I defines and discusses the concept of endogenous development;
* Part II analyzes the processes involved in the mechanics of capital accumulation and local development. It examines the role of institutions, innovation and organization of production in development processes, and the functions of cities in globalization;
* Part III argues that a new generation of development policies is beginning to take shape, based on the fact that greater competition and globalization increases spatial diversity and stimulates strategic behavior.

This work will be of essential interest to academics and policy-makers in planning and development and development economics.

Antonio Vázquez-Barquero is Professor of Economics at the Universidad Autónoma de Madrid. He was Director of the Instituto del Territorio y Urbanismo in Madrid and worked as a consultant for the EU, OECD and several Municipalities and Regional Governments. His research interests focus upon matters of economic growth, organization of production, innovation and local development policy. He has published over fifty articles and books.

Routledge Studies in Development Economics

Endogenous Development

Networking, innovation,
institutions and cities

Antonio Vázquez-Barquero

LONDON AND NEW YORK

First published 2002 by Routledge
2 Park Square, Milton Park, Abingdon, Oxon, OX14 4RN

Simultaneously published in the USA and Canada
by Routledge
605 Third Avenue, New York, NY 10017

Routledge is an imprint of the Taylor & Francis Group, an informa business

Copyright © 2002 Antonio Vázquez-Barquero

Typeset in Baskerville by Wearset Ltd, Boldon, Tyne and Wear

British Library Cataloguing in Publication Data
A catalogue record for this book is available from the British Library

Library of Congress Cataloging in Publication Data
A catalog for this book has been requested

ISBN 13: 978-0-415-28579-7 (hbk)
ISBN 13: 978-0-415-40645-1 (pbk)

To Gloria, Paco and Gloria

Contents

Illustrations

Figures

Tables

Preface

This book began to take shape over the years of teaching courses and seminars on local economic development in Europe and Latin America in the 1990s. It is essentially based on the material and notes on endogenous development that I prepared in order to answer questions posed to me by both students and colleagues. These courses and seminars have involved a wide variety of teaching experiences and research topics and I was able to share ideas with students and colleagues from far and near who brought with them diverse backgrounds and valuable practical knowledge.

Besides doctoral courses at the Autonomous University of Madrid (UAM), I have taught seminars in the postgraduate course on Local and Regional Development organized by the University of Barcelona and at the Inter-university Cooperation Program on Economic Development funded by the Erasmus Program of the European Union and hosted by the University of Pavia in Italy. I have also instructed seminars within the LIDER courses organized by the Economic Commission for Latin America (ECLA) in Santiago de Chile and Santa Cruz de la Sierra, Bolivia, in the Masters Program in Local and Regional Development of the Catholic University of Uruguay, in the Center of Development Studies (CENDES) doctoral program at the Central University of Venezuela and in the Master Program in Local Economic Development, a joint teaching effort of the Autonomous University of Madrid and the National University of Rosario in Rosario, Argentina. Because many of the Latin American and European students and colleagues brought with them practical experience in local development, the discussions were always fruitful and stimulating. Thus, over the years, I have come to clearly understand that endogenous development is a relevant concept in economic analysis and policy implementation in times of globalization.

Globalization is a process characterized by increasing internationalization of the production of goods and services and international trade and particularly by growing interdependence of financial markets. Its present form has evolved with the creation of large economic regions such as the European Union, the North American Free Trade Agreement or the Southern Cone Common Market (Mercosur). Globalization is associated with trade liberalization, the growing role of private, generally multinational, firms and the surge of needs and demands for new institutions to regulate the process. Some feel that social concerns are not being addressed and inequality is on the rise. This view has led to an anti-globalization movement which demands new approaches to the questions of development.

Since the mid-1970s, important transformations have taken place that affect economic growth and development policies. Firm organization has become more flexible and integrated into the territory, while location patterns and, with them, regional development models, have changed. Moreover, European and Latin American countries have undergone political decentralization processes leading cities and regions to assume, to a greater or lesser extent, new competency over economic policy. Finally, local economic policies and tools have been implemented in cities and regions, first in Europe and more recently in Latin America.

The purpose of this book is to show that endogenous development provides an interpretation for understanding economic dynamics and change within this environment of economic, organizational, technological, political and institutional transformations. It deals with the mechanisms that shape capital accumulation processes and argues that innovation, organization of production, urban development and institutional dynamics are all processes that determine capital accumulation and explain economic growth. Interaction between these forces produces a synergetic effect that conditions growth and progress in cities, regions and countries. Local development policy stimulates these processes and helps provide a local response to the challenges of increased competition and globalization.

The book begins with a discussion on globalization and development in which the concept of endogenous development is presented. The contents are then organized into three parts. The first, Chapters 2 and 3, defines and revises the concept of endogenous development. After identifying endogenous development processes and conceptualizing local development strategy, this part launches on a discussion of the similarities and differences of this approach with some of the traditional economic development theories (the big push theory, dualistic growth and dependence theory) and of territorial development theory. The theoretical roots of endogenous development and its main characteristics can then be defined.

The second part of the book, Chapters 4 to 7, carefully analyzes the processes involved in the mechanics of capital accumulation and local development. First the formation of firm and institutional networks (industrial districts, strategic alliances) that improve territorial competition are described and interpreted. Then the creation and diffusion of innovations is analyzed and the relations of firms with their environment are stressed. This part also includes a discussion on the role of institutions in development processes, specifically in local development, as well as an analysis of the functions of cities in globalization and the formation of multiple hierarchies in the urban system. Interaction between technology, organization of production, institutions and cities is portrayed and their combined effect on endogenous development is discussed.

The third part, Chapters 8 to 10, argues that a new generation of development policies is beginning to take shape. After describing the advance of local development policies since their initial appearance in the early 1980s in Europe and more recently in Latin America, the question of a new generation of development policies is taken up. This idea is based on the fact that greater competition and globalization increases spatial diversity and stimulates strategic behavior on the part of economic agents and public and private actors. Some initiatives aim to promote quality human resources and the diffusion of innovations and know-how, some target sustainable development of cities, other tools are designed to improve the organization of production and networking while still others propose to stimulate the institutional dynamic and facilitate alliances between economic, political and institutional actors.

This book has benefited from my friendship with a number of colleagues who have made comments on previous drafts and have provided ideas and information that have enriched my work. I wish to thank María Teresa Costa Campi of the University of Barcelona, Javier Alfonso Gil and Antonia Saez Cala of the UAM, Francisco Alburquerque of the Council of Scientific Research in Madrid, Sergio Boisier of the ECLA, Carlos A. de Mattos of the Catholic University of Chile, José Arocena of the Catholic University of Uruguay, Sonia Barrios, director of CENDES, Oscar Madoery of the University of Rosario and Israel Cifuentes of the Cuchumatanes project in Guatemala. Special mention and gratitude must be made to Ricardo Brinco of the Foundation for Economics and Statistics of Porto Alegre, Brazil with whom I maintained an on-line conversation about local development in Latin America throughout the writing of this book and, last but not least, to Gioachino Garofoli of the University of Pavia, Italy who read the manuscript and made precise and helpful comments, that I did not always follow. I also wish to thank Cathy Dunn for the translation. The process was most fruitful, thanks to her skill, experience and patience and our interaction during the various revisions of the manuscript helped me improve the text.

Finally, I wish to acknowledge Taylor and Francis (www.tandf.co.uk) for their permission to use parts of my paper "Inward investment and endogenous development. The convergence of the strategies of large firms and territories?" published in *Entrepreneurship and Regional Development*, Vol. 11, 1999.

1 Globalization and endogenous development

Over the last decade, a new paradigm haunts the world: the globalization of both the economy and society. Productive systems and markets steadily acquire global dimensions, states relinquish leadership to innovative firms (generally multinational) as new information, transportation and communications technology facilitate and reinforce interaction among organizations.

The globalization process means increased market competition, which calls for continual adjustments in the productive systems of countries, regions and cities immersed in the process. Since firms do not compete alone, but rather within the context of their productive and institutional milieu, globalization fosters new modes of organization in city and regional systems, in accord with the new international division of labor.

While the new scenario of competition among firms and territories is being defined, firms and organizations introduce innovations, more flexible forms of productive organization are created and new productive spaces appear as cities and regions provide strategic responses to the challenges of increased competition in the markets. Thus, they find they must once again respond to the question of productive dynamics and development, that is, of what factors determine capital accumulation processes, in such a way as to satisfy the needs and demands of the citizens.

From a context of economic, organizational, technological and institutional transformation, the notion of endogenous development emerges as an effective instrument for analysis and action. We will begin by attempting to answer the simple questions. What factors make it possible for the endogenous development approach to explain capital accumulation processes in times of globalization and what is the relation among them? What is the role of the state in processes of accumulation and development? To what extent are local initiatives useful instruments in stimulating urban and regional development?

The process of globalization

Let us first discuss the question of globalization itself. Generally, globalization is described using indicators of increasing economic integration.

Among the main trends are an increase in foreign trade and economic openness, the internationalization of productive systems, the reduction in the economic role of the state and the leadership of multinational firms. The various forms of regionalization and integration of national economies, such as the European Union, the North American Free Trade Agreement, the Southern Cone Common Market or the Association of Southeast Asian Nations, can be understood as the institutionalization of globalization processes.

An intense controversy as to the meaning of globalization, its importance, dynamics and effects is currently taking place. Dabat (2000) identifies five main interpretations: globalization as a world without frontiers (Ohmae, 1990 and 1995), globalization as a fantasy far-flung from reality (Veseth, 1998; Wade, 1996); globalization as liberalism's present tendency (Fukuyama, 1992); globalization as internationalization (Oman, 1994; Ferrer, 1996; Chesnais, 1994); and globalization as a historical process (Castells, 1996; Scott, 1998; Waterman, 1998). Discussion about the notion of globalization often leads to certain skepticism as to its meaning and implications (Hirst and Thompson, 1996). However, it can be accepted that there has been a strengthening of economic, political and institutional relations among countries over the last decade that could lead to the formation of a global system.

Some of the factors responsible for globalization have been proposed (OECD, 1996a). Changes in economic and commercial policies have greatly expanded the liberalization of goods, service and factor markets. New strategies of multinational firms take advantage of location opportunities arising from integration. Innovation in transportation and communications facilitates market integration and multinational production, while reducing production and exchange costs.

As Ferrer (1996) points out, globalization, associated with international exchange of goods and services and the internationalization of capital and production, is not new. However, the novelty of present-day globalization is the fact that the internationalization of markets and production is associated with the increasing use of new information technologies. Globalization today clearly differs from former experiences characterized by the search for raw materials or new markets (Oman, 1994). The new process is reinforced by more flexible forms of organization of production, the formation and development of firm systems and international strategic alliances, which, in turn, lead to the creation of global networks.

Globalization may give rise to a new international order and a new international division of labor (Ugarteche, 1997). Leadership of the global economy would be in the hands of the OECD countries, the new industrialized countries of Eastern Asia and some Latin American countries. These have free market policies, they are open to foreign capital flows and their productive systems are linked through the exchange of goods and services, capital and labor force. The economies of the rest of the countries would be excluded, unless they were capable of joining the group by accepting the rules of free competition and trade liberalization (Ohmae, 1990).

Globalization is a process rooted in the territory, not only because it affects nations and countries but, particularly, because productive adjustment and economic dynamic depend on the investment and location decisions of the economic actors and on the attraction factors of each territory. The process of globalization, therefore, conditions the economic dynamics of cities and regions which, in turn, are also affected by the behavior of local actors.

Firms compete in markets along with the productive and institutional milieu of which they are a part. Hence, we can speak of competition among cities and regions and it can be said that the international division of labor is an urban and regional phenomenon. Improvement in competitiveness and productivity of cities depends on the introduction and diffusion of innovation among firms, the flexibility and organization of the productive system and the existence of institutions that facilitate market performance. The formation of firm networks, the introduction of more flexible organizational forms in large firms and the externalization of production systems have led to improved productivity and competitiveness in innovative cities and urban regions (Scott, 1998).

But, as Castells (1996) maintains, and in sharp contrast to the old center–periphery paradigm, the global economy is highly asymmetrical and polycentric. Moreover, the north–south categories have lost analytic capacity since the centers and the peripheries in the new international order are not symmetrically located on either side of the hypothetical line dividing "North" and "South." There are cities and regions in southern areas linked to the global economy and there are cities and regions in the northern areas that are not. Furthermore, poverty not only affects the South. Low income levels, weak technological capacity and unequal income distribution also mar some cities and regions of the North, even though inequality and poverty levels in the North and the South are not comparable.

In short, globalization and productive restructuring affect the productive systems of both developed and backward regions, as well as cities of all sizes. In an increasingly global world, some cities and regions are winners and others are losers (Benko and Lipietz, 1992); their status depends not on their belonging to a predefined northern or southern category, but rather on their supply of human and natural resources, the structure of their productive systems, their institutional framework and their position in the global economy.

Increasing competition and economic growth

Although the concept of globalization may be rooted far back in history, the new processes have only become fully manifest since the mid-1990s.

The restructuring of production distinguishing the international economy since the beginning of the 1970s had come to an end, the technological and information revolution was well under way, and new ways of regulating the economy and society were gradually being implemented in developed and developing countries. In short, a new long-term economic cycle was on the drawing board (OECD, 1999).

What is the effect of entrepreneurial and economic integration into international markets on economic sectors and territories? Putting aside the controversy as to the meaning of globalization for the time being, one can acknowledge that the phenomenon involves increased market competition. Consequently, firms and local economies demand new services to help them adjust to increasing global competition (Welfens *et al.*, 1999). Therefore, the productive restructuring of countries, regions and cities is bound to continue in coming decades as can be seen in the case of the European Union and Spain (Martín, 2000).

In this setting, as in the past, the central question of structural change in local and regional economies resides in identifying the capital accumulation processes, which stimulate economic growth. Therefore, it is a matter of how to deal with diminishing returns which, according to neoclassical thought, would lead to the steady state (Barro and Sala-i-Martin, 1995).

In the mid-1950s, Solow (1956) and Swan (1956) proposed the production function as the centerpiece of economic growth. Increasing productivity and per capita income come about as a result of exogenous technological progress and an increase of the capital/labor ratio. This theory has two limitations. One is that economic growth is determined by an element that is outside of the model. The other is that its concept of equilibrium is, as Nelson (1995) points out, "mechanical" and out of touch with reality, since economic agents do not act in a predetermined way and the results of their decisions do not always lead to equilibrium in the system.

Modern growth theory (Romer, 1986, 1990; Lucas, 1988; Rebelo, 1991) is a step forward in answering these questions since it considers that the law of diminishing returns is only one of the alternatives in economic growth processes. Economic growth can continue over the long term since investment in capital goods, including human capital, can generate increasing returns as economies grow through diffusion of innovation and knowledge among firms and the creation of external economies.

New knowledge would emerge as a consequence of R&D activities. But it would also be generated through the learning process that takes place during production tasks. On the other hand, the know-how required to use the new knowledge comes about through job-practice and formal education. Thus, the process of learning-by-doing is endogenous. Romer (1986) in the formulation of his model links Arrow's (1962) idea to the assumption of instant and costless spillover of knowledge.

The introduction of technological progress into the production function brings up the question of equilibrium in the growth model, because it incorporates increasing returns to scale into the production function. The answer to this question can be found in at least two ways: by assuming the existence of production externalities and by discarding the perfect competition assumption (and the acceptance of oligopolistic rents).

The first mechanism implies admitting to the existence of increasing returns to scale in the aggregate production function, although with diminishing returns in that of each firm. A production function that shows the existence of externalities could be written as

$$Y_t = AK_t^\alpha L_t^{1-\alpha} \tau^\eta$$

where A is the level of technology, K_t and L_t are the production factors capital and labor, τ^η represents the externalities and η is a parameter that expresses the importance of the externalities (Sala-i-Martin, 2000).

Each enterprise operates with a neoclassical-type production function and tries to optimize its market behavior. But its decisions to upgrade human resources or invest in R&D bring about a spillover effect in the milieu, which benefits competing firms, without changing their individual behavior. As to the aggregate production function, as a result of the firms' individual decisions to invest, increasing external returns are incorporated, as was proposed by Alfred Marshall (1890), which favors endogenous growth. The externalities generated by the diffusion of innovation and knowledge should neutralize the effects of the tendency for the marginal productivity of capital to fall and this also works under the assumption of constant returns to scale in capital and labor (Valdés, 1999).

Discarding the perfect competition assumption is a way to respond to the question of general equilibrium in endogenous growth models. Although the first approaches were founded on the consideration of spillover effects, theorists of endogenous growth explored other paths, opened by Dixit and Stiglitz (1977), among others. The existence of monopoly rents allows the surplus, left over after the retribution of all the productive factors, to be applied to investments that increase knowledge and innovation in the system.

Endogenous growth models differ significantly with respect to the neoclassical model, as Sala-i-Martin (1994: 30–32) acknowledges. In the first place, endogenous growth models argue that the economy would grow, at least at a constant rate, whatever the level of income and capital and there would, therefore, be no transition to the steady state. Second, the growth rate and the level of income of the economy would not be interrelated, so endogenous growth models do not predict convergence among the various economies. Finally, external impulses that foment increased savings or technological advancement would be transformed into greater income and would foster endogenous growth processes.

This approach, however, seems rather unsatisfactory for understanding the forces behind the "immediate sources of growth" (Nelson, 1999). Economic growth is a process characterized by uncertainty and chance and conditioned by changing market conditions and the decisions of the actors, and it should be understood as an evolutionary process. Thus, for interpreting and explaining economic growth the nature and dynamics of the organization of production, the role and change of institutions, and technology and technological advance should be specified.

Development processes take place not as a result of isolated actions of competing economic agents, as neoclassical thought would have it, but rather as a result of investment and location decisions of firms. When it is a matter of interpreting development processes and, therefore, the relationship of structural and spatial change with innovation, the key economic agents are the firms, the entrepreneurial organizations, who act strategically in oligopolistic markets.

Furthermore, in contrast to the functional view of endogenous growth theory, economic and productive dynamics should be understood from a territorial perspective. The territory is not just a place where plants locate, but rather a place in which economic actors make decisions, production is organized, technology and knowledge is created and accumulated and interaction between economic, social and political actors takes place.

As concerns capital accumulation processes, unlike the endogenous growth theory proposals, organizational models of both firm and territory play a decisive role in development processes. As shown in Lasuén (1973) and Ettlinger (1992), innovative firms are constantly changing their production systems, their internal organization and their relations with other firms. Therefore, the introduction and diffusion of innovation and, ultimately, the economic dynamic depend on the way the firms are organized.

However, not only is it a matter of acknowledging the strategic nature of entrepreneurial organization. There are also strong relations between economy and society, so that economic and productive systems are intensely linked to and conditioned by institutions and, within this relation, firms act as an "interface" between economy and society. In capital accumulation processes, this relationship is expressed by flexibility in the labor market, mechanisms of diffusion of technical knowledge and cooperation among economic and social actors.

Finally, development is also a question of the forces and processes that are within the "black box." Economic growth and the efficiency of the productive system are stimulated by firm interaction within the milieu and the use of the available external economies. As Garofoli (1999) points out, externalities and public goods are created thanks to the interaction of the economic, social, institutional and territorial processes within the local milieu, and local firms use them in the productive process. The production logic can therefore give way to what was called collective efficiency

(Schmitz, 1995). Thus, a broader view than that of endogenous growth theory should be taken in order to analyze the mechanisms accounting for the processes of capital accumulation and, consequently, of increases in productivity and competitiveness in local and regional economies.

The endogenous development approach

In today's scenario of economic, organizational, technological, political and institutional transformation, it is useful, therefore, to embrace a view of social and economic dynamics that takes into consideration the responses of economic actors and identifies the main mechanisms of economic development. Both theoretical research and the analysis of experiences in productive restructuring and urban and regional dynamics have led to the concept of endogenous development.

The endogenous development approach holds that capital accumulation is a key process in economic growth. It argues that economic development comes about as a result of the processes determining capital accumulation: creation and diffusion of innovation in the productive system, flexible organization of production, the generation of agglomeration and diversity economies in cities and institutional development. Moreover, it identifies a path of self-sustained development of an endogenous nature by maintaining that the processes contributing to capital accumulation generate external and internal economies of scale, reduce production and transaction costs and favor economies of scope.

The diffusion of innovation and knowledge

Economic development and productive dynamic depend on the introduction and diffusion of innovation and knowledge, which propel change and renovation in the productive system. In the final analysis, capital accumulation is accumulation of technology and knowledge. Hence, the actors that integrate the local productive system must make adequate decisions as to investment in technology and organization (Maillat, 1995; Nelson, 1995; Freeman and Soete, 1997).

Whatever methodological tendency they subscribe to, economists, sociologists and geographers agree that economic growth and structural change come about as a result of innovation in the productive system. Nevertheless, the economic effect of innovation depends on how these innovations are diffused throughout the productive fabric and what technological strategies are employed by firms in their struggle to maintain and improve the performance of their activities.

Firms make decisions to innovate within an increasingly competitive and global context, and increasing returns on investments and market share are what ultimately constitute one of the key mechanisms in the process of innovation. Therefore, from the perspective of the competitive development of economies, innovation and new technology do not come from outside the economic system but are rather endogenous to the productive system, the economy and society itself, as the OECD report (1992) on technology and economy acknowledges.

As shown by Schumpeter (1934), innovation involves the production of new goods, the introduction of new production methods, the creation of new forms of firm organization or the opening of new products and factors markets. In contrast to Schumpeter's view, however, endogenous development theory considers that these technological improvements include both radical and incremental innovations. That is, innovation also refers to those small engineering changes in products, process and organization that help firms and firm systems respond efficiently to the challenges of increased market competition.

Processes of diffusion of innovation and knowledge are conditioned by the milieu (the system of firms, institutions and economic and social actors) within which firms make decisions on innovation. Firms invest in technology and knowledge in order to increase profits and improve their competitive position, but their needs and responses are conditioned by the context in which their productive activity is carried out. The results depend, therefore, on what their competitors do, the kind of relations that firms maintain within the milieu and, ultimately, on whether that milieu is innovative or not.

The introduction and diffusion of innovation and knowledge reinforces competitiveness and profitability of firms and productive systems (Rosegger, 1996). Innovation leads firms to create larger units and build smaller, economically more efficient plants, thus reinforcing internal economies of scale. Moreover, innovation leads firms to design and carry out strategies aimed at broadening the scope of entrepreneurial operations, whether through horizontal or vertical integration or through a greater variety of products and product differentiation. In short, the introduction and diffusion of innovation and knowledge improve the stock of technological knowledge in an industry or productive system, which creates external economies for the benefit of all firms in the system.

Interaction between the scale and scope of firm operations and the introduction and diffusion of innovations favors the appearance and development of internal and external economies of scale and economies of diversity for each and every one of the firms in the productive system or industrial cluster. That is, innovation is always the collective result of tacit cooperation among firms and generates increased productivity and competitiveness of local economies.

Flexible organization of production

One of the central factors conditioning capital accumulation is the organization of productive systems, as manifested in developed countries and in late developed economies of Europe and Latin America over recent decades. It is not a matter of whether the productive system of a locality or territory is formed or not by large or small firms, but rather of how the local productive system is organized (Becattini, 1979; Fuà, 1983). The organization of the milieu, in which relations among firms, suppliers and clients are established, conditions the competitiveness and productivity of local economies.

Thus, firm networking within local firm systems is one of the mechanisms through which growth and structural change of local and regional economies is brought about. These interrelations produce increasing returns by encouraging the use of one of the potentials of local economic development, scale economies, which are concealed in productive systems and urban centers.

The analysis of the functioning of local productive systems, particularly in the case of industrial districts, has shown that the existence of networking in local industrial firms leads to the generation of multiple internal markets and meeting areas which facilitate the exchange of products, services and knowledge (Becattini, 1997). The confluence of product and resource exchanges, multiple relations among actors and the transmission of messages and information encourage the diffusion of innovation, contribute to increase productivity and improve competitiveness of local firms.

However, in recent decades, local economic growth has not only been stimulated by the formation and evolution of firm systems, but also by organizational changes in large enterprises and the proliferation of strategic alliances and agreements among firms (Bueno Campos, 1992; Amin and Tomaney, 1997; Bramanti and Senn, 1993). More flexible organization in large firms and groups of firms has led to improved efficiency and competitiveness and new territorial strategies involving networks of subsidiary plants that are more autonomous, more integrated in the territory. These new organizational forms and territorial strategies have facilitated a more efficient use of territorial attributes and, subsequently, brought about competitive advantages. Where these events have taken place, the competitive level of the localities and territories where branch plants are located has increased.

Finally, economic dynamics in recent decades are typified by the appearance of explicit entrepreneurial networks, such as local productive systems, and, particularly, strategic agreements and alliances among firms, mainly in innovative industries, such as electronics and telecommunications, and in service activities such as transportation and the financial system. These alliances are established in order to carry out specific projects and they may affect products, production processes or markets. Firm competitiveness in the markets is improved through these alliances, profits are increased and the competitive position and income of local economies are bettered.

The creation and expansion of firm systems, new organizational forms in large firms and strategic alliances lead firms to obtain scale economies (external and internal, depending on the case), not only in production, but also in research and product development when the alliances affect innovation. Moreover, in every case, it is possible to push forward production diversification processes, thus attaining scope economies. Finally, firm systems and strategic alliances reduce transaction costs among firms, branch plants and internal departments.

In brief, the new forms of organization help firms attain external and internal economies and use indivisibilities hidden within the productive system, all of which undoubtedly favors economic growth and structural change.

The territory's urban development

At the onset of the twenty-first century, cities have become the preferential spaces of development, since it is there that the investment decisions are made and industrial plants and service offices are located. The development potential of cities helps firms to face the challenges of increased competition, linking processes of productive and organizational adjustment to the use of local resources, diffusion of innovation and strengthening of relations with other cities.

Cities are actually territories made up of constructed space and a set of actors who decide upon investment and the location of productive activities. Going beyond the idea held by neoclassical thought and new economic geography, cities are more than a point in space because they constitute an organization in which actors interrelate and exchange goods, services and knowledge according to specific rules. That is why one can say that cities continually change as a consequence of learning and acquisition of knowledge by the actors, the establishment of networks and cooperation, and the implementation of strategies and actions by each actor in order to achieve the firms' and organizations' objectives. For this reason, the most important representative factor of cities is not size but rather the functions performed within the city system.

Cities and local productive systems participate in a common process (Vázquez-Barquero, 2000). Decisions to invest in the productive system and in the city tend to favor convergence of productive and urban development when the economic and social actors interact to create new spaces for interrelations, exchanges and the production of goods.

In any case, cities are the space of endogenous development *par excellence*. They generate externalities which lead to increasing returns, they have a diversified productive system that drives the economic dynamic, they provide space for networking, in which relations among the actors lead to the diffusion of knowledge, and they stimulate innovation and learning in firms (Quigley, 1998; Glaeser, 1998).

Cities, therefore, are places for the creation and development of new industrial and service spaces because of their development potential and capacity to generate externalities. The competitive space created by globalization processes induces cities to respond strategically through local initiatives that stimulate endogenous development processes.

Flexibility and complexity of institutions

Development processes do not take place in a vacuum but rather have profound institutional and cultural roots (North, 1981 and 1986; Lewis, 1955): "The central issue of economic history and of economic development is to account for the evolution of political and economic institutions that create an economic environment that induces increasing productivity" (North, 1991: 98).

Economic development is always led by the actors in each society. Every society has its own cultural and organizational styles and mechanisms and encourages the development of these unique forms and institutions, which will either facilitate economic activity or put obstacles in its way. Economic agents must make decisions within that organizational and institutional environment and, of course, they do not always conform to the theoretical prescriptions of economic models.

Globalization compels entrepreneurial systems to interact with the institutions and organizations of each society and to adapt to the conditions of each environment. Greater market competition means that competitiveness increasingly depends on the dynamic of the institutional network that structures the milieu in which firms are located. As Streeck (1991) points out, those cities and regions with institutional systems that encourage the production of public goods and actors who cooperate to promote learning and innovation will be better able to compete.

Economic development, then, is stimulated in those territories with highly evolved, complex and flexible institutional systems. That is why training and research institutions, entrepreneurial associations, unions and local governments can more efficiently use available resources and improve competitiveness when firms are integrated into territories characterized by thick relational networks. Barriers, which hinder self-sustained growth processes, frequently appear due to deficiencies in and poor performance of the institutional network.

As Rodríguez Pose (1998) and Alfonso Gil (1997 and 1999) observe, new institutional theory argues that the strategic significance of institutions in development processes lies in the economies that its functioning provides. Their behavior can lead to the reduction of transaction and production costs, increased trust among economic and social actors, improved entrepreneurial capacity, increased learning and relational mechanisms, reinforced networks and cooperation among the actors.

That is, institutions condition capital accumulation processes and, subsequently, economic development in cities and regions.

Endogenous development policy

What role does the state play in processes of endogenous development? As was indicated above, the reduction of the presence of the state in economic activity, privatization of public productive activities and decreased prominence of industrial and regional policy particularly stand out among the characteristics that define globalization processes. Thus one might be led to believe that the state would only be responsible for maintaining the stability of the macroeconomic framework and for creating the conditions necessary for the adequate performance of capital accumulation factors.

Nevertheless, since the beginning of the 1980s, a profound change in economic policy has taken place as local and regional actors initiate action aimed at influencing growth processes in local economies. Thus, it is the reaction of local communities to the challenges of firm shutdowns, deindustrialization and increased unemployment that ushers in local development policy.

At that time, all cities and regions in Europe, and later in Latin America, were confronting the need to restructure their productive systems in order to meet the challenges of increased competition and changing market conditions. The task was approached through the introduction of organizational, technological, productive and commercial changes. Faced with the passivity of central administrations, local actors spontaneously tried to launch and control those adjustment processes and it is this activity which gave rise to the policy of local economic development (Stöhr, 1990; Vázquez-Barquero, 1993).

In other words, the question facing cities and regions at the end of the 1970s in Europe and at the beginning of the 1990s in Latin America was how to restructure their productive systems in such a way that agricultural exploitations and industrial and service firms could increase productivity and improve competitiveness in both domestic and external markets.

Research on local development policy in Europe (Bennett, 1989; Stöhr, 1990) and on-going studies in Latin America (Alburquerque, 2001; Aghon *et al.*, 2001) show that local response to increasing competition involves the design and execution of a development strategy, instrumented through actions designed to increase productivity and competitiveness of the productive system, improve income distribution and maintain natural resources, as well as historical and cultural heritage.

These actions can be of a very diverse nature. However, the outstanding characteristic of local development policy is that most local initiatives aim to act on the key processes determining capital accumulation. One of the main axes of local development policy is the diffusion of innovation and knowledge, as can be seen in initiatives in territories with varying production dynamics and development levels. Thus in Bari, a city with an industrial tradition in the Mezzogiorno (Italy) which has undergone severe productive adjustment processes, a technological park (Tecnópolis CSATA) was established in 1984. Some of its most important activities entail technological transfer, research applied to industrial automation, the delivery of innovative services and technical assistance to local firms and training for qualified workers.

The same occurs in developed environments such as the region of Upper Austria or in more peripheral rural areas such as the Cuchumatanes Mountains in Guatemala. In the region of Upper Austria, a technological center in which research laboratories, firms and technological colleges collaborate (Kaufmann and Tödtling, 1999), the Software Park Hagenberg, was created in 1987. Its major activities are innovation consulting, research facilities and training. Furthermore, the park acts as an incubation center since many of the new firms are spin-offs of former research projects. The park is funded by the university budget and research contracts.

In the Cuchumatanes Mountains (Cifuentes 2000) over the late 1990s, innovations in productive processes were gradually introduced in order to facilitate the transformation of subsistence farms into market-oriented agro-business. Some innovations were in the areas of modern reproduction and feeding techniques in sheep and improvement of the technological package that led to the conversion of natural coffee production into organic coffee and increased production and quality of coffee and vegetable farms.

On the other hand, the creation and expansion of firms and the formation of networks constitute one of the objectives of intermediate organizations and local initiatives. A good example of response to changes in environment and an adaptation to new firm needs and demands is that of Barcelona Activa, the Barcelona City Council's Local Development Agency, created in 1986 as a firm incubator. In 1999, Barcelona Activa developed a telematic platform for entrepreneurs and small and medium-sized firms in Barcelona. This program promotes the creation and development of firms by on-line consulting, promotion of cooperation among firms, support for the diffusion of innovation and knowledge among firms in the network and the stimulation of permanent learning through new technologies.

In the Gran ABC, a traditional industrial pole in the State of São Paolo in Brazil since 1997, initiatives were launched to create new firms and improve entrepreneurial and organizational capacity in the region through the creation of a "Fondo de Aval" (a fund whose financial agent is the Caixa Económica Estadual) which would encourage better funding for small and micro firms, the revitalization of activities such as furniture through the creation of a Design Center or support for new activities. In the province of Buenos Aires in Argentina, the Bonaerense Institute of

Entrepreneurial Development was founded in the 1990s to design, promote and carry out initiatives aimed at firm start-up and development and the delivery of real services to small and micro firms. Implementation is effected through the network of Local Centers which provide the services to local firms according to the needs of each territory.

Territorial articulation and the recuperation of hidden external economies in cities are the goals of initiatives implemented through strategic and urban policy. This is evident in such initiatives as the Plan Bilbao Metropoli-30, which aims to revitalize the metropolitan area of Bilbao, the plan for the "Reorganization of Transportation in the Region of Munich," whose goal was to modernize facilities and improve coordination, or the Bogotá Strategic Plan 2000 and the Córdoba Strategic Plan in Argentina (Berg *et al.*, 1999; Borja and Castells, 1997). Furthermore, concern in the area of sustainable development has led cities to develop imaginative projects, as in Curitiva, Brazil where a program has recently been launched to integrate actions on urban infrastructure (the building of a road uniting fourteen suburban areas around the city) with business initiatives based on installations (community barracks) in which micro and small firms can be established with the support of services rendered through vocational and entrepreneurial training.

Finally, one of the typical characteristics of local development policy in Rafaela, Argentina, is the city's institutional development (Costamagna, 1999). Over the 1990s, civil society and public and private organizations have created a set of new institutions which have facilitated the governance of the city through economic, political and social agreements. Furthermore, trust and cooperation among firms and institutions have been reinforced, thus encouraging local networks and contributing to increased firm competitiveness. Improvement in the institutional environment has clearly contributed to reduce transaction costs of all kinds and favored the social and economic development process.

Local development policy as implemented in Europe over the last two decades and in Latin America over the 1990s shows perceptible differences with regard to regional development policy of the 1960s and 1970s, differences which affect the concept of development strategy and its objectives as well as the management and operational mechanisms of the policy itself.

Traditional regional policy was based on the concentrated growth model and therefore promoted regional distribution of income and employment by attracting external resources to target areas. Local development policy, however, aims to overcome imbalances by fostering development within all territories with competitive development potential. Thus, local economic policy proposes that polarization is not essential to growth, which can be diffused as cities and regions attempt to develop using available local potential.

The urban/industrial concentration–diffusion model considered economic development in functional terms; the mobility of productive factors would produce redistribution and restore equilibrium between rich and poor regions. However, local development strategy is based on a territorial approach to regional development and assumes that local institutions, development path and local resources condition economic growth processes. For this reason, in order to develop a city or a region, one must resort not only to external factors, but also to endogenous local factors. In any case, local actors who are able to transform the territory through their actions would be at the helm of processes of change.

Hence, one of the priorities of local development strategy is the development of territories with development potential in a highly uncertain and turbulent context. The objective, then, is not so much to obtain short-term results as it is to change the development model. This involves the diffusion of innovation and knowledge in firms and society by incorporating these factors into physical and human capital. It also involves achieving increased flexibility in the productive system, improving the urban environment where people live and produce and favorably disposing the institutional system to the creation and development of firms. Rather than launching great industrial investment projects to obtain these goals, projects of adequate size should be encouraged, which would contribute to gradual change in the local economic system.

Finally, there are important differences between the two types of policies in the areas of organization and management of development strategy. The state administration managed traditional regional policy centrally through direct financial aid to those firms that fulfilled the requirements established in incentive laws. The management of local development policy, however, is decentralized and instrumented through intermediate organizations and agencies, such as technological institutes, business innovation centers and training centers, that render real and financial services to firms. Funds are not simply made available to firms; local productive systems are provided with the services that firms need to improve competitiveness.

Local economic policy, then, is a bottom-up approach to development policy in which local actors play a central role in design, implementation and control. In its most advanced forms, local actors organize into networks through which they acquire knowledge and learning about the dynamics of the productive system and institutions, come to agreements on initiatives and carry out local development strategy actions.

The interaction effect of endogenous development

Globalization implies increased market competition and focuses the discussion of growth and structural change on the dynamics of capital accumulation. Moreover, the process of productive adjustment and restructuring emerges as a result of firms' decisions on investment and location, thus opening the door to local initiatives. The endogenous development approach, therefore, is of use in understanding economic and productive dynamics and also in helping organizations and institutions to design and implement strategies to meet the challenges of competition.

In contrast to neoclassical models, the theory of endogenous development argues that each process and set of processes determining capital accumulation create an environment in which economic transformation and development processes take shape. Furthermore, the theory holds that local development policy leads to efficient local response to the challenges of globalization (see Figure 1.1). This last tenet shows that the theory of endogenous development is an interpretation for action.

Local and regional economies grow when innovation and knowledge is diffused among firms and territories in such a way that productivity and output are increased, production costs are reduced and scale economies are improved. Local and regional economies also develop when the organization of production is more flexible, and networks and alliances are formed which foster internal and external economies of scale and improve the competitive positioning of cities and regions. Moreover, local and regional economies expand when firms are located in innovative and dynamic urban regions, thus facilitating the use of economies and indivisibilities already existing in the territory. Finally, local and regional economies grow when institutional networks are complex and flexible, thus encouraging reduced transaction costs and trust among the actors.

Therefore, diffusion of innovations and knowledge, flexible organization of production, and urban and institutional development generate increased efficiency in the performance of the productive system. Each one of these mechanisms becomes an efficiency factor in the process of capital accumulation, to the extent that they stimulate economies of scale,

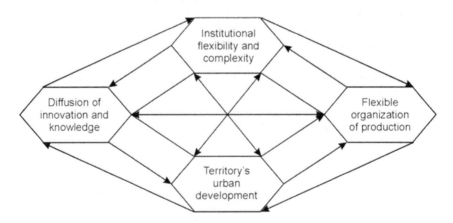

Figure 1.1 The interaction effect of endogenous development.

external economies and reduction in transaction costs, all of which bring about increased productivity and returns.

Cities and regions will probably be more successful in their processes of growth and structural change when all these processes converge to reinforce their effect on capital accumulation. It could be said, then, that efficiency factors form a system capable of multiplying the effect of each individual factor. From now on, we will refer to this phenomenon as the H effect. Consequently, one can argue for the existence of increasing returns when the H factor is activated and the H effect takes place.

To some extent, capital accumulation processes require the combined action of all the factors that determine the H effect. It is not possible for firm networks to perform efficiently and obtain scale economies and increasing returns, if the institutions that condition relations among firms do not encourage trust among the actors and do not guarantee formal agreements among firms.

In turn, the creation and diffusion of innovations will encounter difficulties in reducing production costs and stimulating the presence of firms in the markets if the institutional system does not stimulate interaction among the actors and collective learning through cooperation and agreements between firms and organizations, or if the social and institutional environment does not facilitate the optimal performance of research and knowledge organizations. Finally, hidden economies and externalities existing in cities proliferate easily when the institutional context is flexible and adequate for the needs and demands of the economic, social and political actors and when institutions promote cooperation among the actors.

In the following chapters, the relations between the various forces determining economic growth and structural change are analyzed. It is argued that each and every one of the processes determining capital accumulation act to stimulate or restrict development processes depending on whether the H factor of efficiency facilitates or constrains processes of change. In the final analysis, it is argued that each of the factors acts favorably on the development process only when the rest of them also influence it positively. Therefore, these are interdependent factors that generate externalities through reciprocal interaction and activate development processes.

This would explain the differences that can be observed in the dynamics of cities and regions. The difference between development processes is not only due to differences in development potential or in the efficiency factors of capital accumulation. Differences in the dynamics of cities and regions lie mainly in the interaction among the processes involved in the endogenous development process. Cities and regions have developed thanks to the diffusion of innovations throughout their productive fabric, organization of the productive system, development of adequate institutions and improvement in infrastructures and environment. What truly marks the difference between varying development processes are the externalities that generate interaction among these processes.

Therefore, the H effect comes about as a consequence of the joint economies that generate factors determining capital accumulation as the development process takes place. Optimal performance of the network and interaction of actors and institutions reduces the costs of information and uncertainty; the explicit transfer of knowledge throughout the productive and social fabric improves the quality of resources, makes productive processes more efficient and firms more competitive; learning on the part of the actors improves the results of their actions and decisions; availability of institutions that satisfy the needs and demands of the economic, social and political actors facilitates coordination in the actors' decision-making. The H effect, then, includes the effects of the diffusion of knowledge, learning and coordination, that is, the externalities that are a consequence of the interaction of processes that determine endogenous development.

Local development policy fulfills a significant function in productive adjustment since it acts as a catalyst of the H effect through local initiatives which foster the diffusion of innovation and knowledge, facilitate entrepreneurial development and the creation of firm networks, and stimulate urban development and institutional complexity. That is, local development policy leads to improved behavior of each one of the efficiency factors determining capital accumulation.

The new generation of local development policy also aims to integrate the various types of actions and better adjust them to the needs of productive systems and firms. In this way, its objective is to act jointly on all the efficiency factors in an attempt to improve the H factor of endogenous development and produce the H effect in the locality or territory.

Recapitulating, then, endogenous development theory accounts for capital accumulation processes and identifies the mechanisms that lead to increased productivity and competitiveness of cities and regions. Over the last decades, this approach has become an interpretation for action and local development policy has become civil society's answer to the challenges of increased market competition. The generation of new forms of economic governance through intermediate organizations and public and private networking leads cities and regions to optimize their competitive advantages and thus to stimulate economic growth.

Part I

The notion of endogenous development

2   Endogenous development
An approach for action

One of the important changes that have taken place in economic development theory over the last 20 years is the formation of a new paradigm known as "endogenous development." With the uncertainty, increased competition and institutional change of today's economic environment, more flexible forms of capital accumulation and regulation have emerged to characterize processes of growth and structural change and have become the preferred instrument for development policies.

The spontaneous and independent appearance of both phenomena has brought about, on the one hand, reduced levels of system instability and, on the other, the placing of globalization in the context of territorial development. The main idea of the new paradigm is that the countries' productive systems grow and change through development potential existing in the territory (regions and cities) by way of investment from firms and public actors, under increasing control of the local community.

The new paradigm goes beyond the definition of growth as proposed in models based on the production function and exceeds the modern version of endogenous growth models. Economic growth and structural change are the result of investment strategies and decisions of enterprises operating in the markets and integrated into institutional and cultural milieux. These, in turn, condition the economic dynamics of the territory in that they affect the organization of production, the relational system and innovation and learning processes.

The endogenous development paradigm is presented in this chapter. After looking into its origin and formation, the mechanisms that favor growth and structural change in local economies are analyzed. Some of the most important features and factors, such as diffuse development, organization of local productive systems, diffusion of knowledge and innovation, institutions and culture of the territory and local development policy are described. A summary of the singularities of the endogenous development approach concludes the chapter.

The formation of the endogenous development paradigm

At the beginning of the 1980s, two research programs converged to give rise to the formation of the paradigm known as endogenous development. One was a theoretical approach, which originated in response to the search for a development concept that would define public action in underdeveloped regions (Friedmann and Douglas, 1978; Stöhr, 1981 and 1985). The other was an empirical development model in that it came about as a result of the interpretation of industrial development in southern European localities and regions (Becattini, 1979; Brusco, 1982; Fuà, 1983; Garofoli, 1983; Vázquez-Barquero, 1983; Costa Campi, 1988; Silva, 1987; Reis, 1987).

The proposals of territorial development theory, of self-centered development and bottom-up development are a reaction to the dissatisfaction with the development model, which was the prevalent proposal of the 1960s and 1970s. In the words of Aydalot (1985), territorial development theory is a voluntaristic (and, certainly, utopian) approach to development. It represents the search for a new paradigm articulated on three great questions: the concept of development, the mechanisms that favor development processes and, finally, the most efficient actions of economic and social actors.

Endogenous development pursues the satisfaction of local needs and demands through active participation of the local community in development processes. It is not simply a matter of improving the position of the local productive system in the international or national division of labor, but rather of economic, social and cultural well-being for the local community on the whole. Therefore, this development strategy not only proposes to improve the productive side (agricultural, industrial, services), but also to promote social and cultural dimensions that affect the well-being of society. This view can lead to various paths of development depending on the characteristics and capacities of each local economy and society.

It is a territorial approach to development and to the performance of the productive system. The territory is no longer simply a place where resources and economic activities are located. It can be understood as an agent of transformation because firms and other actors of the territory interact to develop the economy and society. The starting point for development of a region or locality are the resources (economic, human, institutional and cultural), which constitute its potential for development.[1] It is precisely the small and medium-sized firms, with their flexibility and entrepreneurial and organizational capability, who are to play a major role in endogenous development processes.

Finally and above all, endogenous development is a strategy for action. Local communities have their own identities that lead them to launch initiatives for development. Once their organizational capability is developed, external firms and investment may reinforce local development potential and strengthen their development process. This ability to conduct their own development and mobilize the economic potential is a characteristic feature of the notion of "endogenous development."

It was in response to the loss of analytical and policy capacity of the industrialization model, based on large firms located in large cities, that researchers of endogenous industrialization put forward a new proposal. They demonstrated that industrialization in late developed countries, such as those of southern Europe (for example in the Terza Italy, in the region of Valencia in Spain and in the Val do Ave in Portugal) was initiated and consolidated thanks to the development of local industrial systems. This historic approach to development is characterized by specific forms of organization of production, integration of society and institutions into productive processes and response of the territory and its economic actors[2] to the conditions of the new economic, political and institutional environment.

The production of manufacturing goods – generally industrial products – through the flexible organization of production and the intense use of labor is a feature of endogenous industrialization processes. Firms specialize in the production of parts of the productive process or of components that are later assembled to make the final product.[3] The labor force employed in the production process is flexible in the sense that it can perform various tasks and the labor supply can be adapted to the firms' demand for labor through home work and part-time and informal work.

Endogenous industrialization is also characterized by the fact that integration of the productive system into the local society is achieved through the firms. On the one hand, firms find they are destined to cooperate with each other because of the way in which specialization in the local productive system evolved and the fact that their reduced size forces them to cooperate in order to obtain the economies of scale necessary to compete. Moreover, local traditions, values and codes, as well as family, social and cultural structure, are driving forces in the dynamics of the industrialization process. They contribute human and financial resources, facilitate labor and social relations and encourage the formal and informal exchange of goods and services and diffusion of information and knowledge throughout the network of firms and local organizations.

Finally, endogenous industrialization processes are deeply rooted in the territory. They spontaneously emerge in small and medium-sized cities through the activity of local entrepreneurs. Over time, technical know-how accumulates and they form their own relational systems and consolidate cultural habits that generate economies that justify their survival. An economic and institutional milieu is thus created which provides local firms with resources, services and cooperation networks, all of which leads to improved competitiveness in national and international markets.

The convergence of both research programs has given rise to the theory of endogenous development, an approach which significantly differs from traditional interpretations that postulated development through industrialization with large plants located in large cities. Economic viability is possible due to the generation of external economies of scale and the reduction of production and transaction costs in the productive system. Endogenous development theory is also far from some interpretations, such as that of D'Arcy and Guissani (1996), who consider this approach utopian. Still others, such as Blakely (1989), consider it a development strategy rather than a theoretical approach since it refers to initiatives that generate and stimulate capital accumulation processes in specific localities and territories.

Endogenous development,[4] then, can be understood to be a process of economic growth and structural change, which is led by the local community and employs its potential for development to improve the local population's standard of living. Arocena (1995) adds that endogenous development is a process in which social aspects are integrated into economic aspects. Income and wealth distribution and economic growth are not two parallel processes, but rather parts of the same force, since public and private actors make investment decisions aimed not only at increasing firms' productivity and competitiveness, but also at solving problems and improving the well-being of local society.

At least three dimensions can be identified in processes of endogenous development. One is an economic dimension characterized by a specific production system that allows local entrepreneurs to use efficiently the productive factors and reach productivity levels which make them competitive in the markets. Another is an institutional dimension where economic and social actors are integrated into local institutions thus forming a complex system of relations, which incorporates social and cultural values into the development process. Yet another is a political dimension, instrumented in local initiatives, which leads to the creation of a local environment that stimulates production and brings about sustainable development.

Competitiveness of local productive systems

As mentioned above, one of the lines of thought relative to endogenous development originated from research on local productive systems in late developed countries of southern Europe, which made it possible to identify the mechanisms at work in capital accumulation within these systems. What factors account for competitiveness of local productive systems and industrial districts? What processes are behind the emergence of local entrepreneurial systems? What factors and processes account for endogenous development?

First of all, it must be clear that the organization of production is, in itself, a main factor of competitiveness. The organization of firms within specialized entrepreneurial networks makes it possible to obtain economies of scale (which are external to the firms but internal to the local productive system) and reduce production and transaction costs. Available technology allows firms to attain competitive advantages in the market by specializing in segments of the productive process and assembling production at the level of productive districts with significant economies.

The availability of entrepreneurial and organizational capabilities, intensely linked to the productive tradition of each territory, leads to the rivalry of firms in the local market which, in turn, leads to increased internal and external competitiveness of local firm systems. Moreover, local productive systems have historically shown a particular ability to adopt and adapt innovation and technology. But this is not only a matter of the use of machinery and capital goods made in outside productive systems but, above all, the small adaptations and modifications that workers and technical personnel make in these capital goods, which increase productivity and competitiveness. In the local context, industrial development is perpetually in debt to the local environment's capacity to learn and acquire knowledge leading to the introduction and diffusion of innovation.

Finally, both the way in which society is organized and the system of local institutions make for more flexible labor markets, which means that local firms and economies can function with low production costs and, in particular, with relatively low wages. The availability of a less conflictive labor supply, skilled for the tasks it must carry out and sensitive to the firms' needs allows enterprises to obtain comparative advantages in the markets.

These factors refer to the capital accumulation process that drives development of local productive systems. But how do local industrial systems come about? What are the factors that contribute to the birth of an industrialization process in a locality or territory? How can industrial development be accounted for?

An industrialization process begins as a consequence of a crisis in or loss of vitality and performance of the local economy's agrarian productive system, and the appearance of new market opportunities. There is a wide range of possibilities in this respect. There may be a change in the tastes and needs of consumers for those products, in which the local economy has a competitive advantage – due, for example, to the availability of specific raw materials and natural resources. Or the local community may be responding to a crisis in the productive system or a loss of traditional markets for local products. These factors lead local entrepreneurs and firms to seek new initiatives in expanding markets.

On occasion, as Krugman (1990) points out, a local productive system can arise by chance; on other occasions, as Bernabé Maestre (1983) suggests, it may come about in reaction to successful industrialization experiences in nearby or contiguous towns that lead a local economy to imitate them with their own resources. In cases of endogenous industrialization investigated in Italy and Spain, for example, it has been noted that this initial push that sets off the structural change eventually leads to a process of industrialization and development. This occurs thanks to the existence of a certain entrepreneurial capability, an abundant and cheap labor force, a developed social structure, local knowledge on "new" products and markets through previous commercial activities, and savings from agricultural and/or commercial activity (Fuà, 1983; Vázquez-Barquero, 1988).

Driven by the firms' need to produce goods and services for an exigent market in which they compete with products of firms from other cities and regions, the local economy spontaneously self-organizes. The firm's pursuit for profit and the improved positioning within the markets in increasingly complex and competitive environments has brought about more efficient forms of organization of production such as the industrial district. This form of organization can bring artisan activities, which played a secondary role in the traditional agrarian economy, into the center of the new local economic system.

Flexible organization of production

At the center of the process of capital accumulation in local productive systems is the formation of external economies of scale and the reduction of transaction costs. Both components are conditioned by the way in which the productive system is organized. Therefore, the dynamics of the local economy revolve around the organization of the environment or milieu and the relationships established among firms, suppliers and clients. The backbone of local productive systems (particularly in the case of industrial districts) is the configuration of the production model, the existence of a network of industrial firms, in which a profusion of internal markets and meeting opportunities facilitate the exchange of products, services and know-how (Costa Campi, 1988; Becattini, 1997).

The industrial network (Hakansson and Johanson, 1993) is made up of actors (the firms in the local productive system), resources (human, natural, infrastructure), economic activities (productive, commercial, technical, financial, social, legal) and their interrelations (interdependence and exchanges). Not only are the relations within the network conducive to the exchange of products and services among the actors, but also of technological knowledge and behavioral codes.

Throughout history, systems of relations and connections among activities and firms have increased and form part of the social and productive culture of the local community, thus taking on a unique form in each locality. As Piore and Sabel (1984) point out, local productive systems are made up of a system of internal networks that give rise to a large number of internal markets and the exchange of information and know-how, which brings about cooperation and competition among firms.

Furthermore, Becattini (1997) maintains that the dynamics of industrial districts lead firms to reconcile competition with internal social reproduction. For this reason, real prices in internal markets tend to remain between two levels. They should not be higher than those existing in markets outside of the local productive system or district, nor should they be so low that a group of firms specialized in an activity necessary for network operation be forced out of the local system. Under free market conditions, this leads to the uninterrupted introduction and adaptation of innovation into the productive system.

Two elements that often cause some confusion in talking about endogenous development are the role of small and medium-sized firms and the importance of local resources in productive processes. Territorial development theories base their arguments on the strategic advantages of small firms in development processes. As we have seen above, however, the determinant factor in economic growth is not the size of firms, but rather the formation of firm systems or networks, that give rise to economies of scale and scope and reduce transaction costs. As Chandler (1990) has shown, these characteristics are also typical of large firms.

As to the importance of local resources, it must be pointed out that the origin of the resources is not a determinant factor in processes of growth and structural change; in reality, it is quite usual that local and outside factors be combined. What does actually characterize processes of endogenous development is the ability of the local community to control the process of structural change taking place in a locality or region.

As we will propose in Chapter 9, large firms and industrial groups from other territories can play a strategic role in local development when the goals pursued by these firms converge with those of the territory. Technological, organizational and institutional changes affecting large firms and territories seem to have created favorable conditions for endogenizing initiatives and inward investment (Bellandi, 2001; Vázquez-Barquero, 1999). Increasing competition within the markets would prompt firms to abandon their functional strategies, in which the territory was, at most, a place to locate their plants. They will be substituted with spatial strategies that seek greater insertion of production units into local contexts (Dupuy and Gilly, 1997).

Innovative firms are attracted to locations with quality resources and infrastructure, a productive system (and society) open to innovation and a system of firms susceptible to generating external economies of scale and producing goods and services in conditions of increasing competition. They also look for places with an institutional network supportive of an entrepreneurial climate favorable to cooperation and competitiveness. At the same time, increased organizational complexity and the devolution of competencies to local communities have converted cities and regions into organizations capable of defining and executing development strategies which stimulate local economic dynamics, as will be discussed in Chapter 9.

Strategies of territories and external firms share the same objectives in that they both desire that the attributes of the territory will allow firms located there to enjoy competitive advantages. The convergence of interests contributes to improve competitiveness of both the large firm and of the territory. Thus, competition and the contention for markets make cities and regions partners of large firms and conglomerates. So, when firm and territorial strategies converge, processes of endogenous development acquire their own dynamics.

Learning and innovation

A local productive system is more than an industrial network, however. It is also made up of a network of social actors and is therefore further defined as a system of economic, social, political and legal relations (Best, 1990). The local productive system can be understood as a "milieu," that is, a local environment that "integrates and dominates a knowledge, certain rules, norms and values and a system of relations" (Maillat, 1995). Thus, local firms, organizations and institutions within the local milieux are capable of knowing, learning and acting; they are a sort of "brain" for the dynamics of a local economy.

The concept of local milieu goes beyond the notion of industrial district. It includes the system of relations among the actors in a territory and emphasizes the cognitive dimension of the actors in acknowledging the evolution of firms and local economic performance, and recognizes their capacity to make strategic decisions for themselves and for the productive system on the whole. Added to firms' production and organization capability are learning potential and the ability to intervene in the growth and structural change in local economies.

Economic development and the dynamics of production depend on the introduction and diffusion of innovation and knowledge, which impel transformation and renovation of the local productive system. Aydalot (1985) maintains that local firms are the instrument through which innovations and knowledge are introduced into endogenous development processes. Their creativity is conditioned by the territory's experience and tradition. In other words, knowledge, accumulated in firms and organizations, is one of the mainstays of development.

Firms in local productive systems produce goods and services under competitive conditions. Therefore, their presence in the markets depends on the introduction of changes and transformations in production processes and in products, which will allow them to continue being competitive. Innovation takes place when firms, through relations within the milieu, discover that changes affecting their results have occurred.

This brings them to make investment decisions leading, eventually, to adoption and, finally, to the creation of innovation.

In local productive systems, and particularly in those specialized in traditional activities such as textiles, clothing, footwear, wood and metal final goods, the innovation process is limited to the diffusion of capital goods, intermediate products and raw materials on the part of firms from other sectors (Pavitt, 1984). The most relevant local innovations are those improvements made in manufacturing plants by specialized workers, that is, incremental innovations, as well as those in the area of organizational and market innovations.

Incremental innovations, then, are all those changes and adaptations of technology that entail progressive improvement of products and processes. Small engineering modifications in productive processes in order to employ available raw material more efficiently, changes in product design and specifications to bring final goods closer to client demand: these innovations are aimed at improving the articulation of market and production. When this goal is attained, the result is improvement in productivity and firm profits.

The development of incremental innovations is based on firms' ability to learn when, faced with the challenge of competition in the markets, they must necessarily apply efficient solutions in order to maintain productive activity. Accumulated knowledge as a result of constant adaptations and solutions in the production plant means improved efficiency and "profit" for the firm.[5]

Diffusion of innovation and knowledge within local productive systems is, admittedly, a slow but continuous process and usually comes about in a hierarchic form throughout the firm network. Once leading firms have adopted an innovation to meet production or demand needs, a process of technological diffusion within the productive system spreads by way of formal and informal relations in the district as described above.

Facilitating the diffusion of technological innovation and knowledge are the organization of local productive systems, the concentration of a great number of firms in a single area, productive specialization in the district and the characteristics of the labor market's skills (Pecquer and Silva, 1992; Garofoli, 1992). Worker mobility from one firm to another is common and facilitates the transfer of innovations from one firm to another by specialized workers and management. Moreover, the circulation of information about process, product or market innovations is quite rapid since firms are immersed in a social fabric which encourages the circulation of ideas and knowledge. Finally, increased face-to-face relations, particularly between suppliers and consumers of intermediate products and services for firms, favor the diffusion of technological and organization improvements.

Imitation is also a mechanism of diffusion of innovation and knowledge among firms in the network and among the territories in which they are located. Competition and the demonstration effect lead firms to adopt innovations in order to maintain and increase their market share and returns on their investments. This phenomenon happens rather quickly when imitators see that the introduction of innovations has brought profits to the firms that first adopted them.

The imitation process in local productive systems transcends the dynamics of local firms because productive specialization in cities and regions where they are located leads them to act as innovative centers in the area of influence. Thus, once the diffusion process begins in one of the cities, it spreads to other nuclei in the urban network specialized in the same kind of activity. When these processes of diversification of productive activity toward auxiliary industries occur in industrial cities, or when product, process, market or organizational innovations are introduced, spatial diffusion usually operates according to the mechanism described above.

Development, culture and institutions

Endogenous development takes place in an organized society whose institutions and cultural forms determine processes of structural change, which are subsequently influenced by the conditions in which development has taken place. Therefore, studies on local productive systems assign a strategic value to the institutional and cultural components of endogenous development (Fuà, 1983; Vázquez-Barquero, 1988).

The emergence and consolidation of local productive systems have come about in areas in which social and cultural systems are strongly rooted in the territory. A social model, in which effort and work ethics are rewarded, entrepreneurial skill is of social value and social mobility is encouraged, can account for positive performance of local labor markets and explain community reaction in the face of technological change and the challenges of increasing competition in the markets.

Local firms are a vehicle to the integration of local productive systems into the social–cultural relations in the productive system or district. Since firms belong to a productive system and are located in a city, they frequently maintain exchange and cooperation ties within the district itself. Social and cultural conditions and behavior codes directly influence productive activity. It is the intense relation established in local productive systems among firms, culture and territory that can account for the internal dynamics of local economies. The feeling of belonging to a differentiated local community is sometimes so strongly rooted that it can triumph over class sentiment, altering industrial relations and reducing local social conflict.

One may ask to what extent family structures and local cultural values influence local development and what mechanisms are at work in the consolidation of these processes. Throughout history, the family has contributed singularly to the performance of local productive systems and industrial districts, in particular. Not only is the family an institution – along with others such as schools and the religious community – specialized in education and the transmission of social values. It has also played a significant economic role in the creation and development of firms in that the family provides human, financial and entrepreneurial resources to a good share of business endeavors.

In local development processes, the dynamics of the productive system are conditioned by the standards that orient society. A strong local identity along with social recognition of the business activity can account for the birth of productive activity and its continuation, even in times of need and high risk. Trust among entrepreneurs favors cooperation and assures transactions among local firms, which, in turn, lead to economic growth and reduced costs. Finally, the work ethic contributes to upgrade human resource skills, reduce the potential for social conflict and, ultimately, stimulate capital accumulation.

Pecquer and Silva (1992) point out that the existence of mechanisms leading to territorial solidarity are characteristic of areas in which endogenous industrialization processes have taken place. Specific links are formed among the actors within the milieu which usually lead to a response on the part of the local community, particularly when the external environment changes as a consequence of increased competition in the markets and macroeconomic policy changes. Local entrepreneurs tend to adapt to these changes in the milieu by establishing cooperative relations with one other.

Furthermore, the existence of local and regional social organization systems, in which trade and monetary exchange developed throughout the pre-industrial period and in the initial stages of industrialization, have fostered the emergence and consolidation of endogenous development processes. When flexible cultural devices, open to new ideas, new firms and modern production methods are also present, then one can conclude that the cultural environment has contributed to endogenous industrialization.

Finally, economic dynamics and new production methods have contributed to the evolution of social organization, culture and ethical codes of the population. The internal dynamics of local productive systems have gradually strengthened entrepreneurial culture, accumulated technological knowledge, both productive and commercial, and improved training and skill of workers and entrepreneurs. The institutional system in cities and regions, where endogenous development processes have taken place, has also been modified.

Urban development

Endogenous development, then, is a process of growth and structural change determined by the organization of the productive system, the relational network among actors and activities, the dynamics of innovation and learning and the institutional system. However, it is further characterized by its territorial dimension, not only due to the spatial effect of organizational and technological processes, but also to the fact that each locality, each city, each region, is the consequence of its institutional, economic, technological and organizational history, shaped over time.

From the perspective of endogenous development, each economic space has its own configuration, defined by successive productive systems, technological and organizational changes in firms and institutions and transformations in the system of social and institutional relations. Historically, each territorial community has been molded by interest relations and ties among its social groups and actors and a unique identity and culture, which differentiate it from other communities. The territory can be understood as the territorial community's grid of interests. Thus it is perceived as an actor for local development, interested at all times in maintaining and defending territorial integrity and interests in processes of development and structural change.

Massey (1984) maintains that each local economy has played different and specific roles in the international division of labor. The productive system, labor market and social and production relations possess unique traits which make it different from the rest. Therefore, each territory interacts within the international economic system in function of its particular history which confers upon it specific possibilities for productive restructuring and economic dynamic.

Development, therefore, acquires significance within the territory and, in organized societies, is articulated through the urban system. Research studies on processes of endogenous development and the dynamics of industrial districts show that medium-sized cities are a preferred space for local productive systems. External economies are established in these locations where conditions also concur to reduce transaction costs among firms and local organizations.

The system of relations among firms of a productive system and with clients and suppliers is generally based on a well structured urban system and adequately developed infrastructures. A well structured urban system, made up of city networks, encourages the exchange of goods and services, stimulates the performance of firms and promotes satisfactory evolution of the labor market, while the presence of adequate economic (transportation, communications, energy) and social (health and education) infrastructures facilitates the appearance and development of external economies and, therefore, sustainable development. Physical infrastructures and urban development, then, influence the economic dynamics of cities and regions.

The formation of local productive systems has contributed to the continued diffusion of development in the territory. Furthermore, the processes that characterized urban cities in the 1990s have weakened the idea that development is diffused through the urban hierarchy, as will be seen in Chapter 7. The hierarchical level of present-day urban systems tends to blur as a consequence of anti-hierarchical elements in the new economic and territorial processes. The location pattern of industrial and service activities tend to be less and less concentrated; production plants are smaller and smaller, thus reducing the need to tap large labor markets; decreasing transportation costs and widespread use of the automobile have meant a departure from the principles of market areas.

Nevertheless, as Camagni maintains, one cannot deny that the hierarchic factor still exists in the urban system. Undoubtedly, though, there is a tendency toward less urban hierarchy or the emergence of multiple hierarchies in the urban system. This can be conceived in terms of polycentric urban models, of a sort of urban armature, which tends to function more and more as a network, Cappellin suggests. Cities with local productive systems constitute one of the basic networks of new urban models.

Local development policy

According to territorial development theory, endogenous development is also an approach geared for action. Local and regional communities facing the challenges of increasing competition and problems associated with productive restructuring (increased unemployment and structural change) design and implement strategies and policy action and respond to them by employing development potential already existing within the territory.

In an increasingly global world, in which cities and regions compete for specific resources to give them an edge over the rest, local communities (public and private organizations, entrepreneurial associations, firms, unions and local governments) have understood the challenge of economic globalization and have reacted by promoting local development initiatives.

Productive, technological and institutional changes that have come about over recent decades affect the competitiveness of firms, cities and regions. Therefore, the variables conditioning productive restructuring and local and regional development are the regional rate of innovation, human resources skills, entrepreneurial capability of firms, institutional flexibility and the integration of firms, cities and regions in competitive and innovative networks. As Stöhr (1990: 40–41) points out, "the central distributive policies are ineffective [to confront this type of change because] they cannot influence the entrepreneurial climate and innovative capacity of structurally weak regional communities." Above all, they "have not been able . . . to overcome the problem caused by the functional economic and labor-market segmentation" which international productive restructuring processes have brought about in local and regional economies. Moreover, redistribution policies "are seldom effective in inducing local innovation in places where it would not happen anyway."

Faced with a global problem of restructuring production, in recent decades cities and regions have attempted to respond to their problems by trying to stimulate adjustment in local productive systems. Local and regional governments in Europe and Latin America have increasingly intervened in the processes by promoting policies aimed at solving problems associated with productive restructuring.

Some local public administrators were aware of the severity and relevance of the changes and of the negative effect at the local level (firms closing down and unemployment). They were also aware that measures aimed at controlling macroeconomic imbalances (inflation, public deficit, deficit in the balance of payments) launched by central administrations were not sufficient to reconstruct local productive systems. Therefore, it was necessary to intervene in the restructuring processes and stimulate the creation of local initiatives and jobs. Local development policy spontaneously began to take shape as strategies, objectives and actions were gradually defined. Their objective is to achieve sustainable and enduring development. Cities and regions therefore attempt to promote the economic, social and environmental dimensions of development. Local initiatives are aimed at the efficient allocation of public and private resources, the fair distribution of wealth and jobs and environmental balance in the territory.

In general, local initiatives are conceived in order to improve employment conditions and advance restructuring conditions in cities and territories. But their orientation varies greatly since some are mainly economic-based while others have a more social orientation, while environmentally oriented initiatives have proliferated over the last decade. There has, in fact, always been an animated debate as to which of these orientations should prevail in local development policies and, in any case, which direction is the most adequate for each economy.

Frequently, the initiatives are clearly economic in nature, aiming to promote local entrepreneurial capability and the adoption and adaptation of necessary technological innovations. The initiatives, then, endeavor to create and develop firms. It is also common to find initiatives whose fundamental objectives and actions have a distinct social orientation. These seek to provide jobs, assist the physically, socially and culturally disadvantaged or fulfill the needs of specific social groups such as youth, the elderly or women. That is, their objective is to directly improve the welfare of the population. Finally, other types of initiatives are designed to maintain historical and cultural heritage and conserve the environment.

In fact, all of these actions contribute to the development of cities and territories. The goals of each one complement all the others and should therefore be stimulated together. Local development strategy is actually designed to solve economic and social problems in a city or region which means that priorities are set as a function of local needs and agreements defined by local actors. Whatever is useful in strategic terms is also useful in operational terms. Feasible actions should be prioritized since available resources are limited.

In any case, when designing strategy and initiatives, it is advisable to define clearly the type of goals one expects to reach since this will lead to specific actions. Promoting competitive and innovative firms is quite a different matter from favor-developing initiatives in an informal economy or helping young drug addicts through subsidized job-insertion programs. All of these are desirable and possible from the point of view of local development, but each one requires unique measures.

When endogenous development strategies are aimed at promoting production restructuring processes or improvement of the competitive positioning of a city or region, they should be oriented toward reaching the economic objectives. Its actions are aimed at improving infrastructure to produce and to live, upgrading the non-tangible factors of development (learning, knowledge, entrepreneurship and information), and strengthening the organizational capacity and the adequate use of non-renewable resources.

Each territory requires specific treatment and appropriate instruments in order to overcome any obstacle to optimal performance and firm competitiveness in the local economy. Encouraged are the diffusion of innovation, entrepreneurship, skilled human resources, flexibility in the organization of production, formation and development of networks and relations among actors, protection of natural resources and the recuperation of the historical and cultural heritage.

Finally, the definition, design and promotion of the new strategies and actions of regional development policy has received strong support from international organizations such as the OECD and the Commission of the European Union, and recently from the UN Economic Commission for Latin America and the Caribbean countries (ECLA) and from the Inter-American Development Bank (IDB). Although proposals are sometimes branded as vague and indefinite, they significantly influence change in industrial and regional policies.

The ILE-OECD program has lasted for over a decade. In July of 1982, the OECD Council targeted local employment initiatives with a new Program for Cooperation and Action. The program's most important goals were to promote the exchange of experiences and information on entrepreneurial development and local employment, improve means for evaluating local initiatives and provide technical assistance to member countries when defining intervention programs (OECD, 1987).

The Program for Local Economic and Employment Development (LEED) has expanded and reinforced this line of work since the mid-1990s. LEED is part of the Territorial Development Service of the OECD to further social and institutional innovation in order to promote entrepreneurship and job creation in member states. Some of the services offered by the LEED Program are: the study of innovation in local development, the assistance of bilateral cooperation on job creation, entrepreneurship and local development, the organization of study missions aimed at broadening knowledge on policy implementation, the mobilization of a LEED Program member club and the transfer of experiences among OECD member states.

Local development and the promotion of job creation in the European Community is dealt with more pragmatically and efficiently than in the OECD. European Union programs are less ambiguous and essentially fund specific local economic development projects. Although not all the programs have this pragmatic approach, as occurred with the LEDA (Local Employment Development Action) Program, the availability of structural funds (European Regional Development Fund and European Social Fund) differentiates European Union programs from those of the OECD.

Finally, the Leader Program, framed in March of 1991, received great impetus over the subsequent decade. Its activities focus on growth in rural areas of less developed regions and priority rural zones of the European Union. The program represents a change in direction in dealing with problems faced by rural communities since it promotes territorial-based initiatives leading to integrated development strategies in rural areas, at the same time as it reduces the role of European Community agrarian policy. In today's context, the combination of both policies can, in fact, create mutual synergies.

Recently, the international institutions charged with Latin American affairs have shown an increasing interest in local development, particularly due to the fact that decentralization and modernization of local governments is bringing up the question of the bottom-up approach to development as a feasible strategy for the growth of cities and regions. Thus the Economic Commission for Latin America and the Caribbean countries has begun to study the incidence and significance of local initiatives in Latin America. With the help of the German Agency for International Cooperation (GTZ), it has supported a research project on Local Economic Development and Decentralization in Latin America through the Division of Economic Development in the ECLA. The main conclusion of the project is that recent local initiatives are closely aligned with the economic, political and institutional conditions of each country.

Since the beginning of the 1990s, the Inter-American Development Bank has supported activities in territorial environments that favor competitiveness in small firm systems. At present this organization is investigating some of the most significant experiences in local economic development in Latin America in order to discover to what extent the demand for this type of industrial development initiative is met by present availability in the operations of the IDB.

Finally, some NGOs, the development agencies of European Union countries such as Spain, Italy, Germany and the Netherlands, and international organizations occasionally support specific local initiatives in Latin America. For instance, the United Nations Development Program is carrying out an important joint project in the area of participative management and local development in Brazil with the National Economic and Social Development Bank (BNDES), an important federal development entity in Brazil.

Endogenous development, a much-debated concept

The above discussion indicates that the endogenous development paradigm combines propositions from territorial development theory with those derived from the analysis of endogenous industrialization processes. The approach thus defined is an alternative to the model of urban industrial concentration/diffusion, which has been the axis of development policy and programs for decades. It is an interpretation of growth and structural change that also aspires to be a viable development strategy.

In recent years, some aspects of the theory of endogenous development have been under fire. In most cases, this criticism is aimed at certain parts of the theory, such as the viability of endogenous development strategy or the consistency of the industrial district development model. In some cases, critics point to its ambiguity or its scant effectiveness. Some authors such as Amin and Robins (1990) and Harrison (1994) argue that the endogenous development approach is not able to respond to social and institutional change in the market. Local production systems would, therefore, have a limited future in a world in which development is increasingly global and where there are great forces at work that tend toward concentration and integration.

It is true that some authors who embrace endogenous development theory, as Becattini (1997) recognizes, have undoubtedly exaggerated when maintaining that the industrial district is a model of flexible organization of production more efficient than and alternative to the Fordist firm. In fact, the endogenous development approach only argues that the way production is organized leads to the flexible use of local and entrepreneurial resources as well as recondite external economies of scale, and to a reduction in production and transaction costs.

In any case, it must be acknowledged that the endogenous development approach facilitates interpretation of recent changes in the mechanisms of capital accumulation. Since this model admits that organization of production tends to be more flexible and less hierarchical, it can reason in terms of external economies of scale and not only in terms of the internal economies of scale that characterize the Fordist firm. Furthermore, for reasons advanced above and analyzed in later chapters, the territorial strategies of large innovative firms should indicate that the production system does not necessarily tend toward concentration in times of globalization.

Because the endogenous development model takes an interactive view of innovation and technological change, it not only recognizes that incremental innovations play a strategic role in economic development process but also that local productive systems can become innovative milieux when local actors decide to invest in innovation and organization. Furthermore, by pointing out the role of the adaptation of technology and change in process technologies in local productive systems, it acknowledges that production can be increasingly adjusted to demand and less standardized and, therefore, that local firms can maintain their market share.

Since endogenous development theory admits that diffuse industrialization is a feasible model for economic growth in increasingly competitive environments, it can argue that urban systems and medium-sized cities can also provide agglomeration economies to firms while in large cities agglomeration diseconomies are taking place.

Finally, the endogenous development approach is an interpretation that benefits from the contributions made during the last two decades by an important number of research programs. The theories of industrial districts (Becattini, 1979) and diffuse industrialization (Fuà, 1983) have been enlarged by works on clusters within less developed countries (Schmitz, 1995), and on networking and learning (Maskell *et al.*, 1998). Evolutionary theory of innovation (Nelson and Winter, 1982; Nelson, 1995) and the innovate milieu approach (Aydalot 1986; Maillat; 1995) have been expanded with works on local and regional innovative systems (Asheim and Isaksen, 1997) and learning regions (Morgan, 1997). Institutional Economics (North, 1990) has given way to the theory of proximity (Gilly and Torre, 2000; Bellet *et al.*, 1993). Finally, research programs on city networks (Camagni, 1991; Cappellin, 1990), specific resources (Colletis and Pecqueur, 1995) and urban milieux (Crevoisier and Camagni, 2000) have enlarged the territorial development approach.

Whatever the value of the critiques, it is important to remember that endogenous development is an approach characterized by a specific mechanism of capital accumulation, based on flexible organization of production, an innovation and learning system, institutional flexibility and urban development of the territory. All of these factors bring about unique dynamics and give local communities an instrument for action (Vázquez-Barquero, 1992).

3 On the theoretical roots of endogenous development

The concept of endogenous development is often linked to endogenous industrialization processes, that is, to the economic dynamics of cities and regions. Its growth and structural change would be founded on the expansion of industrial activity and the use of development potential existing in the territory (D'Arcy and Guissani, 1996; Bianchi, 1998). At least two approaches can be identified among the authors that investigate and theorize on endogenous industrialization, one whose analyses are related to the organization of production and another that considers endogenous industrialization one of the paths of development for cities and regions.

The first approach, founded on industrial organization theory (Becattini, 1979 and 1987; Brusco, 1982; Costa Campi, 1992; Costa Campi *et al.*, 1993; Piore and Sabel, 1984; Porter, 1990), analyzes the theoretical and empirical aspects and effects of the organization of production. It also studies the mechanisms in how local productive systems become clusters and industrial districts and defends this model of industrial organization as a substitute for the Fordist model.

The approach from the point of view of development theory (Fuà, 1983 and 1988; Vázquez-Barquero, 1983 and 1988; Garofoli, 1983 and 1992; Coffey and Polèse, 1984 and 1985; Arocena, 1986 and 1995) examines the mechanisms that drive local economic growth. This approach recognizes that local productive systems are one of the various forms of organization of production leading to improved productivity and competitiveness of firms and territories. Economic development is subject to the laws of capital accumulation and endogenous industrialization constitutes one of the possible paths within the capitalist mode of production.

Both approaches acknowledge that endogenous development is a paradigm that adequately interprets the economic forces at work in cities and regions today. This chapter argues that the main propositions of local economic development[1] (as to increasing returns, capital accumulation, institutional flexibility and local initiative) are rooted in the main paradigms of economic development theory. Thus, various rationales and views of development converge in the theory of endogenous development.

The chapter begins with a definition of local economic development and the identification of specific features. The main theories of development are then discussed (the theories of the big push, transitional growth, dependence theory and the theory of territorial growth), in an attempt to identify the concepts and relations that have survived on into endogenous development theory. Finally, some comments will be made on the features that differentiate and characterize endogenous development theory.

The concept of local economic development

Local economic development can be defined as a process of growth and structural change, which provides more well-being to the inhabitants of a city or region, as a result of the transfer of resources from traditional to modern activities, the employment of external economies and the introduction and diffusion of innovation. The development process that takes place when the local community is able to put its development potential to work and conduct structural change, can be considered local endogenous development or, simply, endogenous development. The concept is based on the idea that localities and territories possess economic, human, institutional and cultural resources, as well as hidden economies of scale, which constitute their development potential. A productive system capable of generating increasing returns by applying available resources and introducing and diffusing innovation guarantees the creation of wealth and improved local well-being.

This concept of development combines various characteristics and features to give it a unique configuration. First of all, it must be emphasized that local economic development refers to processes of capital accumulation in specific cities and regions. Factors contributing to accumulation of capital in local productive systems are a labor supply adequately skilled for the tasks to be carried out and with a low conflict level, along with an entrepreneurial and organizational capability and a productive system where technical innovations and knowledge are diffused.

These processes of economic development are characterized by a flexible organization of production. The organization of the local productive system into firm networks contributes to generate economies of scale and reduce transaction costs, thus increasing returns and economic growth. Processes of local endogenous development arise from the productive use of development potential, which is expedited when the territory's institutions and regulatory mechanisms function efficiently. The way production is organized, the institutions, social and cultural structure and behavior codes all condition development process, promote or restrict economic dynamics and, in short, determine the specific path of development of cities and regions.

Besides these features, local endogenous development arises from a non-functional territorial view of the processes of growth and structural change. This view rests on the assumption that the territory is not merely a physical support for economic factors, activities and processes, but rather an agent of social transformation. Firms, organizations and institutions of each locality or territory are actors that stimulate processes of local growth and structural change through investment and control of these processes.

The environment in which agents make decisions concerning investment and control is transformed as processes of capital accumulation define the economic dynamic. At a given historic moment, a city or region can undertake new investment projects on its own initiative, which will put it on the path of competitive development.

The high theory of development and increasing returns

> **Proposition 1.** Endogenous development processes take place as a result of the use of externalities in local productive systems, which is conducive to increasing returns and economic growth.

This proposition is not among the assumptions of neoclassical growth theory of the 1950s and 1960s, but it has recently been restored following Romer's (1986) seminal studies.[2] But high theory of development, as Krugman (1995) likes to call it, already considered scale economies as one of the foundations of economic growth. The basis for a defense of economies of scale as promoters of local well-being through externalities can be found in Rosenstein-Rodan's (1943 and 1961) big push theory, Hirschman's (1958) interpretation of forward and backward linkages, and Perroux's (1955) theory of growth poles.

Given the fact that investors do not usually consider the external effects of their actions, Rosenstein-Rodan indicated that, from the perspective of development, "the whole of the industry to be created is to be treated and planned like one huge firm or trust" (Rosenstein-Rodan, 1943, p. 204). He proposed that the success of a development strategy depended on a minimum amount of resources being assigned to it. That is, a minimum number of coordinated investment projects must be carried out, thus forming a system of relations which would lead to the creation of a sufficiently dense network of exchanges in the economy.

The emergence of a system of complementary firms would reduce risk and ultimately constitute a special case of external economies which would therefore result in a drop in costs of each individual firm. Moreover, Rosenstein-Rodan argued, two more kinds of external economies would arise "when a system of different industries is created": strictly "Marshallian" economies external to the firm, which are generated by the growth of industry, and external economies to one industry due to the growth of other industries. He pointed out that this kind of economies would produce the same amount of profits as those of the firms. Thus, private investment would be stimulated.[3]

Rosenstein-Rodan argued that the big push theory "seems to contradict the conclusions of traditional static equilibrium theory" for three reasons. In the first place, the existence of indivisibility generated increasing returns and technological external economies due to increased technological efficiency. Second, the allocation of resources necessarily occurs in an imperfect market, in which there are often pecuniary external economies that save firms money outlays. Finally, in underdeveloped economies, markets are imperfect, and therefore the price mechanism does not provide the indications that lead to an optimum position under perfect competition.

Rosenstein-Rodan implicitly indicated that external economies come about through the relations that arise between (new) enterprise and (new) industries in the region as well as through the externalities that can be generated by new investment. It is Hirschman (1958), with his definition of forward and backward linkages, who answers the question of how external economies evolve. His main proposal indicates that the best development strategy is the one that mobilizes available resources through mechanisms, such as forward and backward linkages, that stimulate investment and channel new energies into the development process with such force that the vicious circles of development are broken. For this reason, he recommends priority be given to basic and intermediate industries since they are capable of inducing more forward and backward linkages than other productive activities.

As Krugman (1995) points out, backward linkages encourage economies of scale and pecuniary externalities when the investment of one industry produces such an intense increase in demand for goods and services from its suppliers, that these activities are, at the least, able to rise above the minimum economic scale. Forward linkages favor the rise of scale economies when an industry's investments allow customers to produce at lower cost and at a dimension that provides them more returns.

Perroux's (1955) theory of growth poles describes the mechanisms that favor the formation of technological economies. The central element is the propulsive firm, which exerts a driving force over other firms due to its innovative capacity and leadership. Its location within a specific territory creates productive and spatial imbalances and promotes development. The propulsive firm's investment decisions (in capital goods, technology and organization) exert an induced effect on associated firms. In turn, these firms make their own investment decisions. The decisions of the propulsive firm encourage diffusion of innovation horizontally and vertically throughout the network of dependent firms. Propulsive, dependent and subcontracting firms tend to locate near each other, which favors the rise and expansion of technological external economies.

The pole becomes, then, a group of firms linked together who exchange and diffuse knowledge under the influence of the decisions of the propulsive firm. The pole stimulates the diffusion of innovation and economic growth and accounts for the concentration of productive activity.

The high theory of development constitutes, therefore, one of the theoretical references of the endogenous development paradigm. They share two principles: one, that the existence of externalities is a necessary condition to the development of a city or region and the other, that relations of industrial firms give rise to a multiplicity of internal markets and, consequently, to external economies. But the theory of endogenous development differs from that of high theory of development in that the important factor in economic development is not the dimension of the firms but rather the existence of a system of firms linked through intense relations and exchanges (Becattini, 1997).

Although the high theory of development is not always explicit here, it can be admitted that both also share the idea that relations within the network not only lead to exchange of products and services among firms, but also of technological innovation and knowledge and behavior models. However, the theory of endogenous development goes on to point out that relations in local productive systems are based on the knowledge that some actors have of others, on the mutual trust that has gradually been built up and on benefits from commerce and exchange (Ottati, 1994).

Finally, endogenous development theory differs from high theory of development in that local productive systems are characterized by a system of internal networks of cooperation and competition relations among the firms (Piore and Sable, 1984). It also considers that the industrial network is a form of regulation and governance of the productive system, whose stability depends on the strength of the system of relations and exchanges within the district (Hakansson and Johanson, 1993).

The theory of transitional growth and capital accumulation

Proposition 2. Endogenous development involves processes of capital accumulation that come about as a result of the pull of resources from mature to more modern activities and the use of surplus generated in the productive process.

This proposition has its origins in classical thought, which transitional growth theory appropriates as its own with Lewis (1954 and 1958) and Fei and Ranis (1961, 1974).[4] It is based on the assumption that there will be an unlimited supply of labor at the wage level of the modern sector (identified as the industrial sector). This level is considered higher than that of the traditional sector (agriculture), which remains at a subsistence level.

Fei and Ranis contend that the central question in development resides in the gradual displacement of the center of economic activity from agrarian to industrial activities. The most typical indicator of this process would be the transfer of available labor from the subsistence sector to the modern sector. It is the difference in wages which stimulates labor mobility from one sector to another (Lewis, 1954).

The dynamic forces of the growth process are capital accumulation, technological change and labor force. The integration of these forces into the productive process of the modern sector is only possible due to the generation and availability of surplus (agricultural and industrial). According to Fei and Ranis, the fundamental causal factor of growth in the long run is the evolution of labor productivity, which depends on capital accumulation and technological change. Lewis considers that the only dynamic force is capital accumulation; technological change would be secondary to capital accumulation. The combination of both forces stimulates processes of economic growth[5] and increases the demand for labor and employment.

Transitional growth occurs due to the formation of surplus in the industrial and agricultural sectors. This surplus, once invested, leads to the absorption of labor force from the agricultural sector and generates increased production, which, once sold, gives rise to new surplus. Lewis and Fei and Ranis consider that returns originating in the industrial sector are the greatest source of funds invested in the modern sector. However, they point out that the amount of agricultural surplus (which is transferred to the industrial sector through landlords) benefits the absorption of superfluous labor from the agricultural sector[6] by industry.

Transitional growth theory constitutes a theoretical reference point for endogenous development. Studies carried out in late developed countries in southern Europe (Fuà, 1988; Vázquez-Barquero, 1988; Garofoli, 1992) show that both industrialization in non-metropolitan areas and accumulation at the local level are related to dualistic transition growth processes described by the transitional growth model, but they also incorporate other elements into the analysis.

Endogenous development and transitional growth theories are founded on the assumption of the existence of an abundant and cheap labor supply and partially share the thesis that growth and structural change in an economy often come about through the evolution of production activity from traditional to modern activities. Nevertheless, where transitional growth theory holds that there is one path of development, made up of various stages, which all economies must necessarily go through (Rostow, 1960), endogenous development theory postulates that local development can be articulated around any type of activity (agrarian, industrial or services), as long as its production units are competitive in the markets.

Contrary to the proposals of traditional development theories, studies carried out in Spain, Italy and other late developed countries demonstrate that endogenous industrial development has taken place in rural areas or, in any case, outside the influence of metropolitan centers. Development comes about through entrepreneurial initiatives based on the use of development potential already existing in the territory. It therefore constitutes a different model and, for some, an alternative to the industrial growth model based on large firms located in large cities.

Endogenous development theory coincides with transitional growth theory in observing that industrialization is frequently grounded on the existence of a proto-industrial culture of artisan and commercial activities and the availability of savings from commercial and agrarian activity.[7] However, it does not assign a strategic role to landlords in structural change, but rather emphasizes the importance of entrepreneurial capability at the local level. Small entrepreneurs emerge in favorable local conditions and proceed from commercial activities, immigration and, particularly, from agricultural activities. These primary sector activities, carried out under landholding formulas, take place in conditions favorable to the diffusion of entrepreneurial culture because it was necessary to generate surplus from the land in order to pay rent to the landowners.

The theory of endogenous development and transitional growth theory both consider that capital accumulation and technological change are the forces that foster processes of growth and structural change in local economies. But endogenous development theory argues that one of the factors accounting for accumulation processes in local economies is often the use of human resources with relatively low wage levels. Flexible labor (such as home work, temporary jobs or informal work) the use of female labor, the diffusion of cooperatives and the low-conflict behavior of unions (workers are very integrated into the local culture) keep labor costs relatively low. This of course means that the rate of returns of local firms can reach a level that favors accumulation in the local environment.

Dependence theory and local control of development

> **Proposition 3.** Endogenous development is characterized by the use of existing development potential through the initiative and, in any case, under the control of local actors.

To a large extent, this proposition is also shared by the high theory of development and transitional growth theory, particularly in closed models. However, dependence theory rejects this proposition in regard to local control of development processes. The theory of dependence (Cardoso, 1971 and 1972; Frank, 1966 and 1967; Santos, 1968 and 1970a; Sunkel, 1969 and 1973; Furtado, 1964 and 1970; Amin, 1970 and 1973)[8] considered that the international economic system was a result of a historical process. Economies (and social groups) were integrated into this process as capital accumulation progressed. Countries, regions and cities joined this process in a hierarchical manner, thus establishing the center and periphery of the system.

The fundamental characteristic of peripheral economies is a dependent structure, which incapacitates them to follow an autonomous and self-sustained development pattern.[9] Industrial development depends on the importation and adaptation of technology, which is created and controlled by large multinational firms in advanced economies. Thus, dependent theorists conclude that technological dependence is the dominant form of dependence at present.

The rationale of dependence theory rejects the possibility of local endogenous development. Its most radical version (Frank, Amin and Santos) did not allow for spontaneous development processes in peripheral cities, regions and countries since insufficient internal demand, technological dependence and a productive system oriented toward external markets would impede capital accumulation.[10] But, the moderates (Cardoso, Furtado, Sunkel) maintained that specific forms of dependent development could be possible in certain conditions, even though they could not be extended to all the periphery.[11]

This age-old discussion recently arose again when globalists (Harrison, 1994; Amin, 1989 and 1993; Amin and Robins, 1991) and localists (Piore and Sabel, 1984; Sabel, 1989; Hirst and Zeitlin, 1989a and 1989b; Zeitlin, 1989; Pyke *et al.*, 1990) debated as to whether flexible specialization systems were an organizational alternative to the Fordist model, in crisis since the mid-1960s.

The globalists, defenders of the thesis of the "blockade" of dependent development processes, indicate that globalization has stimulated the centralization and concentration of capital and markets and that small and medium-sized firms (including those that form local enterprise systems, clusters and industrial districts) are still under the technological and commercial control of large firms. This means that changes that come about through the restructuring of cities, regions and countries are conditioned by the globalization process and, therefore, by the strategy of large multinational corporations.

When the discussion is defined in terms of local economic development and the dominant mode of development, which Castells (1996) calls "informational," the analysis should be broadened. It should deal with questions such as change in the ways production is organized and the contribution of organization of production to economic dynamics, the meaning of technological dependence today, the control of transformations in the international economic system and the distribution of power on a global scale.

The central area of conflict between both visions lies in the role of social forces in leading economic transformation. Where the reductionist position of dependence theory maintained that external firms dominate capital accumulation processes, endogenous development theory holds that local productive systems, a network of economic and social agents, are founded on a system of economic, social, political and institutional relations capable of stimulating growth and structural change.

The first implication of this fact is that the industrial network of local firm systems and industrial districts provides the productive system with the conditions necessary to generate economies of scale and increasing returns. Furthermore, the territory responds strategically to the challenges of competition and the city or region comes to agreements with outside firms and organizations through the network of local actors, thus limiting the negative effects of dependent development.

In today's scenario, the location of large external firms in a city or region does not necessarily imply that inward investment will have a predatory effect on the territory. As will be shown in Chapter 9, some innovative firms (such as those producing quality goods with high-tech content, differentiated goods or specialized services for specific tastes) have been led by globalization and increasing competition to abandon functional strategies, in which the territory was, at most, a place where their plants could be located and local resources exploited. They have substituted them with territorial strategies that seek places with specific resources and pursue a greater adaptation of the operating units to local contexts. Consequently, in certain conditions the territorial strategies of external firms and the economic strategies of the territory may converge.

Dependence theory and endogenous development theory share the belief that technological dependence becomes an important constraint on the development of peripheral economies. However, the concept and assessment of the relation between technological change and economic growth differ.

The theory of endogenous development recognizes the difference between radical and incremental innovation and contends that case studies prove that local development processes profit from the adaptation of technology and gradual improvement of products and processes. Often small engineering changes integrated into productive processes in order to incorporate available resources more efficiently, or changes in product design and specifications in order to meet customer needs, offer an adequate solution to adapting local production to the markets.

The diffusion of technology has traditionally followed a hierarchical pattern both in terms of production (the relations of large firms with small firms) and space (large urban centers as opposed to small and medium-sized cities and rural areas). Recently, this pattern has been altered and firms in local productive systems have direct access to international product markets and technology-producing centers, and they import equipment goods directly. That is to say, in these times of globalization and increasing market competition, the integration of local productive systems into the international division of labor leads them to break, to a great extent, with hierarchical relational patterns and perform within a space of multiple hierarchies.

Dependence theory and endogenous development theory both consider that each territory has its own economic trajectory and that not all territories will always behave in an innovative way. For local production systems to be innovative, they must be able to introduce and develop new productive paradigms within the local productive system. For this reason, local firm systems must behave creatively and deploy their learning capacity, something not all territories are able to do.

However, endogenous theory adds that all cities and regions, whether they be in the North or the South, center or periphery, will gain or lose in function of their human and natural resources and of their links to the global economy. Given that the global economy is asymmetric and polycentric (Castells, 1996), the path of development is determined by their ability to respond and adapt to the challenges of market competition. The fact that a city or region is located in the South or on the periphery does condition economic dynamics to some extent, but does not determine them.

This brings us to one of the central questions in processes of endogenous development, that is, the balance of power between large external firms and territories. Endogenous development theory maintains that the way local productive systems are organized contributes to making local economic development processes efficient. This is not necessarily incompatible with the proposition of dependence theory, which states that some multinational firms are at the center of power and therefore lead and control momentous transformations in the global economy. These two views refer to different dimensions of the analysis. One refers to growth and structural change in local economies and thus to the mode of development, while dependence theory relates to political and institutional factors of the capitalist mode of production. Therefore, at least theoretically, there is nothing to prevent local actors from controlling the local economic dynamic as long as it is compatible with the evolution of the economic system.

Territorial development theory and local initiatives

Proposition 4. Endogenous development refers to economic and social transformation generated as a result of the response of cities and regions to the challenges of competition, in which local actors take up strategies and initiatives aimed at improving the well-being of local society.

This proposition revolves around a central idea in endogenous development policy: the dynamic and transformation of local economies are necessarily anchored in the forces for change within the local community. Territorial development theory considers that development from outside is a strategy that has been demonstrated to fail in all kinds of economies. For this reason, the only feasible solution is local response to the specific challenges of increasing competition in each locality or territory (Gore, 1984). Territorial development theory (Friedmann and Weaver, 1979; Stöhr and Tödtling, 1979; Sachs, 1980; Stöhr and Taylor, 1981) is built on the idea that each territory is the result of its history. Over time, the institutional, economic, organizational environment has gradually been shaped to give the territory a unique identity. It is this identity that guides it in the search for strategic answers to the challenges of globalization.

Economic development of cities and regions (and the reduction of regional imbalances) is greatly facilitated by the recent transfer of competence to local communities. Stöhr and Tödtling (1979) argue that international experience in developed and underdeveloped economies demonstrates that when decision-making capacity is given to local organizations and institutions, they are then able to employ the local development potential and integrate the factors and forces coming from more developed regions.

In this way, an alternative road to development from outside is opened to cities since they can adopt their own development strategies. Friedmann and Weaver (1979) advocate change in the development paradigm, abandoning the functional view that considered the territory a mere spatial support for investment and adopting a territorial view. Thus territories take on an active role in development processes through their investment initiatives and the participation of the population in the design of development policies. In this line of reasoning, Stöhr and Taylor (1981) advocate "bottom-up" development strategies, which open a wide range of opportunities to individuals, social groups and local institutions and communities, and allow them to mobilize their potentials and resources. Development, from this point of view, integrates initiatives of local firms and institutions with those pushing in from outside.

The greater part of the proposals of territorial development theory defend those local development policies capable of overcoming the negative effects of industrialization and of fostering those activities that will fulfill the basic needs of the population. To this purpose, they propose initiatives aimed at keeping the population in the territory and maintaining links with the local community, initiatives that encourage the creation and development of small and medium-sized firms and promote peasant agriculture. In the final analysis, territorial development theory constitutes an alternative to the traditional model of industrial development.

Territorial development theory is, therefore, one of the basic theoretical references of endogenous development theory. Both theories share two key methodological principles: they have the same concept of economic space and they give priority to bottom-up action in development policy.

Both theories describe territory as a network of development actors, who actively safeguard the interests and integrity of the territory as it undergoes growth and structural change. Both theories consider that the territory does not necessarily have to accept external decisions that global firms try to impose, but rather is able to react strategically in the face of challenges and take action aimed at achieving its own objectives. It is possible to regulate relations between external firms and the territory and stimulate local economic development through planning agreements between large firms, associations of small firms, central and regional administrations and the highest level of management of the city/region.

Furthermore, both theories agree in accepting that each and every territory has its own development potential, which makes a different path to growth. Thus, each city or region has a unique productive system, a labor market, a specific way to organize production, entrepreneurial capacity and technological know-how, an endowment of natural resources and infrastructures, a social, political and institutional system, tradition and culture through which local economic dynamics evolve.

However, the proposals of the territorial view of development run the risk of subsiding into localism, as occurs with Friedmann and Douglas' (1978) agropolitan development strategy. These authors postulated the creation of local economies, with unique local markets, independent of the export production systems typical of most economies of developing countries. These local economies would integrate rural with urban development, the country with the city.[12]

Like dependence theory, the position of endogenous development theory differs from the territorial view in that it approaches the analysis in terms of an open model and considers that economies are integrated into international relations systems. But endogenous development theory further argues that the economy of each city or region is embedded within the country's system of economic, social and institutional relations, though it agrees that the local growth path is dependent on its endowment of resources and the local cultural identity.

Contrary to endogenous development theory, territorial development theory does not explicitly define the model of capital accumulation. Rather it offers a body of proposals, often of a voluntaristic nature, that do not contribute to understanding the mechanisms behind growth and structural change nor the financial resources through which policy measures will be implemented.

Finally, endogenous development theory conceives development in strategic terms. The capacity for self-organization leads cities and regions to respond in a unique and differentiated way to needs arising within the economic and social environment, through the strategies of economic, social and institutional agents in the local community.

The complexity of endogenous development

The foregoing discussion shows how endogenous development theory is deeply rooted in the main paradigms of economic development theory which, over the 1950s, 1960s and 1970s, have dominated theoretical debate and inspired policy in the area of economic development. It shares a large part of the content of these paradigms and incorporates several of their propositions and ideas.

From the theories of high development and transitional growth it retrieves the mechanisms which facilitate capital accumulation and growth in market economies. From dependence theory, it takes the idea that approaches to development must necessarily include a systemic view of the processes that link economic, social, political and institutional aspects into an organized structure. From territorial development theory, it reclaims the idea that development agents (not social classes) are the actors who make investment decisions and control the processes of change through local initiatives. (See the summary presented in Table 3.1.)

In reviewing the various development paradigms, some of the elements of endogenous development theory have been identified. As opposed to the theories of the big push and transitional growth, endogenous

Table 3.1 Theoretical roots of endogenous development

Endogenous development characteristics	The high theory of development	Dualistic growth theory	Dependence theory	Territorial development theory
Development potential				
Resources	X	X	X	X
Indivisibilities	X	–	–	–
Capital accumulation				
Application of surplus	X	X	X	–
Innovation	X	X	X	–
Flexible labor market	–	X	X	X
External economies of scale				
Organization of production	X	–	–	–
Networking	–	–	–	–
Urban relations	–	–	X	–
Institutional context				
Institutional flexibility	–	X	X	–
Organization of society	–	X	X	–
Local action				
Local initiatives	–	–	–	X
Local control of development	–	–	–	X

X = Convergence between the main development paradigms and the endogenous development theory.

development theory understands economic growth not as a succession of equilibria as proposed by neoclassical theory, but rather as a process characterized by uncertainty and chance. Thus, depending on the firms' technological trajectories and the decisions of local actors, the economic dynamics of the city/region can follow alternative development paths.

In contrast to dependence theories, endogenous development theory holds that the growth of a city/region is not determined by its peripheral nature or the level of development at a given point in time. It is path dependent, but it involves the array of natural and human resources and the firms', cities' and/or regions' ability to react and respond to the challenges of competition at each historical moment.

Finally, endogenous development theory differs from the position of territorial development theory in that it contends that cities and regions move within a global strategic environment where they compete within the international economic system. Cities and regions are organizations with strengths and weaknesses, and they carry out their activity within a changing external environment, which presents new challenges at every turn. In order to achieve their development objectives, they define strategies for action that lead them to satisfy the needs and demands of their firms and citizens in the face of these challenges.

The foregoing discussion leads us to consider, as Arocena (1995) proposes, that endogenous development is a complex concept in which various rationales and views of development come together. Without a doubt, at the heart of endogenous development is the rationale of the capitalist mode of production, with the laws that govern processes of capital accumulation and income distribution. However, we are dealing with systemic processes in which the structural components act as constraints, although, as the environment is transformed, the value of resources and relations among variables change, making it possible to identify alternative development paths. This is feasible because the local actors behave strategically in function of the opportunities that appear in the competitive scenarios of an increasingly global economy.

Part II

The mechanisms of endogenous development

4 Networking and the organization of development

One of the central issues of endogenous development theory is that local productive systems and firm networks constitute one of the mechanisms through which processes of growth and structural change in local and regional economies take place. It was argued in foregoing chapters that increasing returns to scale can be generated when relations and interaction among firms allow them to employ economies of scale which are hidden in productive and urban systems. This is one of the potentials of local economic development.

The question, then, revolves around the way local firms are organized. The notion of network can be applied here since the organization of local firms reflects the relation between entrepreneurs and firms. Research carried out on entrepreneurship in small and medium-sized firms, on the one hand, and on production and market organization, on the other, has assigned an analytic value to the concept of network. This value converts network models into a useful instrument to account for certain phenomena such as the dynamics of entrepreneurial organizations and local productive systems.

This chapter attempts to show how the concepts of network and networking allow us to analyze some basic mechanisms of endogenous development processes and discover to what extent categories such as the industrial district are of use in understanding endogenous development processes. But it will also be argued that when large firms adopt more flexible forms of organization they too can play an active role in endogenous development processes.

The chapter begins with the definition of the concept of network, which will then serve to account for processes, such as the emergence and development of entrepreneurial capacity or exchange of goods, information and knowledge, which are a product of relations between firms and territory. Next, after commenting on the formation of networks and strategic alliances among firms, the chapter turns to some thoughts on the importance of fostering networks through local development policy. Finally, interactions that exist between flexible organization of production and the other processes that explain endogenous development are examined.

Networking, competitiveness and innovation

Economic, social and institutional activity is based on relations among individuals, firms and organizations. Therefore, a great variety of networks can be specified. On the one hand, there are personal networks and networks of firms with agents in the immediate environment; here relations, although commercial at times, tend to be informal and casual. On the other hand, local productive systems show a special type of network defined by their deep roots in the territory and commercial relations mainly built on trust. Moreover, alliances and agreements have in recent decades proliferated among firms whose relations are of a contractual nature.

A network can be defined as a system of relations and/or contacts that link firms and actors together and whose content can refer to material goods, information or technology. From the perspective of economic activity, a network is the set of relations among firms or entrepreneurs, which facilitate the exchange of goods, services and information (Malecki and Tootle, 1996).

Whatever the definition adopted,[1] relations among entrepreneurs and actors may have the following features, among others (Grabher, 1993). In the first place, a network refers to transactions within the context of reciprocity (not to market exchanges or hierarchical relations within a firm). Second, these are interdependent relations between actors and firms; they are not relations of independence, as in the market, or of dependence, as in the hierarchic firms and organizations.

Furthermore, networks refer to systems of multiple interconnections and of responses and reactions of firms and actors. Networks are characterized by a series of weak links whose interaction strengthens the network through access to information, interactive learning and diffusion of innovation. And finally, relations among firms and actors can be asymmetric, of a hierarchical nature, when power becomes a functional element in the network's performance.

Networks can vary greatly. Therefore, in order to describe precisely their content and importance, it is necessary to classify them according to the kind of relations established among the firms and actors (Monsted, 1995). First, relations can be formal, that is explicit, related to decisions on strategic goals of persons and organizations, or they can be informal, that is, tacit or spontaneous, specifically, personal contacts among actors and firms. The former would refer to relations with organizations such as banks or service firms, while the latter would involve interaction of a casual nature with families, friends, colleagues or ex-employees.

Firm networks may also refer to commercial transactions, that is, to the exchange of goods and services, which facilitates relations with suppliers and clients, or to technical relations based on the exchange of codified information on technological applications, and of product, process, organization or market innovations. Since the latter depend on technical cultures, the contacts and relations are based on specific rules that govern professional and personal ties.

From the specific point of view of economic development and entrepreneurial activity, it is important to establish the distinction between personal networks and firm networks (Brown and Butler, 1993; Johannisson, 1987; Johannisson and Nilsson, 1989). Personal networks formed by individuals provide information and, over time, resources that are necessary for the emergence and start-up of a firm, but they also favor the exchange of goods and knowledge within local productive systems. Firm networks, on the other hand, provide technical advice and information on business, financial and material resources and they even lead to strategic alliances against rival firms and groups. The notion of network, its characteristics and typology, brings us to the concept of industrial networks,[2] which are of particular interest to local development, as we have indicated in Chapter 2.

Contrary to the behavior of personal networks, in industrial or firm networks activities and resources have a central role. Relations of interdependence are established among these activities, in the sense that the results of each activity affect all the others within the network. Although changes in activity are usually slow, learning acquired during processes of structural change is strategic because it favors adjustment within the network. When the actors control activities, information and resources in a network, they indirectly exert influence (and eventually power) over the other actors through the interdependence that exists among them.

Hakansson and Johanson (1993) point out that the structure of an industrial network depends on the nature and organization of the connections and relations established among actors and activities. Technical and cultural factors condition the structure somewhat, but its formation and transformation depend on interaction among the actors. Thus, the system of relations and connections among activities and firms evolves gradually. For this reason, it could be said that networks are a product of history. However, the system of economic relations within the network is based on the knowledge that some actors possess concerning others, on mutual trust. Although trust is not likely to figure in the firms' calculations because it is a non-economic variable, it is, however, crucial to economic relations.

As Granovetter (1992) indicates, trust is needed for the day-to-day operation of entrepreneurial productive activity and of institutional activities in general, but it becomes essential to economic exchanges due to temporal and spatial constraints. For this reason, without mutual trust there could be no networks, nor local productive systems nor endogenous development processes, according to Monsted (1995). Relations of trust reinforce business arrangements and cooperation among firms. They depend on personal contacts among the actors and they are reinforced over time due to their positive outcomes. On occasion, mutual trust can play a stra-tegic role in business because it is always a reference and often supplants professional evaluations when initiating or developing a business.

Finally, Hakansson and Johanson argue that the industrial network can be understood as a form of regulation and governance of the productive system in that it controls and directs its activities through decisions made by the actors who condition productive activities.

The decision-making of each firm and actor within a network, as opposed to a market or hierarchy, is motivated by specific interests such as trust, instead of price or norm. External forces that impel actors to make decisions are the specific interactions of firms and actors within the network, as opposed to supply and demand relations in the market or hierarchical relations in the large public or private organizations.

This is a kind of governance within the real world, along with other forms, such as the market or the hierarchy. As we have indicated in the first part of this book, local productive systems and industrial districts base part of their relations and efficiency on systems of multiple exchanges taking place among firms in cities and urban centers. Therefore, in the productive system, networking relations among local firms occur at the same time as trade relations between firms and hierarchical relations within the firms themselves.

Networks have an intense internal dynamic as a result of economic rela-tions arising from exchanges and the open nature of the system. This dynamic involves constant reorganization of the networks and, therefore, structural change. Since changes and transformations come about slowly, networks show a certain stability, which allows the firms to meet market demands and adapt to business conditions in a world in continuous trans-formation. But it should be remembered that networks are a form of gov-ernance, continually off-balance as a result of the decisions made by the actors in their interrelations. Within the network, the difference in behav-ior from one actor to another establishes internal power relations which can strain the performance of the network itself and its efficiency.

Firm networks and endogenous development

The formation of firm networks plays a key role in endogenous develop-ment processes since it conditions the start-up and growth of firms, dif-fusion of innovations and, ultimately, structural change itself. Since Birch (1979) launched his interpretation of the birth and death of firms, a growing part of the literature on local economic development attempts to account for the emergence and development of firms. In the 1980s a significant number of theories, such as the theories of recession push, income growth and technological change, were associated with the behav-ior of variables or factors of a strategic nature in the productive adjust-ment. Keeble and Weber (1986) point out that these three factors provide a convincing explanation for the birth of new firms and entrepreneurial development in Europe since the end of the 1970s. Maillat (1990), on his part, specifies that, while recession push theory admits that the phenomenon of emerging small and medium-sized firms is of a temporary nature, the other two theories are founded on long-term structural considerations of economic transformations.

Those explanations of endogenous development that hold that local firm systems have been one of the decisive instruments in productive dynamics, particularly in late developed countries in southern Europe (Garofoli, 1992), are also to be included among the interpretations of entrepreneurial development in recent decades. Above, it was pointed out that small local firms have specialized in the production of reduced series, adjusted to the demand for modern products, by employing the technology necessary to compete in the markets. Normally, their strategies are based on the differentiation of production and the speed of their commercial response. Local firm systems become one of the forms of flexible organization of production, particularly in the most advanced cities and regions.

All these interpretations show the variety of the factors accounting for the birth and development of firms and the way in which they are associated with the characteristics of local productive systems (Keeble, 1990; Chisholm, 1990). At any rate, the birth of entrepreneurs and small firms depends upon the existence of a personal network, as Johannisson (1995) points out. Made up of an increasing number of trustworthy persons, people known before the idea was born and evolved into a project, the network helps mature the firm project and initiate development by providing information and personal support.

The context in which the entrepreneurial undertaking takes place facilitates the reinforcement of firm relations with the external (eventually global) environment, for the following reasons, among others (Johannisson *et al.*, 1994). First of all, the local context provides the resources and relations necessary for the development of productive activity. Moreover, it reduces the degree of uncertainty that characterizes productive activity and provides entrepreneurs and managers with the self-esteem necessary to take the risks involved in entrepreneurial projects. Finally, the economic, social and institutional context provides local firms with the elements necessary to identify and take advantage of opportunities arising in the markets.

This approach is opposed to the neoclassical view which considers entrepreneurs as rivals who relate to each other through market signs (price/costs) in their pursuit of profit. The emergence and growth of entrepreneurship and organizational capability within a territory is the result of a joint process, in which the network of personal contacts and strategic actions leads entrepreneurs to develop business projects. On the other hand, these networks of contacts and relations among firms have become strategic in attaining greater productivity and competitiveness in an economy, since the processes of technological change and diffusion of innovation are increasingly interdependent and interactive. As Malecki (1991) has pointed out, networks offer multiple means to learn and generate new knowledge.

At present, firms more often improve their technological capacities through direct learning from clients and suppliers, by seeking out new technologies and, in general, by employing the knowledge from firms with whom they relate (Malecki and Tootle, 1996). Therefore, the characteristics and structure of the networks that support local firms condition endogenous development.

Interactive learning has three dimensions: technical, communicative and social learning (Lundvall, 1993b). Technical learning takes on different forms for users or producers. On the one hand, users must first know about technological opportunities, then understand their potential utility and, finally, develop their own know-how. Throughout all of these steps, the relations with the producer play an important role. Producers, on the other hand, must be aware of the needs of users, how they can satisfy these needs with specific technology and, finally, how they can learn from the problems that users encounter in incorporating the technology. To be smooth, efficient and beneficial, relations between producers and users should be based on adequate and sufficient communication in which both share technical knowledge and organizational strategies. For this reason, users and producers must learn to communicate through technical and organizational codes. Moreover, users and producers need to know each other's goals and economic situation and agree on the norms that will govern the relation if technical learning is to take place and develop.

The introduction and diffusion of innovation is, therefore, a process involving significant uncertainties in firms as to information on new products and processes, how to apply them and the results that will be obtained, and the performance of relations between users and producers. Innovation means new spending, which also increases the risks faced by firms. For this reason, the context in which the firm operates and the structure and relations of the network converts decisions by firms to invest in and adopt innovation into a "collective, socialized process," thus reducing the risks and costs of introducing innovation (Camagni, 1991).

Informal exchange of information that takes place among firms in a network facilitates the acquisition and filtering of technology and market information. Networking also generates a collective learning process on the part of decision-makers, technicians and workers of the various firms in the network and produces informal coordination of decisions through personal relations. All of this leads to reduced production costs, improvement in economic results and greater efficiency in those investment decisions concerning technological change. The network ultimately contributes to diffuse innovation within the local productive system. Therefore, since the neoclassical model attributes many of these functions to the market, one could say that the network is an extension and concretization of the market.

In sum, as Rosenstein-Rodan and Hirschman anticipated, relations among firms facilitate the exchange of products and services as well as of technological knowledge and behavior codes. Due to mutual trust, firm networks stimulate interaction among firms and entrepreneurs, which leads to the cropping up of hidden external economies of scale. As a consequence, therefore, of economic transactions among firms, formal and informal information exchange within the network and collective processes of diffusion of technological innovation, increasing returns to scale can be generated in local economies thus reinforcing growth and structural change processes.

Industrial districts

The birth and growth of networks of industrial firms is of interest in the analysis of endogenous development processes because of its strategic value in improving productivity in local productive systems and competitiveness of cities and regions. Thus, the revitalization over the last 25 years of local and regional economies whose productive systems revolved around networks of small and medium-sized firms awoke great interest.[3]

In particular, cases from late developed countries in southern Europe, such as the Terza Italia in Italy, the Valencia Region in Spain or the Val do Ave and Northern region of Portugal have been identified and analyzed. But other cases have also been studied in various kinds of territories. In Latin America, studies were carried out in Rafaela in Santa Fé, Argentina, Novo Hamburgo in Río Grande do Sul in Brazil or León in Guanajuato, Mexico. In economies currently undergoing processes of industrialization, areas such as Sialkot in Pakistan, Tiruppur in India have been examined as have been industrialized territories, such as Baden-Württemberg in Germany, Jutland in Denmark, Smaland in Sweden or Silicon Valley, Orange County and Route 128 in the United States.

The functioning of local productive systems was interpreted in terms of industrial districts as described by Marshall (1890 and 1919). In Italy and in late developed countries in general, local productive systems were formed by networks of small and medium-sized firms specialized in the production of the same kind of goods. Technology and designs were gradually introduced into the local productive system as a consequence of firm performance. Although firms sold their production in national and international markets, firm networks in small cities were rooted in the local culture and artisan tradition.

The analogies with Marshallian industrial districts led to the recovery of this concept, once it was adapted to the facts revealed by the case studies. It is understood as a cluster of many similar, small firms, located in a common defined territorial settlement (the industrial city), which interact to form a system of relations leading to the generation of external economies of scale. This definition contains two dimensions, one of an urban nature, associated with the clustering of firms in a city, and a sectoral dimension, manifested through relations among firms. The concentration of firms in a territory facilitates the sharing of the same workforce, the same public social services and transportation and communications links, which leads to the reduction of the firm unit cost of production and the use of agglomeration economies, external economies formed in the city.

One of the most characteristic features of the notion of district is the organization of the local productive system, that is, the way production is organized through a network of small and medium-sized firms. The virtue of the local productive system is not the size of the firms, that is, the fact that the firms are small, as the most Utopian would have it. Rather it is the fact that relations have spontaneously been built up and a network of firms has been formed to make productive organization efficient and competitive.

Network specialization in a product or line of related products and firm specialization in the various stages of the productive process or of the finished product leads to the formation of a system of multiple exchanges. These are conducive to scale economies in the network as a result of the formation of scales in the production system. Moreover, the actual physical exchange of information and products means reduced transaction costs for firms and favors the diffusion of knowledge, all of which generates non-commercial scale economies.

These advantages are not a consequence of the internal organization of local firms but rather of the organization of the entire local productive system. They lead to improved competitiveness of the local production system in the markets, just as large firms are able to produce a great quantity of goods and services and internally obtain scale economies and reduce transaction costs. Local firm systems, however, are linked to a territory in which exchanges among firms in the productive system and relations with the milieu take place.

In this way, the industrial district becomes an integrated system of firms, which means that each one of them will benefit from economies associated with productive specialization and proximity. Although the role of proximity for Marshall is not clear, Camagni's (1991) interpretation can be accepted. He states that physical proximity facilitates the exchange of information, homogeneity in cultural and psychological attitudes, frequent personal contacts and cooperation, and mobility of the factors in a relatively reduced framework.

A central element in Marshall's analysis is the beneficial effect on the network of establishments when they are located in areas with a specific industrial atmosphere (Grabher, 1993). There is an availability of labor qualified for the tasks at hand and firms can benefit from the exchange of ideas and knowledge generated within the network through personal contacts and the exchange of resources and products. A great supply of labor with specific skills within dominant productive activities is concentrated in industrial districts and skills are upgraded as the district develops and knowledge is accumulated within the local firms and productive network. This constitutes one of the most significant endogenous resources and is an important pull for inward investment. Moreover, the industrial atmosphere encourages the diffusion of information on techniques, materials, processes, optimal use of machinery and capital goods, and markets, all of which leads to an improvement in technical knowledge and diffusion of innovation among the firms. As Bellandi (1986) maintains, although Marshall's studies did not include a theory of innovation, it could be said that they anticipated some of the ideas that characterize present-day theories on the diffusion of innovation.

Industrial atmosphere constitutes, without a doubt, a critical element for local development due to the advantages it provides to all the firms, but, as was stated in earlier chapters, it is the social and institutional factors that are decisive in the performance of local firms and productive systems.[4] The organization of the firm system, external economies and the industrial atmosphere are grounded in historical and cultural structures of the district, as Courlet and Soulage (1995) remind us. That is to say, it is precisely the articulation of economic, social and cultural dimensions of a territory that characterizes the concept of industrial districts. Becattini (1997) maintains that local firms are the interface through which the productive system is integrated into the system of social and cultural relations of the district.

Industrial districts are, then, made up of a system of internal networks in which relations of cooperation and competition take place. The core of its performance is the organization of the productive system into a firm network. Networking fosters the emergence of externalities through multiple internal markets and meeting points where relations among firms, suppliers and clients are established.

If districts endure over time, it is on account of the intense links established among enterprises, culture and territory. But, belonging to an industrial district and benefiting from external economies of scale does not guarantee a permanent competitive edge, since globalization of the economic space increases competition, reduces relative advantages provided by external economies and forces local productive systems to adjust. Industrial districts, then, find they must renovate and specialize, in the constant pursuit of diversification and articulation of old and new activities (Becattini, 1987).

The large firm and endogenous development

Industrial districts and local productive systems, then, are efficient ways to organize production that lead to economies of scale and scope and reduction of production and transaction costs. Thus, in contrast to some proposals, the most important conclusion to the debate waging over the last two decades is that firm size is not the most relevant factor, but rather whether the organization of production is flexible and allows firms to respond strategically to the needs and demands arising from the economic dynamic in the present stage of the economic cycle.

Therefore, one can propose that large firms are also able to play a dynamic role in endogenous development processes when their organization is flexible and when their strategies stimulate relations between the operational units of the spatial network and the territories where they are located. In fact, the organization and strategies of large firms have gradually moved in this direction over the last few decades. Increased market competition has modified the organization of large innovative firms and opens a new direction for their strategies. These firms have abandoned functional strategies in which the territory was merely a place to locate their plants, to adopt more flexible forms of organization and territorial strategies that seek greater integration of the operating units into local contexts (Dupuy and Gilly, 1997).

Modern industrial enterprise has grown larger and has improved organization in order to reduce costs, increase efficiency in purchasing and marketing, improve their products and processes and allocate resources more effectively in order to meet the challenge of competition. This was possible due to the introduction of organizational and technological changes, which led them to exploit economies of scale and scope and reduce transaction costs (Chandler, 1990). These changes came about gradually as increased competition required that enterprises adapt to changing technologies and markets. At first, investments were marked for enlarging production facilities, then for the creation of marketing distribution and purchasing networks and, finally, to recruit and organize the managers necessary to oversee these activities. This gave rise to managerial hierarchies along functional lines, each function assigned to a different department.[5]

Leading firms in the various activities and products acquired competitive advantages and power which made them oligopolistic and, occasionally, monopolistic. In order to expand market share and reduce production costs, modern firms have implemented various production and organizational strategies,[6] among which decentralization of productive activities to other cities and regions by means of direct investment stands out.

Thus, for decades large firms were preferentially organized following the Fordist model, which is characterized by a highly hierarchical organization, division of labor according to clearly defined and limited functions, vertical integration and functional and productive decentralization. The need to attain scale economies in production, purchasing and sales, following the logic of hierarchical organization of firm functions, limited the integration of branch plants into the local production system. The direction of branch plants had very little maneuverability in promoting endogenization of production activities within the local milieu.

In recent decades, new competitive conditions have required large firms to introduce innovations, principles and practices that lead them to increase organizational efficiency (Cotorruelo Menta, 1996). Examples are: organization according to enterprise objectives and not according to the functions of the departments; management of the time required for supplying raw material and intermediate goods, as well as for the delivery of products to clients; production according to firm capacity along with subcontracting of tasks and functions in which the firm is not specialized. Large firms have instrumented more flexible modes of organization and strategies that allow for more efficient relations among the enterprise's various operating units and between the firm and its suppliers and clients. Thus, the branch plant's ties to local firms and institutions of the host cities and regions are strengthened (Veltz, 1993).

At present, large innovative firms have adopted complex organization structures[7] (Bueno Campos, 1992). The Fordist model of the centralized, functionally departmentalized or the "U-form" structure was abandoned in favor of more flexible forms of organizations. Initially, firms adopted the "M-form" organization with various divisions (Williamson, 1981; Chandler, 1982). M-form organization introduced a divide at the management level and at the level of the firms' value chain and decomposed complex business structures into operating units (see Figure 4.1).

The process of evolution of the enterprise structure led to the formation of conglomerates and multinational enterprises.[8] Finally, this process led to a variety of organizational modes among which could be emphasized the federal organization model, the quasi-arborescent organization, the clover-leaf organization and the molecular organization related to market segments (Aoki, 1990; Handy, 1990).

The adoption of more flexible organizational models has led to improvement in the efficiency and competitiveness of large enterprises and development of the territorial dimension of firm strategies. Thus, networks of subsidiary plants now show greater functional autonomy and more integration within the territory. As Amin and Tomaney (1997) point out, firms that operate in highly competitive market segments employ strategies based on integrated production, reduce the separation among the functions of management, production, marketing and R&D, and establish stronger and better linkages with suppliers.

There remain firms with hierarchical structures whose organization follows the old Fordist model. But when innovative firms are organized

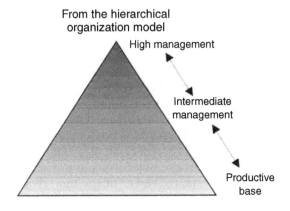

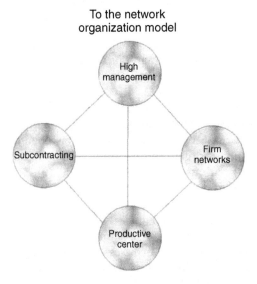

Figure 4.1 Changes in the firm organization model.

more flexibly and adopt competitive strategies, integration into local productive systems and stronger relations with local firms and institutions become priority objectives for the outside firm's branch plants.

The most flexible forms of organization allow branch plants greater autonomy and responsibility in product definition and development, control of production processes and in marketing and distribution. They reduce vertical relations between departments and encourage cooperation among the various units and of these units with headquarters. Thus, the management of branch plants acquires greater freedom and actively participates in decision-making affecting the local productive unit.

The new forms of organization, production and management have significant territorial implications since the competitive strategies of large enterprises have become a factor contributing to the location of external operating units (Cotorruelo Menta, 1996). Innovative firms tend to locate their plants in places where the local attributes of the territory provide competitive advantages. They are attracted to locations with high-quality resources and infrastructures, innovative capacity, a local firm system susceptible to generating external economies of scale and to producing goods and services in increasingly competitive conditions, and an institutional context that favors the development of an entrepreneurial climate inclined toward cooperation and competition. In general, these attributes of host territories lead firms to improve efficiency and maintain or increase their market share. In turn, the large enterprises would protect the local environment, contribute to the upgrading of human resources and facilitate diffusion of innovation and entrepreneurial know-how among local firms.

One could conclude that modern large enterprises may be catalysts in local economic development. Inward investment would aid the start-up and development of local firms through their relations with local suppliers. Branch plants would give rise to widespread diffusion of innovation as a result of more functions being carried out locally (including at times those of R&D) and of local exchanges. They would also foster sustainable development through their interest in the availability of quality local resources.[9]

Networks and strategic alliances

A great variety of types of networks can be described from the point of view of their complexity and the way interrelations are formalized. These range from personal networks to informal and explicit firm networks, explicit networks of firms with communication codes and others where the members of the network know each other well and also use communication codes (Bramanti and Senn, 1993). The first two cases refer to more tacit networks incorporated into the territory with low intensity power relations, while the last two refer to functional networks and strategic alliances in which members have made substantial commitments.

In recent years, strategic agreements and alliances among innovative firms in industries such as electronics, semi-conductors, software or telecommunications have increased. This has given rise to networks whose goal is to synergize firms in order to respond to the formidable challenges of innovation in times of the informational mode of development (Castells, 1996; Harrison, 1994; Camagni, 1991; Grabher, 1993).

Strategic alliances are not new in the world of entrepreneurial organization and management; cartels or agreements among oligopolistic firms have existed for a long time. But different and more sophisticated forms of cooperation, instrumented through joint ventures, mutual capital sharing and agreements on joint research, have greatly multiplied since the 1980s. These alliances are formed to carry out specific projects affecting products, markets and production processes over fixed periods of time (Dunning, 1993). They give rise to functional firm networks located in different regions and/or countries.

Strategic alliances are more and more frequent in technology-intensive productive activities because the economic dynamic and the development of technology markets impose new forms of technology production. Shorter innovation periods, increasing R&D costs, the need to integrate applications from various innovations and the constant appearance of new technological opportunities prompt firms to cooperate.

As Camagni (1991) points out, cooperation agreements among firms have given rise to networks that improve competitiveness of firms in national and international markets and lead to increased returns and market share. Strategic networks make firms and productive systems more efficient, facilitate the control of the creation and diffusion of innovation and, particularly, transform production organization in order to create new innovative capacity. Through strategic alliances, firms can obtain scale economies in production, in research and development of products and in marketing, and they can differentiate production and reduce technology production costs. When firms and the network reach agreements, they are able to obtain these economies. Along with them, competitive advantages improve, which, in turn, allows them to increase profitability, performance and market share. Furthermore, networks and strategic alliances facilitate the control of technological trajectories and processes by members, hence reducing risks (Gordon, 1991). They also increase members' capacity for innovation through greater access to reserved information, the use of complementary technological developments and the incorporation of knowledge and external resources.

Perhaps the most significant factor is that if strategic alliances endure over time, relations among firms become true networks that actually transform business culture and practice and tend to reduce rivalry and increase cooperation. Technical cooperation agreements propose common strategic goals for all firms. This fosters interaction between management and research teams of the various firms, the sharing of confidential business information and, on some occasions, long-term cooperation eventually leading to long-term planning.

However, as Castells (1996) maintains, linking of firms through alliances and agreements of a temporary nature does not reduce competition among firms. Not only do strategic alliances not exclude competition for market shares in areas not covered in the agreements. Today's members may become tomorrow's rivals once the agreement has fulfilled its goals.

Strategic networks and agreements are made up of very diverse firms, each one pursuing specific goals (Hakansson, 1987; Dickens, 1992; Harrison, 1994). In recent years, alliances among large enterprises (for example, in the automobile industry), that normally compete in the same markets have increased to the point that their global strategies are actually founded on strategic agreements instrumented through joint ventures. In other cases, agreements among small firms or between large and small firms with complementary productive dynamics (as occurs with biotechnological activities) are aimed at cooperating on common projects. Finally, agreements and strategic alliances also affect subcontracting firms, on which large firms rely when launching strategies of territorial deployment. This kind of alliance is usually instrumented through formal cooperation agreements with limited operational validity, since the arrangement is made in order to develop projects in which participating firms share knowledge and non-tangible goods. Control of these goods is difficult to regulate and, therefore, mutual trust among firms, organizations and people that work on the projects is critical for these networks to operate.

Implications for local development policy

The above discussion shows that firm networks have become one of the ways to organize production that characterize the mode of development. Networks provide the flexibility needed for local productive systems to respond to changes induced by increasing competition and globalization and they encourage increased productivity and improvement in market position.

Therefore, when a city or region attempts to define a strategy for local economic development, one of the core tenets is to build on the organizational capability of existing economic agents and institutions to attain greater productivity and competitiveness (OECD, 1993). One of the principal axes of the strategy will be to reinforce cooperation among agents and institutions through actions that promote the creation and development of firms and networks of private agents and institutions. The other strategic axis of local development policy is to stimulate learning capacity within the network of local actors, thus helping them to respond adequately to the needs and demands of the local economy.

In today's competitive scenario, each locality and region has its strengths and weaknesses. If a diagnosis is made, following Maillat (1995), in terms of the two strategic axes proposed by theories on networking and industrial districts (learning and technological knowledge on the horizontal axis; entrepreneurship and organizational capability on the vertical axis), four types of productive and territorial networks can be identified (see Figure 4.2).

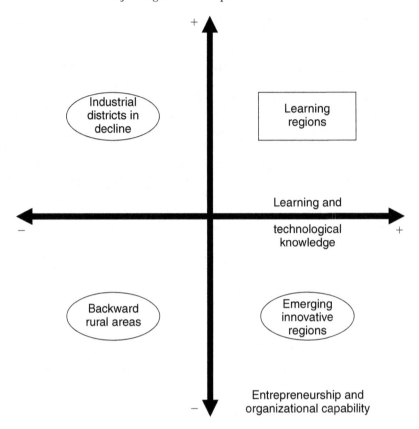

Figure 4.2 Networks and development: typology of regions.

- Territories that show shortcomings both in entrepreneurship and technological knowledge, as is the case in many rural areas in Europe and Latin America.
- Territories that have a sufficiently well organized firm system in the territory but need to incorporate technological knowledge so that local firms can improve their competitiveness. An example would be local productive systems facing productive restructuring processes, as in the industrial districts of Italy and Spain in the 1990s.
- Territories that show weak entrepreneurial and/or organizational capability in the local productive system, but have reinforced their position in recent years due mainly to technological policy that has endowed them with projects aimed at diffusing innovation.
- Finally, territories whose strengths are entrepreneurship and organizational capability and the potential ability to respond to the challenges of competition in an innovative way. This case may be referred to as learning regions.

This typology of various territories, based on two of the local development strategic axes, allows us to propose a strategy. The objective would
be to convert a territory into a milieu in which entrepreneurship and
organizational capability and the innovative responses of firms and local
actors were positive within the setting in which the region or city competes. To reach this goal, it would be necessary to launch actions that
would enable the territory's strengths and neutralize its weaknesses.
These actions would often target technological knowledge by fostering
diffusion of innovations and interaction of local actors. In other cases,
measures would stress entrepreneurship and organizational capability
within the milieu. Thus, one of the dominant lines of action in local
development strategies is to encourage whichever forms of cooperation
among firms may stimulate an enterprising climate within the local productive system and in each one of its firms, as well as ties to national and
international markets.

Finally, the implementation of local development strategies requires
that agents rely on support from formal and informal networks to bring
institutions and organizations to be more receptive to changes involved in
the local development strategy. In this way, the negative effects of excess
administrative bureaucracy can be minimized and the support of national
and regional administrations attained when dealing with the implementation of local initiatives.

Interaction between the organization of production and endogenous development

The way in which production is organized conditions the mechanisms that
facilitate increased productivity and competitiveness in local economies.
As occurs with large firms, firm networks are forms of organizing production through which scale and scope economies as well as reduction in
transaction costs are obtained. However, as has been argued throughout
this chapter, efficiency in the organization of local productive systems
improves when innovations are diffused rapidly throughout the productive fabric, when the city becomes more attractive to firms, infrastructures
make it more accessible and when institutions respond to the needs of
firms and organizations.

Innovations condition the organization of production in the productive
system. The introduction of new products and production methods
requires new forms of internal organization of firms to make them more
efficient. On the other hand, in the case of both industrial districts and
networks of firms around large firms, the application of new technologies
permits the division of the productive process into parts, productive
specialization of firms and reconstruction of the final product at the level
of the productive system. This produces an exchange system within the
firm network which generates economies of scale and facilitates the

differentiation of production and economies of scope in the firms and networks.

Cities are the physical space of firms and local productive systems. Cities provide a labor market, public and private services and a transportation and communication system which allows firms and productive systems to reduce average costs and use the agglomeration economies generated. The physical proximity provided by cities encourages the exchange of information and knowledge within firm networks and the sharing of cultural and behavior patterns, all of which reduces uncertainty and lowers transaction costs for firms. In sum, it is in the city where an industrial atmosphere is created, technical knowledge is diffused and meeting places for firms are established leading to all kinds of economies and reduction of firms' costs.

Institutional development in the territory where firms carry out their activity conditions the organization of production in the productive system. When strong links have been built up between the population and firms, trust grows, thus stimulating the exchange of products and information and the diffusion of knowledge among plants and local firms; this, in turn, leads to decreased transaction costs and activates the ability to create and diffuse technical knowledge. On the other hand, economic transactions and exchanges take place and organization dynamic is implemented through formal contracts and agreements among firms. Strategic alliances formed between firms trigger the mechanisms leading to economies of scale in production and marketing of goods and services, economies of scope through the differentiation of production and lower production costs due to increased innovative capability.

Finally, the main goal of local development policy itself is to feed this continual process of improvement of entrepreneurial and organizational capability in the territory. Among the priority objectives of local initiatives are the start-up of new firms and the improvement of entrepreneurial and organizational capability of the economic agents. To this end, firm incubators, business innovation centers and initiatives favoring specific social groups, such as young people and women, have been strengthened. Over the last few years, there has also been a revitalization of the policy for attracting external firms that are willing to endogenize their activities in the territory through new ways to regulate relations between external firms and the territory.

5   Innovation and development

At this point in the discussion, it has become clear that innovation is one of the central forces in economic development processes and, consequently, one of the factors determining economic change and social well-being. Economic growth and structural change come about as a consequence of innovation being injected into the productive system through investment decisions. However, the economic effects of innovation depend on how it is diffused throughout the productive fabric and what technological strategy firms employ to sustain and improve the results of their activity.

This chapter focuses on the analysis of the process of innovation and technological change in order to link new interpretations of innovation to the endogenous development approach. It begins with a discussion of the paradigms of technological change and the importance of evolutionary theory in interpreting the creation and diffusion of innovation. Next the chapter examines the innovative milieu approach and the mechanisms that account for the diffusion of innovation in local productive systems are explored. Finally, after discussing the implications that this approach has had on technological policy and, subsequently, on local development policy, the chapter ends with some conclusions on the interaction between innovation and the other processes that explain endogenous development.

The emergence of new paradigms of technological change

Technological progress is a necessary condition for the economic development of countries, regions and cities. As we have seen earlier, economic growth is a result of capital accumulation, and capital accumulation always incorporates technological change. Therefore, it could be said that economic growth is, ultimately, the accumulation of technology.[1]

In today's increasingly competitive and global world, innovation has become a differentiating factor for firms and economies. Innovative firms have a competitive edge over their rivals if they are able to satisfy consumer needs and demands as expressed by the market. Therefore, the conception and development of innovation is associated with the dynamics of the competitive struggle of firms in product and factor markets.

The new competitive scenario, in which there are multiple markets and various efficient ways to organize production, has revealed the limitations of paradigms that have disputed the interpretation of innovation processes for decades. Other paradigms have been launched in an attempt to adjust theory to the new reality.

For decades, the dominant view considered innovation a functional phenomenon of a sequential and hierarchical nature. The neoclassical model and Schumpeter's view, expressed in his earlier works, have given rise to an almost "metaphysical" interpretation of the innovation process. Always considered to be external to production, research – particularly of a scientific nature – was the foundation of innovation. Each organization, including firms, was charged with a specific function and the introduction of innovation was "natural" in economic growth.

The neoclassical view reduces technological change to an element dependent on the passage of time, associated with some of the forms of investment in capital goods or as one of the components of the residual in the production function (Rosegger, 1996). The limitations of this view go beyond the fact that the distinction between factor substitution and technological change (displacement through the isoquants) is fictitious and irrelevant. The range of technologies that can be applied to the productive process is restricted and, at any rate, there must be investment if additional scientific or applied knowledge is to be produced.

In this respect, the neoclassical model scarcely applies and, in any case, it is inadequate to analyze technological innovation processes (Nelson, 1995; Metcalfe, 1998). Technological change depends on the decisions of innovative firms; it therefore does not take place in conditions of perfect competition and shows uncertain results. The strategic behavior of firms, in search of greater returns and an improved position in the market, forces the market structure to undergo constant change. Furthermore, this uncertainty can only be resolved once the products have passed through the market, that is, after the firms have overcome the test of market competition.

As Freeman and Soete (1997) point out, a good share of traditional economic theory, in accordance with the assumption of *ceteris paribus*, excluded the analysis of technological and social change. And when it was taken into account, as it was in neoclassical growth models, capital and labor factors were at the core of the analysis. Technological change was relegated to a residual factor, an amalgamation of growth elements such as education, innovation, scale economies and entrepreneurial management. Particularly remarkable is the fact that neoclassical thought only referred to process innovation while overlooking product innovation.

Schumpeter's contribution undoubtedly constitutes a powerful interpretation for a more realist analysis of innovation processes. Not only was he one of the first economists to acknowledge the importance of product innovations[2] in development, but he also placed the phenomenon of innovation at the center of development processes (the principle of creative destruction). He also admitted that innovation is conditioned by the results that innovators perceive in the market and that innovative processes take place in conditions of dynamic competition, that is, of imperfect competition (Freeman *et al.*, 1982).

Schumpeter (1934), however, is not able to perceive innovation in all its dimensions. He distinguishes between invention, innovation and imitation but, in his first works, innovation, which is introduced at irregular intervals by charismatic and visionary entrepreneurs, is the only one assigned the relevant capacity to increase productivity and promote economic growth. Other activities associated with technological change are considered less important. Invention, such as scientific discoveries, would fall outside the productive process, and imitation would be an irrelevant activity, acting only as a diffuser of new technology. Yet, in his later works, Schumpeter (1943) qualifies his position and acknowledges the endogenous nature of scientific and innovative activity, at least of that taking place in the laboratories of large firms.[3]

The difference between technology – all knowledge[4] leading to the production of goods and services – and scientific knowledge is very useful in economic terms since it allows us to consider scientific knowledge as a public good and, as such, available to all firms and organizations. Technology on the other hand, is a private good which individuals and firms can appropriate (clearly so, when it is a matter of new technical knowledge) and, therefore, restrict the use that others can make of it.[5]

One of the main ideas underlying Schumpeter's thought, as pointed out in recent advances in the theory of innovation and technological change, is that innovative activity is an economic activity. Firms and economies, in their competitive endeavor, face challenges and problems whose solutions require new ideas leading to the production of new goods and services, the use of new production methods and the implementation of new forms of production and firm organization.

In this context, inventions – which are really no more than discoveries in a pure state – can be economically feasible and become innovations when they are found to be useful in solving firms' productive problems. As Freeman (1988) indicates, when ideas on products, production methods or organizational forms are no longer discoveries but rather applied to the productive reality, they become what is called "innovation." Through investment, firms apply new knowledge to the productive process in order to employ available resources more efficiently. They manufacture new products, organize in more efficient ways and move into new markets.

Thus, innovation is an economic activity in the most traditional sense. It emerges as a result of competition among firms, who need to increase returns and improve market share. Innovation is implemented through the application of financial resources with the expectation that profits will be gained in the future.

This logic takes us to another of the topics of debate in recent years (Davelaar, 1991), that of the factors that propel technological change. There is no one right answer to the question of whether innovation takes place due to the effect on firms of increased scientific knowledge (*technology push*) or due to demand that stimulates new applications (*demand pull*). In his earlier works, Schumpeter seems to support the idea that innovation is driven by the development of knowledge. This view was also proposed in traditional models of technological change. However, if innovation is considered an economic activity, demand would be the engine of innovation processes (Schmookler, 1966).

However, perhaps the greatest limitation to Schumpeter's thought lies in the nucleus of his most significant contribution, because his concept of innovation does not allow him to view economic development in its full extension. His rationale revolves around radical innovations (Freeman, 1987), that is, innovations that cause considerable ruptures in the productive and industrial system or that generate the creation and development of new industrial activities. He disregards the role of incremental innovations in development processes. These small improvements in products and processes, due to the work of production engineers, technicians and skilled workers in manufacturing plants, improve economic and technical feasibility of the processes and bring products nearer to market demands. In fact, both types of innovations are intensely linked, in that incremental innovations are actually improvements of radical innovations. Often, these improvements cause more economic impact than the initial invention.

Hence, Schumpeter's thought matured throughout his scientific works and found its final expression in a new paradigm of technological change (Vence Deza, 1995). Innovation, stimulated by firm investment decisions, is a process that emerges in conditions of imperfect competition. It is an economic activity, which integrates various stages of knowledge[6] and transforms an idea into a product. Innovation is, therefore, a constant process and is endogenous to productive activity and development itself. It appears at a certain point in time and space and, through continual improvements, is diffused throughout the entire productive system.

According to Nelson (1995), the features of evolutionary thought facilitate the analysis of innovation in environments of uncertainty and have, therefore, made it possible to understand the new paradigm in some depth. It attempts to account for technological evolution over time and identify why the use of specific technologies at a particular moment is conditioned by earlier developments. It analyzes the mechanisms that lead to the selection and identification of innovations embedded in the productive process. Finally, evolutionary theory identifies those factors, characteristic of the old generation of technologies, that remain within the evolutionary process and provide some continuity to reality after decisive changes have taken place.

Modern innovation theory integrates the economic perspective of technological change with the views of sociology, psychology and knowledge-theory, leading it to acknowledge that innovation resides in learning, which is fundamentally interactive and rooted in the productive and social fabric. According to the theory of innovative milieux (Bramanti and Ratti, 1997 and Lundvall 1992 and 1993a), innovation comes about as a result of collective learning processes developing in a given social, institutional and cultural context. This allows firms to access innovation through their network of contacts and relations, thus defining an interactive innovation model as an alternative paradigm to the linear model of innovation (Asheim and Isaksen, 1997).

Endogenous evolution of technology

The works of Rosenberg (1976, 1982), Nelson and Winter (1977), Dosi (1988) and Freeman and Soete (1997) demonstrate that technology evolves in an unpredictable way because the results of innovation are uncertain.

According to Metcalfe (1998: 22), all evolutionary processes are characterized by three basic principles:

- the principle of variation, which indicates that the members of a population vary, with respect to at least one significant selection characteristic;
- the principle of heredity, which demonstrates that copy mechanisms exist which guarantee that the form and behavior of entities in the population will continue over time;
- the principle of selection, which indicates that the characteristics of some entities adapt better to prevailing evolutionary pressures and, therefore, their relative significance is greater in relation to less adapted entities.

The theory of the endogenous evolution of innovation outlined in the works of Schumpeter is founded on the idea that firms (and not individual economic agents) are the strategic actors in processes of technological evolution since they make the investment decisions as to new processes and products. Nelson and Winter (1974 and 1982) point out that firms are organizations that differ from one another and have varying levels of returns yet, nevertheless, they are the true incubators of innovation. Firms "transport" technologies and all of those practices determining what they produce and how they do it. That is, they are the carriers of what Nelson and Winter have conceived as "routines."[7]

Besides knowledge about technology, markets and management,

routines also incorporate other firm-specific knowledge, which differentiates it from their rivals (Rosegger, 1996). Three types of routines can be identified:

- operational processes that determine how and how much a firm produces in various circumstances as a function of the capital and technology stock employed;
- systems and criteria that firms follow to make decisions on investment in technology based on the returns and profits they expect to obtain by marketing the products that incorporate new knowledge;
- the learning mechanisms within the firm, aimed at creating and improving production techniques and whose results affect their profits in the long term.

As has been pointed out elsewhere, firms do not act in isolation. Rather, they operate within a specific environment made up of a network of firms, through which they carry out commercial and technical exchanges, and a series of institutions and organizations, that provide all kinds of services. This environment or milieu, and the strategies of competing firms, will condition their results and, therefore, their profits. In an increasingly competitive environment, such as that created by globalization, firms deploy their strategies in order to maintain market share and improve returns. It is in this environment that a selection process takes place, in which market results define those technologies that are to be rewarded and those that are to be penalized.

The unit of selection is the firm or the "business unit," in Metcalfe's terminology. Each firm carries particular technological and organizational characteristics and routines, which are ultimately submitted to competition in the markets and, therefore, subjected to the process of economic selection. Hence, this process has an indirect influence on firm activity. The endurance of the firm is only possible when it is the carrier of virtuous routines that allow it to maintain or increase its market share and profits. Only continuous learning can foster adaptation of firms to the changing conditions in the markets and give them the capacity to respond to the strategies of rival firms. However, firms resist making changes in routines that have allowed them to be competitive over long periods of time.

In the competitive struggle of firms, innovations emerge that, according to evolutionary theory, can be considered *mutations* of existing technologies. They usually endanger the survival of existing technologies and always alter the routines employed up to then by firms adopting the new technology. It is the firms who decide if they will introduce them or not, who have the last word concerning innovations. Returns are a good indicator of the technology's fitness and of the firm's good health (fitness).

Undoubtedly, the success of an innovation implies change in the evolutionary process, but it does not mean that the dominating technology is necessarily superior to competing technologies. This powerful conclusion of evolutionary thought indicates that the evolution of innovation does not always necessarily fit the criteria of optimization proposed by traditional neoclassical theory. Everything depends on the conditions at departure and which historical factors condition the evolution of technologies (Nelson, 1995).

On the one hand, evolutionary theory considers that for a technology to be successful, that is, adopted by a set of firms competing in the market, its incorporation must be fortunate. But it must also be accompanied by a series of improvements in the firm and in the milieu which are decisive in the competitive battle with rival innovations (the dispute between Beta and VHS video systems comes to mind). According to Silverberg *et al.* (1988), for a potentially better technology to displace a rival technology, efforts must be made to improve firm learning routines and diffuse use of the new technology in the industry. The result is uncertain; the less productive technology may finally prevail because the necessary investments in learning and application are made, while competitors do not make sufficient efforts in these areas.

Moreover, once the innovation has been consolidated in the market, mechanisms associated with *path dependence* come into play that allow the less productive technology to continue dominating the market, even when its advantages have been surpassed by other innovations.[8] Substitution is expensive because of the appropriation of economies associated with skills acquired by the human resources or links established among firms. The cost/benefit relation between use of an older technology and its new, technologically superior, rival can make change unfeasible.

The principle of selection works because a successful technological innovation generates long-term profits for the firm which impulses investment in capital goods, the use of skilled human resources for the new tasks, increased productivity, wages and profits. These events have a strong impact on the productive system because more profitable techniques tend to displace less profitable ones. Since firms using the most profitable techniques tend to grow, rival firms are forced to imitate them by abandoning less efficient technologies to adopt those that have demonstrated their profitability. The process of selection, therefore, promotes diffusion and growth mechanisms within the productive system.

Innovation, then, constitutes a great challenge for firms competing in the markets. New products and/or production methods, changes in the market and the response of competitors drive them to respond strategically. Depending on available resources, management capacity and historical trajectory, firms can choose from various strategies,[9] which could be classified as those of leader, challenger, imitator or follower.

There are few firms who choose to adopt offensive strategies, that is, of commercial and technical leadership, based on the introduction of new products and processes. Most firms adopt defensive strategies, some challenge leaders while simultaneously introducing innovations, others follow along, searching for market niches in order to maintain their market share in specialized markets, imitating leading firms and specializing in specific product or market areas.

As with offensive strategies, imitative and defensive strategies include mechanisms that favor the rapid incorporation of innovations at various times and in diverse ways, depending on the strategic interests and capabilities of the firms. The strategies of traditional followers are not usually innovative; they try to maintain their share in captive markets using cheap and easily accessed resources and by low prices and, at best, they limit themselves to using process technologies already common throughout the industry.

Diffusion of innovation

When processes of structural change and economic dynamics are analyzed, it is not isolated innovations that are particularly significant, but rather innovative processes and the emergence of clusters of innovation in various areas of knowledge and productive activity. In fact, research into the historical evolution of technology has found that these innovations occur in clusters and give rise to expansive phases in economic cycles (Freeman and Soete, 1997).

As Schumpeter anticipated, the appearance of innovation, particularly radical innovation, causes an intense disturbance in the economic system because it must adapt to all of the technological changes necessary to incorporate the innovation into the productive system. Radical innovations show up from time to time and require many improvements and adaptations to reach full development and finally transform the technical and commercial relations of firms. The diffusion of innovation, then, comes about naturally as a result of the appearance of innovative activities. Diffusion is an essential stage in technological evolution and is feasible in a favorable social and institutional context. As Carlota Pérez (1986) states, when innovation is accompanied by institutional change and modified social and political rules, we witness the birth of a new "techno-economic paradigm" as the basis for a new long cycle of the economy.

From this point of view, we can agree with Freeman *et al.* (1982) that expansion waves in economic activity are due to the emergence of technological systems made up of series of innovations issuing from the same technological nucleus. These innovations lead to the formation of groups of firms that produce new goods and services and give rise to new consumer behavior.

Innovation fostering new products and services is not a random, static diffusion process, such as those heralded by epidemiological-type models,[10] but rather flows along specific paths. Dosi (1984) calls these paths of progressive innovation *technological trajectories*, analogous to what Nelson and Winter (1977) call "natural trajectories." Thus, technological systems are formed as a result of the combined appearance of a series of technological trajectories producing basic innovations. Groups of firms are created and developed around these innovations. Through the production of goods and services, they attempt to obtain returns to their investments in an environment of increasing market competition (Davelaar, 1991).

The emergence of a new technological system unleashes the diffusion process through new technological trajectories linked to multiple radical innovations and organizational and institutional change. The new technological setting provides opportunities for new businesses and attracts a great number of firms throughout the various stages of the technology life cycle. These firms will be the producers of new goods and services (Davelaar, 1991).

In the initial stages, diffusion is not merely imitative but also creative. Many firms, attracted by low entrance costs and potentially high profits, maneuver within the technological trajectories in an attempt to be competitive and create new products through improvements that approach goods to market demand. At this point, technology is unstable and firms are continually experimenting. Davelaar calls the incremental innovations taking place in this period a *creative diffusion process.*

As the learning process is developed along the new trajectories and the characteristics of demand are determined, new products tend to standardize. For this reason, competition among innovative firms no longer centers on product innovation but rather on ways of organizing production. Process innovations aim at attaining scale economies that improve competitiveness and profitability for firms. Hence, some of the firms that were particularly creative in earlier stages, abandon production, while other firms show greater ability in organizing production and marketing products.

These changes indicate a transformation in the dynamics of diffusion. In the first stages, diffusion seems to lag behind the production of innovation. But, as demand is gradually defined, innovative activities tend to be market-oriented. By the same rule, the type of innovation varies throughout the stages. The emphasis is gradually shifted from product to process innovations as the standardization of goods and services is consolidated. In the diffusion process, standardization emerges in response to the need to reduce production costs and, ultimately, product prices. In later stages, this means that competition among firms resides more in the price than the novelty of the product. However, when process technology becomes commonplace and is within reach of all the firms, new options introduce new product improvements, through product differentiation, and, once again, bring the product closer to demand.

The evolution of technology goes hand in hand with the selection process. The market establishes which innovations will be successful and rewards firm efficiency, as commented above. In each one of the stages, firms make decisions to invest in technology based on expected returns and these determine what firms enter and exit the market. Profits also account for the evolution of technology and, therefore, the productive dynamic of the industry and, ultimately, economic growth.

However, the diffusion of innovation is not an automatic phenomenon, but is rather conditioned by the firms' internal functioning and by the relations it maintains within its milieu. On occasion, the effect of diffusion encounters resistance within the productive fabric because firms have not developed sufficient learning capability. According to Dosi *et al.* (1992), firms use "packages of routines," which form a very structured, rigid whole and include routines that facilitate entrepreneurial learning. The lack of flexibility creates barriers to the adoption of innovations, which in extreme cases can lead firms and organizations to change activities or disappear.

The diffusion process is also conditioned by the behavior of organizations and institutions, with whom innovative firms exchange goods and services, such as research centers, universities, government offices and institutes or unions and entrepreneurial associations. Pérez (1986) points out that the diffusion of innovation requires institutions to adjust to the new situation and become facilitators to technological change. Greater adaptive flexibility encourages technological and structural change and, in turn, economic development processes.

Innovative milieux

The notion of local "milieu," as formulated by the research teams in the GREMI association[11] (Aydalot, 1986; Aydalot and Keeble, 1988; Perrin, 1991) broadens the analysis of innovation process. This notion discusses the role of the territory within the process of innovation and endogenous development and helps pinpoint some of the factors that condition the response of firms and territories to the challenges of globalization and, therefore, in interpreting present-day economic dynamics.

A local milieu is made up of a network of local actors and the relations that shape the productive system, through which collective learning forces are generated. In networks, economic, social, political and institutional actors possess specific modes of organization and regulation and a unique culture (Crevoisier *et al.*, 1990; Perrin, 1990).

The notion of local milieu is defined by three characteristics. First, it refers to a territorial unit, but does not have clear-cut boundaries. The territory is not merely a support for productive activities, resources and economic and social relations, but rather the place in which local actors are organized, use material and non-tangible resources and produce and exchange goods, services and knowledge.

Second, the local actors (inhabitants, firms, institutions, local authorities) also "network" by way of their social, commercial, technological, political and administrative relations and contacts, through which links of cooperation and interdependence are established. Internal organizational logic allows the local milieu to cooperate in innovation and competitiveness.

Finally, a local milieu involves collective learning processes[12] which help it react to changes in the environment through job mobility in the local market, the exchange of product, process, organization and marketing technology, the provision of specialized services, informal informational flows of all kinds and strategies of the actors.

Aydalot (1986) adds that local milieux are incubators of innovation. Since firms are decisive in innovative processes, and since they are not isolated economic agents but rather a part of specific local milieux, the creation and diffusion of innovation will depend on the organization of the territory, the interaction of the agents, learning mechanisms and, therefore, on local history itself. Innovation becomes, therefore, a collective learning process.

The most original contribution of the milieu approach, then, is having shown the relation between territory and innovation, which allows us to assert that development is of a territorial nature. Innovation and technological change emerge from the territory and are associated with local know-how, human resource skills and institutions of knowledge involved in research and development (Quevit, 1991; Perrin, 1991). The creation and diffusion of innovation originates in the interaction of firms with the milieu. The circumstances of local firms, economies and societies, the innovative capacity of firms, the creative and productive culture of the milieu, the economic and technological history of the area determine how firms and organizations learn and how they respond to the challenges of competition at a given historical time.

However, the complexity and quality of relations that innovative firms can establish with their milieux is crucial to the process of innovation. The closer and more continuous the links that are formed (associations among local firms and with other local actors, for example), the greater the integration of the firm into its milieu. By the same rule, the more dependent and infrequent these relations (for example, subcontracting), the less integration there will be.

Innovation processes in local productive systems

The innovative milieu approach and the interactive innovation models in general argue that innovation in local productive systems is based on cooperation among firms and institutions that embody the productive, social and institutional fabric of the territory. From this perspective, innovation is a learning process among the actors within the milieu in which the firms make investment and location decisions.

Thus, we are dealing with learning processes, rooted in society and the territory, in which coded knowledge,[13] or production "recipes," and tacit knowledge incorporated into human resources are diffused within the network as a result of relations among the actors. Consequently, processes of technological change and innovation are interactive, not linear.

District firms choose to pursue very diverse innovation strategies. In fact, few firms make investment decisions incorporating innovation. According to Asheim and Isaksen (1998), the following typology can be established:

- leading innovative firms capable of developing new products, processes or markets as a consequence of the entrepreneur's creativity and skill and the organization of the firm;
- low intensity innovative firms whose creative capacity involves the introduction of small changes and improvements in existing products and processes in response to the need to innovate in order to be more competitive in the market;
- non-innovative firms that do not effect innovations of any kind because they work for captive or informal markets in which innovation is not a factor in competitiveness.

Radical innovation, that is, an alteration in the evolution of technology, is not the most significant kind of innovation in local productive systems. Rather it is incremental innovations,[14] that is, all modifications, usually made by engineers and skilled workers, leading to gradual improvement in products and processes. Firms accumulate knowledge acquired through continual problem-solving within the plant and in the daily management of production and marketing of the goods produced. The use of available technologies and adaptive R&D bring about small product and process changes which allow firms to respond better to market demand.

In local productive systems, the technological strategies of firms and the innovation process itself are conditioned by the sectoral context. There are great differences in opportunities, incentives, R&D investment and innovative procedures from one industry to another (Dosi, 1988). Moreover, each sector has a different value chain, which determines its internal organization and its relations with other sectors. In turn, organization and relations condition the type of innovation introduced and the location within the productive chain, as well as the hierarchy of the innovations and technological transfer.

If districts are classified as to productive activity, the resulting typology[15] will be very diversified. In districts whose dominant activities are those normally called "high-tech activities" (activities in the areas of electronics, pharmaceutical, biotechnology and aerospace), the innovation process is linked to scientific advancements. Also, investments in product innovation are relatively intense and the search for new discoveries and innovations is essential to firm strategy (Saxenian, 1994; Maillat *et al.*, 1995). High-tech firms are inserted into a context of intense competition in which survival is only possible when innovation in the firm and in the district network is constant. In these productive systems, entrepreneurial strategies aim to create new markets by continually introducing new products. Hence, they must experiment with new products and new techniques and generate internal learning in the firms and within the entire system, which gives rise to multiple technological trajectories.

Innovation occurs in all segments of the industrial value chain (in the case of the computer industry, for example, innovation takes place in chips, software, disks, screens, networking instruments). A single firm could not innovate in all of the components of the production line and must therefore rely on other firms specialized in complementary activities and work together within a network of innovative firms. Each firm tends to specialize in what it is able to make and buys everything else from the local productive network. This not only means less cost and time invested in the development and production of the new technologies. It also means that only those innovations of interest to the firm network will be developed.

However, when local productive systems are analyzed, one usually encounters districts specialized in traditional activities (such as textiles, clothing, footwear, wood and metal products). Frequently, the innovation process is imitative and investment in innovation mainly involves the intro- duction of capital goods, intermediate products and raw materials from firms in other sectors. But local firms realize their creative capacity in the improvements carried out in factories and in management offices (Sáez Cala, 1999).

Local productive systems are made up of a group of firms that are adapters of technology, under the leadership of a few innovative firms that compete in markets with many firms where production costs and prices are the critical variables, and in market niches, where production differentiation is strategic. Technological strategy varies from one firm to another, but, in any case, concentrates on incremental innovations.

- Sometimes these involve the adaptation of well-known production processes and methods, through the installation of new equipment and computer systems to guarantee quality and reduce production costs.
- In product innovation, local products are sometimes differentiated to take advantage of market niches in which a certain competitive advantage can be exploited (such as hiking shoes or track shoes in the footwear industry). Sometimes firms improve and adapt products already in the market (through a new design) and sometimes they attain scope economies by manufacturing new product lines for expanding markets (sleighs and playground material made by toy firms).

- Finally, market innovations of local firms introduce new methods and techniques in the area of marketing and distribution.

The goal of the strategies of innovative firms is to improve their competitiveness and market share. With the introduction of incremental innovations, production costs are reduced, product quality is improved, the product is adjusted to demand and the production process is streamlined.

Innovations typically arise within firms and, in any case, within the local milieu, although, on occasion, clients and suppliers from outside the district can be the catalyst for innovation. The system of relations in the district facilitates the communication of ideas and information about techniques and markets which, ultimately, generate the externalities of the network that benefit the entire system. In any case, geographic proximity facilitates the transmission of knowledge and optimizes the use of informal channels. Yet, it is, perhaps, most important that the strategies of firms in local production systems hinge on cooperation within the district. It is not only a matter of relations among firms, but also with the other local actors, as occurs in the case of the Technological Institutes in the Region of Valencia, or in the intermediary organizations (such as business associations, private technological transfer agencies or banks) in Baden-Württemberg.

Finally, the flexible organization of production, such as industrial and technological districts, exerts a strong pull on large, often multinational, external firms. The clusters that form competitive firm networks and are able to generate agglomeration and network economies, attract firms seeking quality resources and external economies in order to help them maintain or improve their share in increasingly global markets. For this reason, very diverse relational structures can be found in local productive systems.

Subcontracting, one of the most typical relational structures, can have positive effects on the diffusion of innovation in the district. It allows outside firms to reduce their production costs, benefit from supplier specialization, reduce internal costs and improve competitiveness. Yet, at the same time, subcontracting injects new inertia into local productive systems because it leads to an exchange of knowledge and know-how between the external firm and the local firm system. It frequently involves a stable relation between suppliers and the external firm and is operative only when there is an adequate flow of information and efficient coordination among partners.

Innovation policies for local development

The foregoing discussion illustrates that decisions on investment and innovation are based not only on a given internal situation, but also on the relations maintained with other firms in the industry and with institutions and organizations in the milieu. Firms adopt innovation as a function of their specific market position, the technical characteristics of their production methods and products and the productive and institutional context. But each type of innovation requires the availability of skilled human resources. Innovative firms need sufficient internal and/or external financial resources to perform the necessary tasks in R&D laboratories, and management staff who can make insightful and opportune decisions on production, organization and market.

The institutional and cultural characteristics of the milieu are, on the other hand, decisive in the evolution of innovative processes. Innovation can only take place if the institutional system is diversified and flexible and if the network of actors is complex, thus promoting capability for innovation and learning in society and in firms. Innovation processes also require an institutional context[16] (legal and administrative system, social and labor relations, patent system) which supports the creation and development of both radical and incremental innovations.

Thus, innovation is an interactive process led by firms that make investment decisions, but is organized with the entire group of research institutions (university, national research council and other technological centers and institutes). These scientific and technological actors form a network where learning processes are generated. Therefore, the efficient flow of exchanges of knowledge taking place as firms, universities and public and private institutions cooperate, conditions the evolution of innovation.

This view of the innovative processes has brought about significant change in industrial and regional policy, whose objective is to improve technological content and method in the productive fabric. Interest in linear innovation models[17] has subsided as growing attention is paid to interactive models, which strive to provide technological services to firms, strengthen the relational system among the actors and foster cooperation among entrepreneurs, researchers and teachers (Vázquez-Barquero, 1993). (The comparison is summarized in Table 5.1.)

Technological policies based on the linear view of innovation are supply policies which try to remedy some of the market failures by supporting those investments in knowledge that firms would not spontaneously make on their own because of the expectation of limited returns or the economic risks involved. They adopt a functional and hierarchical top-down view of knowledge (science, invention and innovation) and of its diffusion throughout the networks of scientific and technological institutions operating in each country. On the other hand, interactive innovation policy aims to meet the demand for services by innovative firms by providing research and development services. These policies adopt a territorial approach in the sense that services are rendered through the network of local actors to satisfy the demands of local firms. It is therefore a bottom-up policy since it aims to meet local needs and demands locally.

Table 5.1 Change in innovative policy

	Linear policies	*Interactive policies*
Dominant strategy	• Supply policy • Hierarchical diffusion of knowledge	• Demand policy • Bottom-up approach
Objectives	• Favor R&D in large firms • Support radical innovation and high technology • Diffuse knowledge embedded in capital goods	• Promote learning in firms and organizations • Diffuse knowledge through local firm network • Satisfy firm needs and demands
Instruments	• Public financing • Subsidies and incentives	• Rendering of technological services • Rendering of complementary services
Organization and Management	• Centralized management • Public administration of resources • Funding for firms	• Management through intermediary organizations • Sale of services

The objectives of linear innovation policies are to promote research and development in firms and facilitate access to knowledge embedded in capital goods. Target firms are usually large, high-tech firms who produce technology intensive goods and have R&D laboratories. In contrast, interactive policies promote learning and the diffusion of coded and non-coded knowledge throughout the local network of mainly small firms and provide these firms with the technological services which will bring products closer to the market.

Linear policies are instrumented through direct technological support to each firm by providing public funding in the form of incentives and subsidies to R&D programs or to infrastructure. Interactive policies, on the other hand, are implemented through intermediary organizations which, for a price, offer an on-going supply of services to clients. Besides the technological services related to generic or specific technologies of a sector or activity, services offered include the formation of human resources, information and advice on capital goods, raw materials and marketing, all of which complement each other and are essential in order to obtain satisfactory results.

Finally, one must add to these differences in principles, instrumentation and objectives, other organizational and management dissimilarities between the two policies. Linear policies are managed centrally through central (or regional) administration offices that apply the legislation on incentives to innovation. Conversely, interactive policies are decentralized in that intermediate organizations are in charge of rendering the services. Firms, their potential clients, and other local actors interested in the initiative, participate in their management. One of the objectives of these organizations is to become financially self-sufficient through sales of the services they provide, although public administrations often collaborate with budget assignments.

The concept and operation of policy has significantly evolved since the beginning of the 1980s. But one paradigm or technological policy is not simply substituted by another. Both models actually coexist and are implemented depending on the characteristics of target firms. Policies based on linear innovation models aim to promote radical innovations and their initial development. Beneficiaries of this policy are usually large firms, or high-tech firms. Policies based on interactive innovation models, on the other hand, target the development of incremental innovations and the provision of technological services. They attempt to meet the needs and demands of small and medium-sized firms and, particularly, of local productive systems.

Interaction between innovation and endogenous development

The creation and diffusion of innovations, as has been emphasized throughout this book, is decisive in increasing productivity and competitiveness of firms and territories. Product innovations expand productive activities and improve firm competitiveness, process innovations lead to standardization, reduce production costs and product price, innovations in organization lower transaction and production costs, while incremental innovations reduce production costs and lead to production differentiation, thus bringing products closer to the market and stimulating scope economies.

However, for the process of creation and diffusion of innovations to take place, the local productive system must stimulate the creation and diffusion of technical knowledge, institutions must respond to the needs and demands of innovative actors and agents and the city must provide a favorable atmosphere for innovation and change.

The organization of production in the territory conditions the way in which innovation processes work. When the productive system is organized into firm networks, the exchange of knowledge and technology and access to innovations through formal and informal exchanges and contacts are encouraged. Furthermore, the value chains through which productive activities are organized condition relations between firms and the type of innovations introduced into productive processes in such a way that technological changes adopted by some firms condition innovation in all the rest. Finally, there will be resistance to the diffusion of innovations within productive systems when firms show low learning capability and when lack of flexibility makes the adoption of innovations difficult.

The introduction and diffusion of innovations are conditioned by the characteristics of the institutional system. Thus, the more flexible and the greater the quality of the actors' networks, the more powerful the mechanisms of innovation will be. Creation and diffusion of innovations is an interactive phenomenon based on the collective learning of firms which, in turn, depends on the creative capability and the social and institutional fabric of the territory. The creation and diffusion of innovations is also determined by the disposition of a social and institutional environment (based on the social, cultural and political rules and norms) in the face of the phenomenon of innovation, and by the way the system of organizations and institutions, such as universities, research centers, unions, entrepreneurial organizations or the public administration itself, works. Finally, institutional environments determine how mechanisms of cooperation and formal contracts and agreements work, and they also condition the creation of innovations and the diffusion of knowledge.

Cities are and have historically been the space in which innovations and learning processes, as well as diffusion of knowledge and technology, are encouraged. The concentration of human resources, of firms that produce goods and services and of organizations favors interaction and the exchange of information and knowledge which, in turn, stimulates learning. Agglomeration leads to the economies of scale necessary to produce innovations. Physical proximity and worker mobility between firms facilitate communication and the diffusion of ideas and innovations.

Finally, initiatives aimed at creating and diffusing innovations are one of the key elements in local development policy. For many decades one of the mainstays in the restructuring and modernization of local economies has been to stimulate the adoption and adaptation of technologies in productive systems through instruments such as research centers, scientific and technological parks and technological institutes. Among their goals were to stimulate transfer and diffusion of innovations within the productive fabric, encourage the emergence and development of firms and modern technological infrastructures and, in short, satisfy the firms' needs and demands for technological services when faced with competition requiring improvement in technological responses.

6 Institutions for development

In his book *The Theory of Economic Growth*, Arthur Lewis (1955) pointed out in the mid-1950s, that economic and social institutions play a critical role in economic growth. In the early 1990s, Douglass North (1994) in his Nobel Prize lecture went beyond Lewis' view to argue that "ideas, ideologies, myths, dogmas and prejudices" also play a role in development processes, since beliefs, in fact, become economic and social structures through institutions.

Therefore, it would seem to be commonly assumed today that institutions condition processes of economic growth. Development theory had always upheld this thesis, but neoclassical thought did not adopt it until the new institutional economics acknowledged that institutions are decisive in processes of growth and structural change. In neoclassical analyses of the processes of economic growth through the production function, the role of institutions in allocating the key factors behind growth, (physical capital, human resources or technological change) or in the mechanisms that favor the exchange of goods and services in the markets was not acknowledged. Neoclassical theory operated in an ideal world in which economic transaction costs are non-existent and negotiations leading to exchange do not incur any cost whatsoever.

However, in recent decades the idea that the evolution of economies and the specific growth path of a country, region or city also depend on the working of institutions has been incorporated. Firms and organizations make investment decisions within an institutional context that conditions their activity. But these decisions are also made within a system of relations and interactions with other firms which constitutes an institutional system affecting their investment decisions.

The aim of this chapter is to analyze the role of institutions in development process. The importance of the strategic behavior of the actors in cooperation and competition among firms and organizations is examined. After discussing governance and local development, the chapter turns to a review of the theory of proximity and the significance of the organization of development in local development policy is explored. The chapter offers some conclusions on the relation between institutions and the other processes that explain endogenous development.

Economic development and institutions

Lewis (1955) points out that economic and social institutions are one of the factors determining economic development processes and that variation in the other factors of growth will cause institutional changes. In other words, Lewis holds that there is a mutual relation between economic growth and institutions which causes gradual change in institutions as the economies of countries, regions and cities advance along the growth path.

This general proposition has been the target of specific analysis in neoclassical thought over recent decades when it identifies the mechanisms leading to the establishment of relations between institutions and growth. Thus North (1981, 1986 and 1990) and Williamson (1975 and 1985), building on studies by Coase (1960 and 1984), put forward the argument that the connection between institutions and economic growth lies in the economy of transaction costs.

Exchanges and transactions between economic agents are always at a cost. It is only in the ideal world of the neoclassical model that there is no cost, which means that the question can be dealt with in terms of a model in which agents act with absolute rationality thus obtaining efficient results. Reality is, however, more complex and the exchange of goods and services generates market and non-market costs. As Eggertsson (1990) points out, transaction costs are those arising as a result of the exchange of goods and property rights on goods and on economic assets carried out by individuals, as well as the initiatives they undertake to enforce their exclusive rights.

However, this view of institutional economics is a limited one which reduces the question of institutions to the analysis of the exchange of goods and property rights and transaction costs (Williamson, 2000). It is also unable to conceptualize transaction costs (Hodgson, 1988). In some cases, these costs are vaguely referred to with Arrow's definition: "the costs of running the economic system"; in others, these economists use a functional taxonomy of the various transaction costs which is excessively fastidious and detailed.[1] Finally, this view employs a restrictive concept of transaction in that only economic and commercial transactions are taken into account. Left unacknowledged is the fact that exchanges also involve interpersonal transactions that have nothing to do with the exchange of property rights.

What are institutions? Institutions consist of the set of norms and agreements with which actors, organizations and nations furnish themselves to regulate their economic, social and political relations. These are not only formal rules, such as constitutions and laws and the instruments to apply them, but also all informal norms, which are customs, behavior patterns, codes or conventions, as well as those formal norms which condition the behavior of firms and of the population in a territory. Or in other words, as North suggests, institutions are the rules of the game that structure and determine economic, social and political relations among the actors and organizations throughout the productive activity.

Thus, institutions are a decisive factor in transactions and exchanges among economic agents, actors and organizations. In fact, economic activity is generally immersed in a context of social, cultural and political structures that can help or hinder economic dynamics (Granovetter, 1985). Therefore, relations between firms and actors are not necessarily functional in economic terms, as the neo-institutional view would affirm, but rather interactive, because economic agents and actors belong to networks, and strategic in that the actors make decisions strategically in uncertain environments.

From this perspective, economic development consists of a process of growth and accumulation of capital and knowledge in which the economic and social actors and organizations make decisions to invest, exchange goods and services and reach agreements and sign contracts. All of these decisions are supported by institutions that are created to facilitate transactions among actors and organizations and, ultimately, to reduce the costs involved in carrying out exchanges.

Therefore, there are a variety of mechanisms between institutions and growth that make the productive system more efficient. Exchanges are carried out more efficiently when transaction costs are reduced. Interaction among firms and actors as a result of their strategies generates external economies by formally or informally exchanging commodities, information and knowledge within the networks. The reduction of production and transaction costs and the various externalities and economies generate increasing returns and economic growth by their effect on productivity and prices of goods and services.

Processes of economic growth change the environment in which productive systems are immersed and create new opportunities for the economic, social and political actors. When existing institutions become a constraint to the optimal performance of productive and commercial activities and, thus, to growth and structural change, the actors and organizations leading accumulation processes are compelled to introduce institutional changes that will facilitate the accumulation of capital and knowledge.

From the perspective of neo-institutional economic thought, institutional change would be limited to changes in the laws and customs on which the contract system is based because it is laws and customs that regulate relations among economic agents. Increased transaction costs brought about by external changes of the economic agents stimulate changes that alter the relation between cost and benefits. Therefore, just as it is argued that technological innovation plays a key role in the production of goods and services, it could be maintained that new laws and customs constitute institutional innovations that facilitate the regulation and dynamics of institutions (North, 1991).

However, the dynamics of economy and society demand constant institutional change. The creation of new institutions and the replacement of old ones is a slow, complex process which comes about as a result of negotiations and agreements among economic and social actors and organizations faced with changes in the environment. This process is endogenous to the system of relations generated as a result of a process of cumulative causation between economic growth, the demand for institutional change and the actions of actors and organizations.

Institutions, norms and conventions emerge spontaneously because they facilitate exchanges and market and non-market transactions. Agreements among the actors take place subject to the goals pursued by each one to accomplish their projects. Institutions grow and undergo change because they create the conditions from which the mechanisms that guarantee economic efficiency arise. Therefore, a natural determinism does not exist in the formation of institutions. On the contrary, it is individuals and organizations that ultimately make the critical decisions on the process.

Transformations in institutions, norms and conventions come about in response to new demands generated internally in a society. These changes arise due to initiatives by actors and organizations who feel affected by and interested in change in their environment and, in competitive conditions, find an opportunity to improve their position in the markets and profit rate. Changes in institutions can unleash conflicts and tensions between agents and actors, which generate, in turn, changes in their attitudes and actions.

In sum, this is a social process occurring as a result of the emergence and transformation of institutions, norms and conventions. The process could be considered evolutionary in that "natural selection" occurs based on the effectiveness and efficiency of the institutions, rules and norms in an environment of uncertainty.

Finally, the timing of institutional change is, necessarily, slow. Economic development alters power relations within the society of a country, region or city which requires institutional adjustments whose implementation requires time. Moreover, institutional change involves modifying and adapting formal rules as well as informal norms and application systems. This process cannot be completed from one day to the next but rather requires long periods of time allowing organizations and society to adopt new rules and conventions. Finally, old and new institutions co-exist for some time and often both continue on into the future in such a way that the process of institutional change is drawn out over time and may never be fully consummated.

Trust and cooperation

As argued above, the fact that institutions facilitate the efficient functioning of the multiple markets and exchanges among actors and organizations is what makes them one of the decisive factors in economic development. Firms and organizations form networks of relations and exchanges that evolve dynamically from a set of both implicit and explicit agreements and contracts. Cooperation and competition among firms and actors lead to a convergence of efforts that stimulates economic dynamic and development.

Institutional mechanisms for cooperation

From this perspective, cooperation among actors and organizations takes on a decisive role in processes of growth and structural change. The essential condition for the existence of cooperation among firms and organizations is the existence of a system of social, economic and institutional relations. The more agreements between actors and organizations in the network and the more innovative and creative these agreements are, the better and more adequate will be the conditions for development.

There is a great variety of networks, as shown in Chapter 4. There are personal and firm networks involving agents in their immediate context in which relations are informal, even casual, and occasionally commercial. Local productive systems form a special kind of network because they are deeply rooted in the territory and show explicit, voluntary and commercial relations. Finally, agreements and alliances between firms have recently become widespread. The relations in these cases are explicit, coded and of a contractual nature.

What are the mechanisms that lead to the creation of systems of relations, agreements and exchanges between firms in an economy? How can cooperation among actors and organizations in an economy be explained? These are some of the questions under debate and the answers to them depend on the type of network and the relations established among the actors. When the network involves family or neighborhood relations in a community with few external contacts or when the relations are of a community or group with a unique identity, cooperation among members is founded on the trust arising from personal or cultural ties. In these cases, cooperation refers to personal or cultural relations more than to a system of economic, social and political relations.

However, at the other extreme, when dealing with voluntary and formal relations established among firms to improve their market share, the creation and development of a system of relations complies with a rational strategy oriented by entrepreneurial objectives. Therefore, cooperation emerges from formal agreements which are often expressed in contracts and these contractual relations can also give rise to mechanisms of trust among firms.

Trust is one of the elements on which cooperation between individuals and organizations are founded, as Arrow (1974) acknowledges when he points out that "trust ... saves a lot of trouble to have a fair degree of reliance on other people's work." But trust is a complex concept and may refer to widely varying situations. It can be understood as social capital that emerges spontaneously within a productive system along with mutual cooperation among firms or it can be understood as individual capital based on the reputations of the actors and organizations that effect economic and social transactions.

Relations of trust and development

Williamson (1993) ties the concept of trust to risk analyses in that it would refer to the probability that an individual with whom a relation of cooperation has been established will not act against us. This author takes an extreme stand when he states that trust "is reserved for very special relations between family, friends and lovers." Thus commercial relations cannot be understood on the basis of personal trust.[2] At most, one could speak of institutional trust in reference "to the social and organizational context within which the contracts are embedded."

This position is based on an approach dealing with institutions from a micro perspective, as agreements among economic units, not in terms of the influence of their investment decisions on economic development processes. Therefore, it is entrenched within an approach that reduces the institutional question to analyzing exchanges of property rights and their costs and explaining market organization and contract structure. It also deals with economic organizations, such as firms, as little more than contractual networks. Finally, this approach has a functional view of economic relations which can seem to be clearly unrelated to the fact that firms are organizations immersed in the territory and whose competitiveness depends on strategic relations with the rest of the actors in that territory.

In contrast to this contractual, functional view of the relations between actors and organizations, the notion of trust has been the object of considerable attention in recent decades as a result of research into local productive systems in late developed countries. Ottati (1994) assigns trust an essential role in explaining the mechanisms of cooperation in industrial districts. Cooperation and trust are also characteristic of systems of productive and commercial relations in industrial districts. Trust is based on custom and only refers to those transactions that normally take place in districts. It is, therefore, a collective capital that all members of the district can put to use. In the ultimate analysis, trust is a by-product of a common culture. Moreover, relations of trust based on personal reputation are easily developed in industrial districts because the environment encourages knowledge of all moral and personal characteristics of people and firms.

According to Ottati, if trust and cooperation are maintained, it is because they provide benefits to the members of the district. Reciprocal trust and cooperation facilitates transactions that would not take place if these relations did not exist. In turn, these transactions encourage productive specialization, diffusion of technical knowledge and funding of productive activity through "interlinking transactions of subcontracting and credit." In the case of personal trust, returns are associated with those transactions involving too much risk, as is the case of investment in innovation. Finally, Ottati goes on to maintain that the custom of cooperation still exists in districts due to the existence of controls and social sanctions which local institutions (political parties, local government and even entrepreneurial associations and unions) tend to reinforce with their actions.

This interpretation of the mechanisms of cooperation has the advantage of acknowledging the importance of local productive systems in development processes. It also recognizes that firms belong to milieux which encourage the exchanges and interactions necessary to obtain the expected returns. But it suffers from some weaknesses, particularly because it goes so far as to deal with trust as an alternative to the competitive strategies of firms, and even to uphold this view in terms of social and institutional control of the industrial district. The evidence, however, does not seem to support this interpretation. Over the last decade, the process of globalization has created the conditions for the internationalization of production and increased services in industrial districts, two phenomena that weaken the system of internal relations based on the custom of cooperation and trust. Finally, the organization of local productive systems has steadily changed and informal and personal relations have less importance while formal relations and strategic behavior have become increasingly significant in new productive networks and firm alliances.

Thus, trust becomes meaningful in dealing with firm competitiveness, particularly as regards small and medium sized firms, in a turbulent or uncertain environment and with insufficient information on the economic actors. This concept proves to be functional when associated with an environment in which multiple exchanges take place among actors and organizations, where actors share a common technological, productive and social history, a common cultural heritage as well as the feeling of belonging to the same collectivity (Granovetter, 1973 and 1985). But the absence of formal relations does not imply that non-specified reciprocity or agreements do not exist, nor does it mean that the actors and organizations do not take into account the economic effects of cooperation when making decisions.

Finally, the existence of trust does not guarantee the economic growth of a locality or region. On the contrary, relations of trust are established in an environment where institutions have been created as a result of given historical, cultural and associative conditions at a given stage in the process of economic development. However, as has been pointed out above, institutional needs change as a consequence of structural transformations; thus they may not be the most adequate to continue down the growth path in the future. Moreover, local actors may misinterpret the evolution of the productive system and make incorrect investment decisions and the system of institutions, in turn, would be incompatible with processes of growth and structural change.

Strategic relations and development

As described above, trust is a characteristic of systems of productive and commercial relations in a given locality or territory. This aspect means that trust is very difficult to replicate through initiatives of actors and organizations (Williamson, 1993). But trust is a part of the normal operation of productive activity and reinforces commitments acquired by firms in their productive and commercial relations with other firms. In fact, trust can be understood as one of the mechanisms contributing to cooperation and coordination of the actors and, therefore, to the development of a territory.

In competitive environments, when productive systems and firms are undergoing processes of profound structural change and technological innovation, cooperation based on trust among the actors and firms could be interpreted as the calculated use of a spontaneous sentiment existing in a collectivity. In this sense, some of the analyses of diffuse industrialization experiences in late developed countries in southern Europe discussed in earlier chapters interpret the emergence and development of firms in non-metropolitan areas as a response of local communities to situations of necessity implemented through cooperation and trust among local firms.[3]

However, in turbulent and uncertain environments the analysis should be broadened and cooperation among actors and organizations should be seen as a phenomenon occurring through the exchange of goods and services as a result of competitive strategies of actors and organizations. In this sense, it is helpful to apply game theory in analyzing the functions of institutions and norms as well as to interpret the rationality[4] of the strategies of firms and economic and social actors.

Economic agents select their strategies with the goal of obtaining the maximum payoff. On occasion, as North (1994) points out, cooperation among economic agents arises when a relation (a game) is repeated, there are few actors (players) and they possess information on all of the members (participants). When these conditions do not exist, it should be difficult to maintain cooperation among the members. When the economic dynamic involves a change in power relations among the actors or in the cost/benefit relations, cooperation among actors and organizations requires the creation of economic and political institutions to support it.

In fact, when relations among firms and actors are analyzed from the perspective of game theory, cooperation takes place as a result of the combined effect of the dominant strategies of each of the players. This may lead to a game score that none of the players would have wanted (Eggertsson, 1990; Axelrod, 1984). For example, the distrustful attitude of the members (players) that participate in a project (game), would mean that cooperation would be based on the perception/observation of the behavior (actions and reactions) of each one of the members (of the adversaries), which could lead to reciprocal punitive actions.

However, game theory allows one to interpret the strategic behavior of firms and the multiple actors within a locality or territory. From this perspective, external firms' choice of a place within an industrial district in which to locate a plant is comprehensible because the locality offers certain resources whose use reinforces their competitive advantage. The internationalization of local firms who reduce industrial activity in a city or region while increasing local production of services to firms, such as design, technological innovation, entrepreneurial logistics or marketing, also becomes understandable. It is logical that firms in local productive systems act strategically using mechanisms of trust and cooperation existing in the district. And, finally, it is also consistent that local actors attempt to reach their objectives through initiatives for local development that strengthen the competitive advantage of cities and regions and, therefore, of firms.

From the perspective of strategic behavior of the actors, the question does not lie in whether the relations among actors are formal or informal or whether they are based on contracts or on mutual trust. What is really significant is the confluence of the strategies of actors and firms in a territory, which requires support by institutions rooted in the local culture. Strategic cooperation neutralizes uncertainty in the markets and maintains the competitive position of actors and firms, thus contributing to the development of cities and regions.

Governance and local development

Over the last few decades, the diffusion of institutionalist thought has prompted an important discussion as to the mechanisms of governance, affecting processes of economic development. As mentioned above, the organizational forms of the state and political systems create an institutional environment that conditions economic results because they define and manage political, social and legal rules that regulate the behavior of economic actors and organizations. Moreover, public and private actors and organizations create conventions, behavior codes and norms that govern their economic, social and institutional relations. All of this leads to new forms of governance in the territory that stimulate processes of endogenous development.

The notion of governance has received various interpretations emanating from various methodological positions as well as from the unique approach of each field of study (Gilly and Pecqueur, 1998). The neo-institutionalist economists, for example, define it as those processes of coordination that lead actors and organizations to establish agreements and contracts (Williamson, 1985; 1993). Since the economy of transaction costs is central to institutionalist thought, "opportunism and bounded rationality are the key behavioral assumptions"[5] on which governance relies. This interpretation of governance has a "micro-level focus" which analyzes the institutional arrangements that govern the way in which firms compete and cooperate.

Jurists and political scientists (Kooiman, 1993) understand governance to be an institutional system which arises as a result of the interactions and actions of the actors intervening in economic, social and political processes according to specific objectives and interests. This approach to governance has a meso-level focus since it refers to the capability of public and private actors to define and implement public action and policies through their negotiations and agreements. Moreover, it introduces the notion of network into the concept of governance by incorporating system and interaction categories. It also assumes the changing nature of norms and rules, and, thus, of the institutional system due to changing needs and demands of public and private actors.[6]

When governance is approached from the perspective of local development, one must use a broad concept that integrates the various interpretations and also takes into account the following dimensions:

1   The governance of development refers to actions of actors who behave strategically. It is implemented through the activity of private and public institutions such as firms, financial institutions, chambers of commerce, entrepreneurial associations and unions. Moreover, the more complex the institutional fabric, the more important the role of intermediary organizations, such as development and training agencies and entrepreneurial and innovation centers.

2   Governance refers to commercial and non-commercial transactions among actors and organizations because exchanges between firms and organizations are not abstract economic transactions but rather take place in a given social and political context which influences the relations between actors and organizations. Governance also introduces interactions of all kinds that occur as a result of the configuration of actor networks.

3   Governance is the result of a historical process. Relations between firms and organizations change in response to the new needs of the economic, social and political dynamic. These changes give rise to

new institutions. The productive dynamic and innovation depend on the path of growth ("path dependence"), just as the social and political dynamic is conditioned by a historical component.

4   Governance refers to the process of development in a given territory. The economic, social and political relations emerge within a localized institutional context and therefore, actors and organizations play a specific role in development processes with differentiated power relations and competences that evolve and are transformed throughout history.

Governance of local development involves a process of cooperation and coordination integrating the strategies of public and private actors, their investment decisions and the exchanges they establish with each other. It is, therefore, an institutional process that affects the regulation of economic activity and, indirectly, of production. It is also of a dynamic nature since its objective is to facilitate processes of growth and structural change of a city or region. Growth and structural change are stimulated by mechanisms such as the reduction of transaction cost and network economies. Finally, it refers to the norms and conventions that regulate relations among actors and organizations acting within a territory. For this reason, it is different from the rules of government which affect the macro-economy and the general design of institutions.

Governance manifests a specific form in each territory because capital accumulation and the organization of production are different, because the actors are different, because the economic, technological and institutional history is different, because the culture is different. A typology of forms of territorial governance can be proposed. Colletis *et al.* (1999) define four types of actor/organization that lead the processes of local development.

- *Private governance* involves those situations in which private actors, such as a leading large firm in a productive system or a network of firms, who stimulate the local development process, catalyze public and private investment and create norms, conventions and conditions for regulation.
- *Collective private governance,* in which the key actor is a formal institution which groups the private organizations of a city or region, such as chambers of commerce or firm associations, and serves to foster collective development strategy of a territory and the creation and development of new institutions.
- *Public governance* refers to those cases in which an institution or some public institutions (city hall, regional government, development agencies, research centers) encourage cooperation and convergence of public and private initiatives in the local development project and favor the creation and development of new institutions.

- *Mixed governance* refers to a combination of initiatives of public and private actors that implement mechanisms leading to local development.

Governance of local development, then, is manifested in widely varying forms depending on the characteristics of each territory and the actors that come together in it. However, the capability of creating agreements among actors and organizations and the results in terms of the effect on the dynamic of firms and economic development depend on the existence of an institutional environment and an institutional system which encourage exchanges and economic, social and political transactions. In many countries, recent changes in constitutional design have meant a change in the rules of the game governing the formation of systems of governance. And the flexibility of institutions and their adaptation to the needs and demands of firms and society have become critical in the evolution of the forms of governance.

Change in the rules of the game for national states due to the creation and devolution of competences has had a strong impact on development of territorial governance, because the institutional environment has been created that allows local communities to decide on development processes. In Europe and Latin America over the last 25 years, an intense process of political and administrative decentralization has taken place, channeled through constitutional changes and adjustments in administrative systems.[7]

The functional reorganization of state activities and the transfer of competences and powers to local and regional governments have taken place because of the need to provide an adequate response to new demands. These arise from the management of economic, social and political relations which requires new forms of association of public and private actors and new models of political governance capable of administering the increasingly complex economic, social and political dynamics. The door is thus open for local actors to launch strategic initiatives and more flexible forms of organization leading to new processes of growth and capital accumulation.

Finally, increased competition in the markets associated with globalization requires efficient responses and strategic cooperation of actors and local organizations. Thus the emergence of multiple institutions from the plurality of actors has led to effective strategic responses to the new needs posed by economic, social and political dynamics in times of globalization. In the most innovative cities and regions, institutional relations have become more complex and the number of actors and institutions has multiplied. This has led some authors (Amin and Thrift, 1993) to refer to "institutional thickness."[8]

It is not, however, so much a question of quantity or density of institutions existing in a locality or territory, but rather of whether these institutions are responding to the needs and demands arising from the development dynamic. It is principally a matter of each and every institution facilitating processes of economic and social growth and pursuing the objectives that originally prompted their creation and of not becoming an obstacle to development. Furthermore, the key for development is that institutions be flexible so that they can adapt to the needs and demands originating in the economic and social dynamic. Finally, in turbulent and uncertain environments the critical factor in development processes is not so much the quantity of institutions as it is the strategic cooperation and coordination of actors and institutions.

The theory of proximity

The theory of proximity appeared as a new paradigm in the 1990s (Bellet *et al.*, 1993; Rallet and Torre, 1995; Bellet *et al.*, 1998) which claims to inherit the theories of industrial districts and of innovative milieux (Gilly and Torre, 2000). One of the distinctive characteristics of the theory of proximity is that it introduces the institutional factor into the analysis of economic dynamics.

The point of departure is the notion of the proximity of actors and organizations with one component referring to organizational aspects and another to territorial aspects, according to Gilly and Torre (2000). Organizational proximity refers to links among industrial actors in the organization of production and combines two non-exclusive rationales. On the one hand, it refers to actors who belong to the same firm or the same network. On the other, it refers to actors with analogous types of organization, who share knowledge and technological know-how and target the same kind of markets, which implies that there are areas in which exchanges among them are economically possible and feasible. Geographic proximity particularly involves links associated with the physical distance between the actors. It refers to accessibility factors such as transportation infrastructures and the use of communication technologies.

The concept of proximity therefore refers to organizational links among the actors, to positional and dynamic relations among them and, above all, to institutional relations. Particularly involved are the exchange of goods, services, resources and information among actors and interaction among local and external actors who participate in processes of growth and capital accumulation. However, the notion of proximity also has an institutional dimension that includes the set of norms and rules, whether implicit or explicit, that lead to cooperation and coordination among actors and give rise to social and institutional networks.

Organizational and geographic proximity give rise to static interactions which produce external economies of both a pecuniary and technological nature.[9] Organizational and territorial proximity also fosters interaction between actors and the organizations their strategies have created, thus encouraging the exchange of merchandise, information and knowledge, the establishment of contractual relations and cooperation. Strategic relations influence production costs (reduced transaction costs) and encourages network economies[10] that promote the creation and diffusion of knowledge and information and, therefore, influence productivity and competitiveness of firms and territories.

Interaction of actors and firms with organizational, physical or territorial proximity brings up the question of coordination and integrative capability of proximity actions (Gilly and Pecqueur, 1998). The coordination of actors and interactions accounts for the effects on economic dynamics and acts as a model for the solution of the problems arising in development processes in a local system.

According to the theory of proximity, coordination of the actors and organizations that make up a territorial productive system may come about through a pricing system. But it also occurs through relations of cooperation leading to the exchange of merchandise, diffusion of innovations and knowledge and the information flows required by the actors and organizations to reach their objectives.

A territory's capacity for collective action is defined by the coordination of its actors. Faced with the problems arising in the dynamic of local economies, the learning capability of local actors leads to the detection of productive problems and design of adequate solutions. Collective action of local actors and organizations leads to a more efficient use of the local surplus.

It is essential that the actors share a common view on the problems of the local productive system to provide a local response to the challenges of adjustments in productive systems. Moreover, implementation of the actors' actions demands that the local productive system's institutions, whether formal or informal, come together in such a way that an institutional commitment can be reached to facilitate coordination. This commitment among actors normally requires that "one or several specific institutions act as the engine in the institutional relations of the institutional system constituted by the actors: property rights for an industrial financial group, a system of technical norms..." (Gilly and Pecqueur, 1998, p. 505).

The collective action of the actors, that is, local dynamics, comes about as a result of institutional system. The existence of networks of local actors leads to the collective definition of common norms and rules concerning product property and the exchange of knowledge; relations of cooperation and trust make local dynamics informally feasible; and the explicit rules regulate cooperation among the actors.

In sum, the theory of proximity emphasizes the role of institutions. They are the vehicle through which the foundation of growth and capital accumulation, that is to say, interaction among actors and organizations, takes place.

Local development instruments

As policies and initiatives for local development are implemented, local public managers are faced with the need to provide practical responses to numerous questions that arise. There is a great variety of actions, each pursuing very specific objectives. Some aim to foster the birth and development of firms, others seek to provide funding, technical assistance and marketing or trade services. To achieve these goals, it is essential to develop the projects technically and financially, build the necessary infrastructures, encourage change in the entrepreneurial culture and local mentality and promote interaction among local actors.

Thus, the management of development becomes one of the main foundations of local economic policy. To reach the goals local actors have targeted, it is not enough to have conceived of a fortunate strategy and launched the most adequate actions. It is essential that projects and financial and human resources be managed. Just as important as the launching of a new development strategy is the efficient administration of each and every project through which the strategy is implemented.

In order for the results of local initiative to be optimal, they should provide a response to the strategic and operative needs of local economic policy. That is, the creation of a local organization capable of assuming the responsibility of designing and implementing the development process is necessary. Existing management units within territorial administrations are not always the most adequate since they lack competences in local development issues and functional and financial flexibility or they are too bureaucratized.

European experiences[11] show that local development strategies are more effective when they are implemented through autonomous, flexibly managed development agencies. These are intermediary organizations that put local managers in touch and encourage relations among administrations, firms and society. Their diversity is due to the need to create the most technically adequate organization, that is, the one that best adapts to the unique conditions and characteristics of the local economic, entrepreneurial and institutional system.

The creation and start-up of an agency is a complex task requiring a feasibility study to define the prerequisites as regards technical characteristics, financial aspects and qualification of the promoters and managers. Feasibility studies should clearly establish these aspects to avoid unsuccessful adventures.

Most important, all development agencies or centers for local initiatives must be subject to and conditioned by a development plan for the city or region. Not only is it a matter of identifying what kind of services can be rendered with these tools, the objectives that can be reached and the strengths and limitations of the type of instrument selected. Rather and above all, it is a matter of considering their adequacy to carry out specific actions included in the local development policy.

Feasibility studies for the creation of an agency or tool for local development should specify certain *technical characteristics*, among which are:

1 So that the tool can achieve its objectives, *the relevant economic and social conditions of the locality or territory* should be described, indicating the place that the agency will occupy in already existing public and private service activities.

2 *Description of the present market for the services* to be supplied by the center. On the one hand, it should establish the needs and demands that exist in the territory and identify target groups and firms. Also to be defined are the objectives the center proposes to achieve, the services in which it will specialize and the technical facilities to be made available to clients.

3 *The definition of the project* should identify the method, responsibility and timing of the agency's start-up and define future developments. To do this, it is important to design and foresee the organization, the way services are to be rendered, the funding mechanisms, promotion of the tool, priorities to be observed during the development of the implementation plan and the balance between income from services rendered and anticipated costs.

4 *Location of the agency* involves selecting an adequate location to provide services to firms and headquarters for the agency. These buildings are often representative and symbolic infrastructures of the project.

In regard to the *financial aspects* of the project, it is advisable to consider the following issues, among others:

1 *Business plan.* A meticulous, coherent, consistent and realistic business plan for the agency or tool is necessary if a clear idea of the "adventure" to be initiated is to be obtained to apply for financial assistance.

2 *The promoters' contributions* should indicate the capital, tangible goods, human factors and all other resources that each of them is willing to make available to the center at start-up and throughout the initial period (experimental stage of the center).

3 *Loans and credits.* The agency's funding throughout the initial stage and later usually comes from the promoters' contributions and public and/or private external funding. It is therefore necessary to establish the quantity of loans necessary to set up the center and for its later developments, and the actions that will be carried out to attract external resources.

4 *Financial objectives.* The creation of tools for local development requires a realistic definition of the financial objectives of the project

and the establishment of key indicators that will measure the center's economic results.

5   *Coherence of financial data and strategy.* The promoters of the development agency should have a clear idea from the start of the internal consistence of the financial numbers with development strategy and foreseeable behavior of the local market. The success of local initiatives will depend on the creation of technically and financially viable tools. Therefore, the consistence and coherence of the center's business plan and development strategy is sometimes a challenge for promoters and managers.

Finally, a profile of future directors and managers of development agencies can be of considerable use. The success of local development tools requires the implicit and/or explicit support of institutions, firms and opinion leaders within the high direction of the city or region. But it is the management capability of directors, the entrepreneurial and organizational capability and leadership of the person responsible for management and direction of the agency that are of critical importance for the future of the center. Therefore, for directors and managers, experience in the management of this type of organization and the capability to relate to entrepreneurs and the local population is of vital importance.

Interaction between institutions and endogenous development

Institutional development and change is one of the main processes in economic growth and structural transformation. In particular, institutions facilitate interaction among firms and actors and reduce risk and uncertainty in exchanges, thus contributing to a good performance of the economic system. They lead to lower transaction costs and foster the appearance of external economies, all of which affects the price system and leads to increased productivity. Moreover, trust permits transactions to take place that would not otherwise do so. Also, institutional innovations transform the institutional system and regulation which facilitates economic development and evolution.

   Institutions are born and change as a result of cultural, historical and associative circumstances in a given stage of economic development. Thus they are conditioned by innovation, the way in which production is organized and the specific characteristics of the territory. Technological change directly affects growth which places new demands on institutions to facilitate processes of accumulation of capital and knowledge. Innovations transform the milieu in which productive activity takes place and encourage new opportunities and new ways of doing business which, in turn, require appropriate institutions and new forms of regulation. When innovations generate new activities involving transformations in power relations and new agreements among firms and actors, adequate regulation is necessary for the new business transactions.

Organization and organizational change also requires appropriate institutions which facilitate relations among firms and entities. Production in firms or groups of firms of a Fordist nature, where the hierarchy determines the relations and exchanges to occur between the production units, institutional forms, such as norms and contracts that guarantee agreements, are needed. But when production is organized through firm networks such as industrial districts, custom and trust characterize relations among firms. Here, the explicit and codified relations in agreements and strategic alliances among firms must be implemented through contracts that do not exclude trust mechanisms.

Furthermore, institutions take on specific forms in each territory due to differences in the city or region's culture, technological and economic history and the actors and their forms of association. Cities are constructed spaces where different patterns of production, forms of social organization and cultural and behavior patterns are built up over time. The combination and interaction of different layers of economic activity and social organization condition the evolution and dynamic of institutions during the process of growth. The city is, furthermore, the place for networking, where behavior codes and rules based on trust have been created by interaction and exchange between actors. As the behavior of the actors becomes strategic, agreements tend to become formal and relations increasingly follow explicit rules. Finally, changes in the urban system and increased competition among cities lead to new needs and demands for flexible rules to regulate relations among cities.

Local development policy, then, is based on a new form of regulation of the relations among economic, political and social actors. This form of governance has a mesolevel focus which designs and carries out policies based on negotiation and specific agreements among the actors. Actions are implemented through specific intermediate agencies created and managed by local actors. The development and promotion of formulas such as the partnership and the creation of networks among local actors are characteristics of the new approach to regulation.

7   Cities, a place for development

Cities are, and always have been, the space where changes of the economic and productive system and the organization of the institutional system take place. Therefore, income growth (investment and employment), structural change and innovative processes are associated with urban development. One could say, then, that cities play, and have played, a strategic role in the evolution of societies and economic development throughout history.

The factors that place processes of economic growth in cities are precisely those that characterize endogenous development. Cities foster the generation of externalities and productive diversity, they promote interaction and the formation of networks by creating meeting points among all kinds of actors and they provide incentives for innovation.

Cities and urban regions respond to today's challenges of globalization of production and exchange by improving their competitiveness. They do so by linking the production and organization adjustment to the employment of their own resources, by diffusing innovation, adapting institutions to new needs and demands and reinforcing their relations with other cities. This explains why urban hierarchies, founded on the size of the settlements, tend to weaken and why new functional hierarchies related to the development potential of each city appear. A new space for local development policy has thus unfolded.

This chapter starts by discussing the urban features which facilitate processes of endogenous development. The analysis shows that economic transformations of recent decades take place in cities which are of varying sizes. Large cities and central urban systems are not the only relevant spaces in economic dynamics but city networks also play a strategic role in new processes of change. Next the chapter shows that cities have become key actors in local development policy. The final section focuses on the relations between urban development and the other processes that explain endogenous development.

Cities and endogenous development

Lasuén (1976) points out that one of the key concerns in development theory is determining where investment is located. Empirical evidence shows that investment tends to locate in cities and it has, therefore, been thought that there is a direct relation between economic development and urbanization.

Historical evidence shows that sustained per capita income growth is accompanied by higher levels of urbanization,[1] particularly in its initial phases. Increased productivity in agriculture, and later in industry, as well as changes in demand, associated with income elasticity, tend to bring about a progressive increase in the demand for urban goods and, consequently, for urban production, which creates new job opportunities in cities. The transfer of resources from rural areas to cities would seem to have encouraged urbanization.

Particularly after the industrial revolution in England, increasing productivity and expansion of urban production are driven by the introduction of innovation. Changes in firm activities and city systems can be understood as the temporal and spatial effect of adopting innovation. It was Perroux (1955) who, by means of growth pole theory, argued that economic development and urbanization are the consequence of innovation.[2] Economic development and urbanization are, therefore, two sides of the same coin.

Thus, local productive systems and cities participate in a common process. When agents interact and new spaces are created for the production of goods, exchanges and relations among the actors, investment decisions in the productive system and the city tend to favor convergence of productive and urban development. In any case, cities are a space for endogenous development: they generate externalities that lead to increasing returns, they support diversified productive systems that drive the economic dynamic, they are organized into networks, in which the relations among actors lead to diffusion of knowledge and, finally, they stimulate learning and innovative processes in firms (Quigley, 1998; Glaeser, 1998).

Externalities and increasing returns in cities

Endogenous development processes are benefited when firms and productive systems located in the city are capable of using externalities produced by the city. One of the principles that account for the existence and performance of cities is the capacity to create agglomeration economies, which guarantee efficiency in firms and productive systems by reducing the costs of production, coordination and transaction. Most importantly, firms in many industrial activities can have access to economies associated with the size of plants located in cities, the use of raw materials and resources from urban suppliers and exchanges with other urban firms. Moreover, firms that locate in cities encounter advantages that lead to lower transportation costs of raw materials and products. For decades, transportation has been one of the main economies that cities have provided to firms and, although transportation costs no longer constitute the considerable share of production cost they used to, they are still significant.

In any case, cities, and particularly large cities, encourage exchange, which leads to decreased transaction costs. Geographic proximity and the relationships among entrepreneurs, managers, technicians and workers facilitate all kinds of relations in all kinds of markets. In the labor market, the cost of labor searches tends to be lower because the supply of skilled labor and the demands of firms and organizations are matched much faster. In the service market, it is not difficult to find new, uncommon services that assist firms in maintaining or improving competitiveness. In cities it is easier to match physical capital investment with human capital which improves efficiency and effectiveness.

Diversity in the city

Productive, commercial and cultural diversity in cities attracts firms and workers. A broad range and variety of actors, activities and markets exist in cities, which facilitates interaction and the formation of scale economies and fosters endogenous development, in turn. The diversity of economic activities brings about growth in economies derived from the availability of shared markets of resources and productive factors, lower transaction costs, greater differentiation of raw materials and final products and minimum market stability (Quigley, 1998).

Diversity in the labor market provides important advantages to the local economy by facilitating the division of labor in and among firms, which, in turn, leads to more efficient and competitive firms and local productive systems. Diversity facilitates workers' negotiation capacity, allowing them to benefit from positive investment results. In brief, firms and workers benefit from the specialization of labor resulting from diversified markets.

Growth and development in cities is, then, reinforced by diversity. Undoubtedly, an environment favorable to the appearance of external scale economies is generated in metropolitan areas, particularly in those with varied markets. However, as Polèse (1994) points out, diversification of services and economic activities in general, and of markets, in particular, provides more options for exchange, makes local economies more competitive and reduces the need for firms and local organizations to resort to outside resources. These factors enhance their negotiating capacity and market position.

Interaction and exchange of ideas in cities

Cities are also the space, *par excellence*, for interaction. Places in which economic, political and institutional decision-makers, technicians and workers mingle are located in cities, as are the firms' administrative offices and headquarters where investment decisions are made. Training and research institutions, convention and exhibition centers and leisure and cultural sites are usually located in cities as well.

Here, as Maillat (1998) reminds us, meetings take place among economic, social, political and institutional actors according to pre-established formal and informal behavior codes. The relations among these actors encourage the diffusion of information and ideas and facilitate exchanges and economic transactions. Through these contacts, agreements are formalized and mechanisms of cooperation among firms are defined. This relational system reduces transaction costs and facilitates the agreements that make it possible to obtain economies of scale in research, production and markets. The circulation of ideas constitutes an advantage for cities, analogous to the reduction of costs associated with worker mobility (Glaeser, 1998).

Summarizing, then, it is in cities that cooperative relations and exchanges take place, leading to the formation of networks to obtain economic goals. These networks are obviously based on spatial, cultural and psychological proximity. Characterized by their density, their informality and openness, they give structure to the city (Camagni, 1998). Network externalities reduce uncertainty and facilitate exchanges and, therefore, guarantee greater economic efficiency in firms and local productive systems.

Innovation and learning in cities

Yet, perhaps, efficiency in firm and system dynamics is guaranteed by the capacity of cities for encouraging innovation, promoting learning processes and, ultimately, the diffusion of knowledge throughout the local productive fabric.

Sociologists (Weber) and historians (Braudel) have long accepted that innovation originates in cities, and economists (Lucas, 1988) have associated cities with the gestation of the ideas behind growth processes. Cities and, in general, the urban system play a strategic role in the generation and diffusion of knowledge and innovations because the resources (human and know-how) and the relational and service systems essential in order for firms to innovate are located there. In short, cities foster and accumulate information and knowledge.

The theory of growth centers contends that urban areas are hotbeds for innovative initiatives. Hoover and Vernon (1959) show that large cities provide innovative firms with the scale economies (cheap industrial land, common services, meeting points, skilled labor) needed to encourage innovation. Moreover, scale economies not only reinforce geographic concentration but also contribute to the creation of new firms, as incubation theory acknowledges (Leone and Struyk, 1976). Finally, geographers maintain that innovation is diffused hierarchically throughout city systems, from higher levels (often with strong international ties) down to the lowest levels of the urban system.

Cities also facilitate learning. One must particularly remember that, when market competition increases, urban density and the need to compete lead specialists to increase learning. On the other hand, human capital accumulation tends to increase rapidly in cities because people learn through interaction, which is accelerated by the higher population density in cities (Glaeser, 1997). Also located in urban systems are the institutions essential to the production of learning processes in firms, in that they stimulate the efficient diffusion of information.

Finally, ideas spread easily in cities, where, in fact, the diffusion of information and the spill-over effect, as described in endogenous growth theory, are favored. Worker mobility among firms encourages the transport of knowledge and innovations throughout the local productive system. Moreover, the physical proximity facilitates communication and the diffusion of ideas. Hence, one can correctly state that cities reduce the costs of transaction of ideas and stimulate the diffusion of innovation.

The cities of new industrial spaces

In the foregoing discussion on urbanization and development, it has clearly been established that cities are the space in which development processes take place. When analyzed from the perspective of new economic growth theory and territoriality, it becomes obvious that urban phenomena contain the elements that characterize endogenous development processes.

However, as we pointed out in Chapter 2, the characteristics of the environment in which firms and cities compete today reward cities that are capable of transforming their own development potential into competitive advantages. Thus, after the decline of industrial centers and cities in the 1970s, we have witnessed the birth and reinforcement of new industrial spaces and service cities in the 1980s and 1990s.

What kinds of cities take the lead in transformation processes? Do vertical hierarchies exist in the organization of urban systems in which large, global cities acquire a dominant role? Does the formation of city networks lead to improvement in the competitiveness of smaller cities? How important are the new ways to organize production and globalization in the discussion?

As Sassen (1991) and Castells (1989 and 1996) point out, increasing globalization, the introduction and diffusion of a new wave of innovations (especially, those related to information technology) throughout the entire system and an increasing demand for services underlie present-day economic and urban dynamics. A few large cities lead the main transformation processes. However, increasing flexibility of firms, firm networks, changes in the location patterns of large firms and recent initiatives in local and regional public sectors have brought about less hierarchical, more polycentric city systems.

At present, urban development is determined by two tendencies, which are, to a large extent, contradictory. On the one hand, increasing diffusion of both industrial and service productive activities has been observed, which has converted some innovative small and medium-sized cities into preferred locations for modern activities. On the other hand, researchers have simultaneously observed a tendency to spatially concentrate and centralize management, control and specialized services, particularly those that satisfy the demand of more global productive segments. Hence, leadership of the global economy is bestowed on a limited number of large cities.

The formation of new industrial spaces (Scott, 1988) is linked to increasing urbanization in all kinds of cities, whether large, medium or small, as can be observed in the various models of territorial organization that have been taking shape in recent decades.

Based on the type of product, process and organizational innovation (modern technology approaching the technological frontier or high technology or, in other words, incremental and radical innovations) and the endogenous or exogenous nature of resources (entrepreneurial capacity and financial resources), four types of industrial spaces can be identified: high-tech excellence models, technological poles, development poles and local firm systems (see Figure 7.1).

Excellence models are characterized by productive systems, made up of firm networks, which produce new goods or use new production and organizational methods and have put local potential for development to work in urban cities and regions. The availability of skilled human resources and entrepreneurial capacity, adequate transportation and communication infrastructure and R&D centers, as well as efficient management of the institutional system, have nurtured the emergence and consolidation of these models. Hence, both large agglomerations and medium-sized cities have sparked some of the most dynamic activities in the productive system. Cases in point are the Cambridge Scientific Park, Silicon Valley in the San Francisco area, Route 128 in Boston, the area around Munich in Bavaria, the Scientific City in Paris or innovative milieux such as the Swiss Jura. Some of these are older innovative cities, but others are new centers in which production is organized around firm networks.

Technological poles, or clusters, of high-tech firms have formed as a result of innovative firms locating in spaces with skilled labor supply, R&D

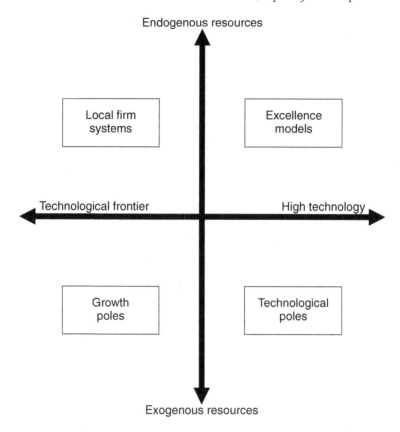

Figure 7.1 New industrial spaces.

centers and good training and research institutions. These spaces are near new expanding product markets and strong financial incentives are offered to firms for locating there. Examples of technological poles are the aeronautical industry in Toulouse, the computer chip industry in Minneapolis-St Paul, Philadelphia or Tucson, aeronautic, software and biochemical activities in Seattle, or the "Silicon Valley replica" in Singapore (under the auspices of Conner Peripherals, Hewlett Packard and some European firms such as Thomson-SGS). All these cities are more or less medium-size that have been specializing over the last decades in high-tech activities because their resources exert a strong pull on leading firms in these areas.

Development poles are clusters of modern technology firms (incremental innovations), formed as a result of branch plants of external firms locating in the area. Affected by urban diseconomies in previous locations, these firms are attracted by the relatively low price of production factors (such as industrial land, labor force) and the existence of financial incentives. In some cases, the concentration of firms comes about as a consequence of specific economic policy and, in others, it is due to the location decisions of the external firms. A renaissance of pole policy is now taking place in the European Union. In Italy, for example, this policy has given rise to planning agreements between the State and firms and the subsequent location of plants in cities of peripheral regions, as occurs with Olivetti and IBM in Bari or with Barilla and Olivetti in Marcianessi (province of Caserta). Or firms may decide to locate and invest in cities of underdeveloped regions, as with Unilever, Unicable and Levis in Olvega (a small town in the Spanish province of Soria with 3,100 inhabitants in 1991), or in declining regions, as with the location of Du Pont in Asturias (an area reconverting from the iron and steel industry).

Finally, *local firm systems* have appeared and become established as a result of endogenous industrialization processes, as previously discussed cases in southern European countries, Asia and Latin America have shown. One characteristic of local productive systems is that they develop in small and medium-sized cities. Marshall (1919) mentions the metallurgic districts of Sheffield and Solingen and cotton cloth production centers in Lancashire; Fuà underlines the bond of diffuse industrialization processes with the "Italia dei Comuni"; Costa Campi places Spanish local productive systems in small and medium-sized cities. The same can be said of the local productive systems in Rafaela in Argentina, Santa Catarina in Brazil, Leon in Mexico, Sialkot in Pakistan or Tiruppur in India.

New industrial spaces, then, are anchored in cities of various dimensions where innovative functions are concentrated. Sometimes, these "new spaces" are older productive, technological and political centers, such as Paris, London, Boston and the Italian and Valencian industrial districts but, occasionally, productive concentration is more recent, as in San Francisco, Munich or Singapore. In any case, production in these spaces tends to adopt new organizational forms through firm networking and even city networks.

Service cities in the global economy

If these new industrial spaces indicate new paths in development and urbanization processes, tertiarization takes us even deeper, if possible, into the economic and urban dimension. The expansion of services[3] and, therefore, of cities as places of production, is due not only to increased demand for both public and private consumer services, but also to the fact that more flexible and disperse ways to organize production depend on the availability of production services. Moreover, geographic diffusion requires greater global integration by means of new service functions.

Services basically contribute to economic development in three ways.

Services produced in the city (tourism, information and production services) may be exported, personal services (such as leisure, health care or commercial services) may be sold to the local and international population and services aimed at improving global competitiveness of the firms may be produced. This last type may be specialized (such as marketing, technical assistance or consulting services) or ubiquitous (such as financial or insurance services).

Location and the factors determining it are, without a doubt, an important question for economic development. Production of services tends to be concentrated in large cities and in the most advanced urban regions. This statement, however, should be qualified in that services have developed rather quickly in medium-sized cities and in areas of industrial diffusion over the last decade.

Large cities and urban regions exert a strong pull on producer real services and financial service activities. The more dynamic functions of the advanced tertiary sector, such as marketing, design, technical assistance, R&D and information, have received a great impetus as firms' increasingly demand these services.[4] Hall (1991) indicates that 93 percent of British service firm headquarters are concentrated in London, 70 percent of all French service firms are located in Paris, 67 percent of Italian service firms are in Rome and 53 percent of German service firms are in Frankfurt.

However, the presence of production service activities in medium-sized cities is on the rise. Although some European cities such as Zurich or Frankfurt are highly specialized in financial services and producer services grow autonomously in Bristol, Lyon and Edinburgh, the fact that some production services follow industrial firms is more significant. Thus, over the last decade, in cities where economic development is based on the model of endogenous development, services to firms have grown strikingly (Vázquez-Barquero and Sáez Cala, 1997).

Finally, institutional change has brought about a perceptible increase in workforce occupied in public and welfare services. Administrative reorganization has transferred more competencies to local and regional administrations (such as the creation and development of the Regional State in Spain and Italy or decentralization in France). Public services have also been decentralized and the prominence of some medium-sized cities has grown, which has not only encouraged the location of public services, but also of production and transportation service firms.

In turn, economic integration and the formation of the European Union have tended to decentralize some of the traditional functions of large capitals, thus fostering new dynamics in city systems. Intense competition has taken place among EU cities to attract some agencies and services (in Alicante, the Patent Office; in Turin, the Agency for Training and Employment; in Lyon, European Television; in Copenhagen, the Environmental Agency). These agencies attract other organisms and reinforce the prominence of cities of varying sizes.

Finally, globalization, deregulation of financial markets and the integration of world-wide markets have not only contributed to the development of service activities in large metropolitan areas of advanced economies, but also in some international cities such as São Paolo, Buenos Aires, Bangkok and Mexico City. The supply of new services to international and global enterprises and of services fulfilling international demand for consumer goods and leisure are on the rise as global markets are formed.

The new processes, then, have emerged as a consequence of the adjustment of accumulation processes and regulation, and have set off contradictory forces. Forces pushing for concentration, associated mainly with the development of modern services, arise even as other forces pushing toward diffusion have been reinforced as a result of the restructuring of industrial and service activities and, in particular, of traditional activities. Since not all industrial and service activities follow the same spatial organization model, new processes have made specific paths to economic development available to cities of varying sizes.

From urban hierarchies to city networks

The discussion of what urban factors facilitate endogenous development and urbanization processes is unequivocal in its conclusion as to the heterogeneity of urban systems. Available resources, development potential and the capacity to attract investment vary from one city to another. Therefore, the creation and evolution of advanced urban functions will be determined, at least in part, by the organization of the urban system (Precedo, 1996).

Nevertheless, there is some difficulty in defining which factors are decisive. The line of thought holding that there is only one hierarchy in city systems, based on the urban dimension, no longer seems to enjoy the same validity today as in the past. From an economic perspective, urban functions are more important and do not depend on city size, but rather on its resources.[5]

When urban areas are perceived as network nodes with multiple economic, social, demographic and informational flows (Smith and Timberlake, 1995), firm and city networks occupy a strategic role in development and urbanization. That is, if the urban system is perceived as a polycentric network of urban centers, it is discovered that there are, in fact, multiple urban hierarchies within the urban system in which cities of varying size perform strategic functions.

The idea that development is diffused through urban hierarchies[6] was quite popular for several decades. Economic growth processes would occur as innovations are spatially diffused through the city systems. Modern productive activities and innovation are concentrated in large cities, then diffused to regional urban centers and, finally, to peripheral localities (Pedersen, 1970; Berry, 1972).

The theory of urban hierarchy and the hierarchic diffusion of production and innovation do not adequately account for the characteristics and processes of urban systems today because the urban environment is subject to constant, unpredictable change which has reduced the hierarchy of economic and social organizations.

In fact, hierarchic structure in the urban system tends to be blurred as a result of the anti-hierarchical elements appearing in new economic and territorial processes.

1 As we have pointed out elsewhere, industrial and service activities location patterns tend to be more and more diffused.
2 A reduced optimal dimension for production plants, the introduction of organizational and process innovation and decreased transportation costs raise the value of territories and locations that firms did not formerly consider attractive.
3 Flexible organization models, such as networking in high-tech firms and local firm systems, become desirable for capital accumulation processes. Hence, non-metropolitan cities, particularly in regions of intermediate development, acquire a strategic role in processes of productive restructuring.
4 Moreover, as Dieperink and Nijkamp (1988) point out for The Netherlands, and this could be extended to all of Europe, the assumption that large cities create and diffuse innovation cannot be generalized to all kinds of products or sectors. Diffusion and adoption of technology depend on the characteristics of the milieu in which firms carry out their activity, the type of production organization and whether it is a matter of radical or incremental innovations. The hierarchical model proposed by central place theory, then, would seem too restrictive.[7]
5 The abandonment of the criteria or principles of market area as a result of decreased transportation costs and the diffusion of the automobile, contributed to reduce hierarchies in city systems.[8]
6 Furthermore, over the last decades large cities have incubated forces that make them less efficient and attractive. The costs of living and producing in a large city tend to increase due to higher housing prices for home and business, the need to commute from home to work, deterioration of the natural environment and increased pollution, as well as less security and higher delinquency and criminality.
7 Finally, one should not automatically identify globalization with urban hierarchy, due to the increasing specialization of cities that form urban, national and international systems and to the organization of urban systems in networks.

However, as Camagni (1993) indicates, one cannot deny that hierarchical factors still exist in the urban systems.

a   Advanced tertiary and other more important functions, related to the qualification of resources and capital requisites, are located in cities within more developed economies, that is, in high levels of the urban system.
b   Castells suggests that the globalization process creates economic power spaces or, as Sassen calls them, global cities where firms and organizations control the global economic dynamic.
c   There are centers specialized in productive activities, such as financial or leisure services which, although not associated with city size, depend on the function and quality of resources.
d   Some spaces are better provided with resources (natural, skilled work-force, etc.), thus equipping them with more relative potential for development. These spaces attract investments and resources from other cities in the urban system.

There are forces, then, which tend to make city systems less hierarchical and more flexible by encouraging horizontal relations among firms and cities in the urban system. And there are also forces that reinforce the concentration of advanced functions, power and global control and, consequently, vertical relations. These apparently contradictory forces require more complex interpretations of the inner workings of city systems and the substitution of pyramidal organization models with more analytic models capable of accounting for horizontal relations and the concept of network.[9]

As Törnqvist (1986) suggests, urban systems can be understood, at present, as the sum of all superimposed, interrelated organizational forms, whether they be older or modern. More important, however, is that the new organizational processes encourage relations among the actors and, therefore, among cities, whatever their dimension. These factors lead us to believe that cities improve their competitiveness when they network and become less hierarchical.

In today's increasingly global context, competition among firms increases, but so does competition among cities where productive processes are rooted. The ability of urban areas to respond depends on the virtue of their functions and services, the quality of their resources and the efficiency of their internal and external networks. When urban systems perform as networks within a polycentric urban organization,[10] cities and, ultimately, their firms become more efficient and competitive.

Each center in polycentric urban systems plays a specific role in the network, depending on its functions, development potential and, finally, its competitive edge. The specific role of each center is determined by its ability to fulfill efficiently and profitably the demand for services or products that other centers in the network are not able to provide. Yet, this does not mean that urban centers must be absolutely specialized which, moreover, is probably not a good idea. In any case, each city performs the functions it is capable of, in order to reach the critical mass necessary to compete in the network's markets.

Network theory's (Camagni, 1992; 1994) view of urban system performance transcends the limitations of the urban hierarchy model, which assigned excessive importance to transportation costs, took into account only vertical and hierarchical relations among centers of various sizes and ranges and disregarded the presence of externalities in urban networks. However, as we have indicated above, existing organization of city systems involves a new relational system among cities in which vertical and horizontal forms coexist. This organizational model brings us to interpret present-day performance of urban systems as a polycentric network in which there are multiple urban hierarchies based on diverse relations among firms and organizations.

Globalization and the territorial model for urban development

Economic and urban growth come about in a context of uncertainty, not only because of technological, productive and organizational change, but also because the economic space has been enlarged as a result of globalization, economic integration and the free circulation of factors and products. Therefore, public and private actors make their investment decisions within a complex productive and institutional environment with new rules.

The new scenario, then, influences the actors' decisions since it determines the way in which productive systems, regulation systems and institutional and organizational systems are related. It is no easy task to define a territorial model within a global environment, because the interpretation must go beyond the sum of the various productive and territorial systems.

The European case provides a good example of the difficulty of building a new stage for competition among cities as a reference for public and private actors' investment decisions. Some of the results of the pioneer research of DATAR[11] (Reclus, 1989) on the European territorial model, show that the European territorial system tends to evolve toward a *monocentric model*, popularly known as the *banana blue* model.

For this approach, the center of gravity of the European productive system would progressively move north and east, thus configuring the European dorsal from London, through Belgium, Holland, Western Germany and Switzerland to Lombardy. Concentrated in the cities of this area would be the most skilled human resources, the most dynamic segments of the productive system and the centers of economic and political decision-making. In the European dorsal more than 70 million inhabitants, with high income levels (GDP of over $900 billion), are concentrated in 18 percent of the European territory.

This perception envisions the formation of an area of diffusion, usually situated around the cities of the Mediterranean Arc (ARCO) running from Valencia to the Emilia Romagna. Some of the territories in ARCO would be witnessing the establishment of innovative urban centers. The rest of the European space would be the periphery. Its territories would not play a decisive role in the configuration of Europe except in the production of tourist services and environmental conservation and would therefore become spaces of assisted development.

This territorial model would be reinforced by three factors (Sénat, 1994): the weakening of the Atlantic façade as a result of the decline of industry and maritime and port activities, the reinforcement of Central Europe as a result of the integration of Eastern Europe and, finally, the definition of the European dorsal zone. There is insufficient empirical evidence to support the thesis that a monocentric territorial model is actually taking shape in the European Union (Meijer, 1993). Paris and London, the great European metropolis, according to the DATAR study, are actually growing as are the large southern cities, Madrid, Rome and Florence, owing to the location of large international firms. But this is not happening with the German and Dutch metropolis where the number of large firms has decreased. Moreover, there is not enough morphological or functional evidence to rationally support the existence of an area of diffusion in the Mediterranean Arc.

In fact, the monocentric model is an imaginary representation, which hypothesizes the existence of a central geographic area, by extrapolating the concepts of central place theory. It disregards the multi-polar and multifunctional nature of the urban system shaping in Europe over centuries. This view actually corresponds to what Europe would have been if it had followed the North American concentration model and independent states had not existed throughout industrial development processes.

As Hall (1993) indicates, the existence of only one urban hierarchy in Europe cannot be justified since, until recently, national capitals were the places for government, finance, commerce, the education system, etc. The structure of transportation and communications (railroad, highways and airports) reinforced the importance of national capitals. One could argue that changes over the last decade and the consolidation of the European Union might favor the emergence of a European center or of a power triangle (Brussels, Berlin and Frankfurt). Nevertheless, it cannot be denied that cities such as Madrid, Copenhagen, Dublin, Lisbon, Seville or Rome are important centers of regional articulation and international exchange.

These observations lead one to acknowledge the polycentric nature of the European territorial model. Two different interpretations of this idea can be made, one of an institutional nature associated with the Commission of the European Union's view, and another, of a historical nature, based on the reality of EU member states.

The Commission of the European Union tends to make investment decisions according to a *decentralized concentration approach* (European

Commission, 1994), which assumes that the European territorial model will continue in the future as it is today. The territorial model, sum of present-day national models, would be reinforced because concentration and diffusion forces would be balanced in the long run. The peripheries would tend to transform their productive activities, attracting the least dynamic industrial and service activities. The decentralized concentration model would be reinforced thanks to measures established by the Commission and national governments, aimed at improving efficiency and strengthening solidarity.

This approach is an institutional view that tries to minimize spatial imbalance in the EU. It is based on an inverted center–periphery approach, using Lasuén's terminology, with political centers that do not always correspond to economic centers. Thus, territorial balance of power would be favored. The multi-polar and multifunctional nature of the European territorial system is acknowledged, as is the role of the protectionist policies of the Nation States and national bourgeoisie throughout the entire period of industrial development. Contrary to the evolution of events in the United States, the European territorial model has led to the polycentric location of dynamic industrial activities in various European regions. However, the Commission's view does not pay sufficient attention to the fact that the EU competes within the global system.

Therefore, a *polycentric view*, with a strategic view of the European Union competing on a global scale, would seem to be more accurate. Each one of the EU cities and regions has a development potential that can be employed to improve the global competitiveness of the Union. Thus, in Atlantic and southern European spaces, there are cities and regions with a considerable history of industrial, technical and research activity that can contribute to this task.

In turn, peripheral regions and territories constitute platforms, which can contribute to the improvement of the positioning of European firms in global markets. The advantageous position of Ireland, Italy or the Iberian Peninsula with respect to the United States, Southern Mediterranean countries or Latin America would lead to increased exports of goods and services, larger direct investments and stronger cultural relations.

In an increasingly global environment and, therefore, one of increasing competition among cities and regions, the peripheral nature of those countries located far from the European dorsal should not be considered functional but rather geographic. The economic, political, social and cultural relations of these territories are multi-polar and multifunctional, hence, likely to be of strategic competitive value to the European Union. For this reason, the response of local and regional actors to these global challenges will be contingent on the competitive value of local resources in the market.

Polycentric and decentralized concentration views are more realistic interpretations of the European territorial model and present-day processes of integration and globalization. Both consider that the urban system is strategic to the dynamics of the European productive system and to improved competitiveness at a global level. The location of investment in cities converts urban systems into the real motors of economic development. These scenarios also introduce significant specifications as to the strategic value of each one of the city systems.

First of all, the polycentric view is not compatible with the proposals of center–periphery models. Within the latter, efficiency is the goal of policies targeting large cities, equity and territorial solidarity are the objectives when targeting medium-sized cities, and ecology and environmental balance when the policy actions are aimed at rural areas. In sharp contrast, within the polycentric approach to the territorial model, all objectives are to be considered as a whole if the ultimate goal is to improve the dynamics of European economies.

Second, the polycentric approach suggests the organization of urban systems into networks, which improve the territorial structure, guide investment and reinforce horizontal relations among firms and organizations. Networking can be applied both within metropolitan areas (in the intra-urban level) and in city systems (at the inter-urban level). There are already some examples such as Randstad in Holland, the Ruhr system (from Bochum to Düsseldorf and Bonn) or the metropolitan areas of Paris and Lyon.

Furthermore, both the polycentric and decentralized concentration views assign a strategic value to medium-sized cities in the economic dynamic. Medium-sized cities constitute the framework of regional space, on which the economic space and institutional system are built. Although not the object of specific policy, in all EU countries medium-sized cities have maintained competitive industrial systems and dynamic service activities (as in the cities of the Terza Italia, Ulm, Freiburg or Patras). They have even become high technology centers, as in the case of Rennes in France or Cambridge in the United Kingdom. It could also be pointed out, as does the European Commission (1994) that cities constitute the framework supporting rural spaces as well.

The strategic planning of local development

Cities are, and have been in the past, the motor of growth and structural change in national and regional economies. As observed above, processes of adjustment and productive restructuring take place in cities and it is there that the economies favorable to endogenous development are to be found. In times of globalization, cities of varying size play a key role because they are the place in which the functions, activities and services structuring the international economic system are located.

Therefore, since the economy is spatially articulated around cities, development strategy must be instrumented through the urban system acting as a support to the system of economic and social relations. Each city possesses certain resources, a given development potential and a relational system as a basis for action aimed at improving competitiveness of local firms. It is for this reason that development strategy that efficiently deploys the urban system competitive potential will not only improve efficiency in the use of resources, but will also take advantage of economies of scale existing in the territory.

As we have pointed out earlier, since the mid-1980s, local development policy as the response of cities to the challenges of globalization is increasingly common in both European and American cities. Recently, public planners and managers have extended the use of strategic planning because it views cities as organizations capable of responding to the challenges of globalization and increasing competition. Cities produce goods and services and compete with other cities in national and international urban systems, that is, they behave like enterprising organizations in the same way as Italian medieval cities.

The possibility of adopting strategic approaches to intervene in the dynamics of cities derives from the analogies that can be drawn between firms and cities and between firm and city systems. Let us consider the city a complex system, acting rationally and coherently in its own interest and relating competitively to other cities in the urban system. Under this assumption, it is possible to make a strategic situational diagnosis and design and implement strategic action to improve the city's position within the urban system.

Thus, cities behave as production and exchange organizations and they are in constant transformation. The internal strengths and weaknesses of their resources and organization condition their competitiveness and performance. Their activities are carried out within a changing external environment in which opportunities and threats, or simply challenges, invariably arise. One could conceive of the city, then, as an organization that incessantly evaluates its strengths, weaknesses, opportunities and threats in order to define strategies and actions aimed at overcoming the challenges and attaining those goals of interest to the local community (Kaufmann and Jacobs, 1987).

Strategic planning helps cities target precise goals with their initiatives. Negotiated among the actors at the highest management level of the city,[12] strategic planning defines strategies aimed at achieving and maintaining competitive advantages for its organizations. According to Cotorruelo Menta (1997), this goal can be attained by mobilizing endogenous potential, attracting resources and external investment and establishing local identity and image.

Strategic planning endeavors to satisfy the needs and expectations of citizens,[13] firms and investors. Its objectives are to:

- increase the standard of living in the city by creating more and better job opportunities, improving the quality of life and promoting social integration;
- mobilize firm competitive advantages and foster the development of productive activities through initiatives such as the diffusion of innovation, the development of productive capacity and the upgrading of human resources;
- guarantee investors a dynamic and secure environment, in which expected economic returns can be obtained through initiatives encouraging relations among firms and institutions and the creation of networks;
- create an attractive urban environment in which to live and invest, through well-defined, efficient urban management, a well-tended historical and cultural heritage and adequate urban infrastructure and social capital.

Strategic plans normally include urban marketing measures aimed at defining, shaping and developing the city's identity and image. A better competitive position is the prime objective of information and promotion campaigns designed to make others perceive the image of the city as it would like to be seen. This portrayal essentially includes all the characteristics that define the identity of the city (resources, development potential, innovative capacity, economic and spatial centrality, infrastructures and symbols) and the communicative messages should efficiently target an objective audience.

Kaufmann and Jacobs consider that strategic planning was often present in earlier planning literature, but they identify important differences with respect to public planning by local and regional administrations in the past.

- Strategic planning is more pragmatic, it is decidedly oriented toward action, the obtaining of results and the implementation of plans.
- Participation of public and private agents is essential to the design and implementation of the plan. It is therefore necessary to reach an agreement among the actors in high-level city management on strategies, objectives and actions.
- The diagnosis of the city's economic dynamics in its relations with the national and international urban system is stressed.
- The economic dynamic of cities is conditioned by an increasingly competitive environment and urban competitiveness may be improved as compared to the other cities in the urban system.
- When proposing plans for action, it attempts to foresee future events in order to compete more advantageously in the market.

Interaction between urban development and endogenous development

As seen above, cities are the place for endogenous development. Cities sustain hidden economies, associated with agglomeration and externalities, and hence there is a potential for lowering production and coordination costs. Firm proximity tends to reduce transportation costs due to greater accessibility and more adequate infrastructures. Transaction costs are also lower since relations among firms are facilitated and because of the diversity of the labor market and the existence of a variety of services. The diversity of actors encourages the formation of networks whose combined action brings about economies as a result of increased efficiency of the organizations.

The economic efficiency of urban development is reinforced by the effect of the other forces that determine the process of accumulation of capital. The diffusion of innovations throughout the productive, organizational and institutional fabric creates a new economic and urban dynamic. The introduction of innovations into the productive system generates increased productivity and income in cities which, in turn, brings about greater demand for urban services to firms and citizens. Finally, innovation in organization, processes and transportation encourage urbanization and diversifies urban functions within the network of cities which ultimately decreases urban hierarchy.

However, the organization of production and productive changes conditions urban development. When the Fordist production model prevails, polarization of productive activity in an urban center is generated and there is increased local demand for labor. This creates greater demand for urban services and increased urban concentration thus reinforcing the mechanisms of urban hierarchy. But when more flexible forms of organization of production are the case, the rules for firm location change and the urban system tends to be increasingly polycentric and dynamic. The organization of production through the diffusion of innovations, then, directly conditions the urbanization process.

Cities are characterized by their history, culture and institutions and these strongly condition urban development. The existence of an institutional context (norms, organization), flexible and adequate for the needs and demands of the social, political and economic actors, reduces uncertainty and attracts investment thus encouraging urbanization processes. The dynamics of economic development require local institutions to provide more and better public and social services which attract private service firms giving rise to urban development. But these processes are not linear. They often meet institutional and social resistance to change, which affects the urbanization process. Finally, cities can be understood as a network of actors who interact and where institutions create the conditions for the agreements that would favor cooperation.

These institutional mechanisms foster investment processes and, therefore, urban development.

Finally, local development policy directly affects urban development. Initiatives aimed at reinforcing urban infrastructures such as transportation and communications, providing firms with urban land, improving social capital, recuperating urban patrimony and improving the environment make cities more attractive to live and produce in. Moreover, the creation of services such as fairs or business centers, and urban marketing through image publicity and emblematic buildings make the city more attractive, generate investment, promote demand for urban services, therefore effectively activating urbanization processes. Ultimately, the adaptation of regulation and norms to the needs and demands of firms and citizens and greater efficiency of public services reinforce the attractiveness of the city, thus promoting urban development.

Part III

The policies of endogenous development

8   Local development policy

In recent decades, a significant change has taken place in development policy. Gradually losing ground are the so-called "top-down" policies which, managed by central administrations, aimed to redistribute economic activity spatially and reduce regional differences in per capita income levels. Simultaneously gaining ground is the "bottom-up" approach, in which policy targeting the economic development of specific regions and cities is promoted and administered by local and regional governments.

Of vast significance, this change of approach represents the instrumentation of a second generation of development policies. Faced with the challenges of adjusting to the new dynamics of the economic system, marked by productive restructuring, regional and local communities decided to have a hand in making their productive systems more efficient. They implemented initiatives encouraging the use of development potential already existing in the territory (human resources, entrepreneurial capability and productive and technological culture) and took on the problems presented by productive restructuring (unemployment and structural change).

In an increasingly global scenario, the diffusion of innovation and upgrading of human resources are strategic factors in fostering productive adjustment. Aware of this fact, local actors (public and private organizations, entrepreneurial associations, worker unions and local governments) have come to understand the challenge of achieving greater competitiveness and responded by stimulating local development initiatives. Since learning processes and organizational capability vary from one territory to another, local responses vary considerably.

A systematic study of regional development policy has not yet appeared. Hence it is not really known how extended endogenous development policies are and how they can be conceptualized. What factors have contributed to the appearance and diffusion of these development strategies? How are local economic policies instrumented?

This chapter focuses on answering these and other questions with information collected from experiences in local development, particularly in late developed countries. After discussing the limitations of traditional regional development policy, the characteristics that local European initiatives and some recent cases in Latin America have in common are described. The chapter then attempts to conceptualize local development strategy with the help of the case studies and a typology of the instruments used is presented. The discussion concludes with some comments on the differences between exogenous development policy and local development initiatives.

Limitations of exogenous development policy

Attracting firms to peripheral regions was one of the main objectives of regional development policy during the 1960s and 1970s (Richardson, 1984; Maillat, 1998). It was understood that growth could be stimulated in less developed regions through exogenous development measures that would induce the diversion of part of the aggregate growth of the national economy to peripheral regions. Inward investment was promoted mainly through subsidies and economic aid, location incentives, public investment in infrastructure and even through direct investment on the part of public enterprise. Such measures were aimed at forming growth poles, which would promote growth in less developed regions.

The policy of development poles or strategy of "concentrated decentralization," as defined by Lloyd Rodwin in 1963, is based on the theory of growth poles (Perroux, 1955; Lasuén, 1969). The focal element is the propulsive firm whose innovative capacity and leadership exert a stimulating influence over the other firms. Its location within a specific territory generates productive and spatial imbalances and promotes local development (Aydalot, 1985).

Growth pole policies became widespread during the 1960s and 1970s in America (Chile, Brazil, Venezuela, the United States and Canada), in Asia (the Philippines, Thailand and Japan) and in Europe (France, Italy, Spain, Belgium). Despite its conceptual ambiguity,[1] the positive effects of pole policy must be recognized. Perhaps its most appealing characteristic is its pragmatism, since it is not possible to take action throughout the whole territory at the same time. Furthermore, it had a positive impact on both employment and income and contributed to productive decentralization, to a reduction in regional disparities and even to growth of national economies.

The evaluation of inward investment in terms of local development is not conclusive, in so far as its effects are not always sufficient to create self-sustained growth processes. The reason lies in the fact that the transfer of resources (capital, technology, skilled labor) between developed and less developed regions can cause dysfunction, which tends to reduce the potential for development in backward regions.

Above all, inward investment alters the normal functioning of labor markets by generating a marked spatial duality between the activities of developed areas and those of retarded regions, which leads to a steady deterioration of labor skills in the depressed areas. Branch plants located in peripheral regions tend to specialize in routine functions of the productive process meaning that the tasks reserved for local employment do not require skilled human resources. In the long term, this generates a negative effect on the area's labor skills.

Moreover, in regions receiving inward investment (such as the Mezzogiorno or Andalucía), there are severe constraints on development of the productive system. On the one hand, branch plants often become economic enclaves with few ties to the local productive system, because subcontracting and the purchase of intermediate goods and services is done through the outside firm network and through suppliers located in or coming from other regions with which the firm maintains economic relations. Also, large firms frequently absorb local entrepreneurial resources (Florio, 1996). In order to enlist qualified local entrepreneurs into management positions in the branch plant, the outside firm offers relatively high salaries, higher, that is, than profits expected in small local firms, thus attracting potential local entrepreneurs. In this way, entrepreneurial capacity in the locality where the branch plant is located is reduced and the city or region's response to the challenge of increasing market competition is weakened.

Branch plants, on the other hand, usually occupy a relatively weak position within the large enterprise network. The functions of direction, finance, sales and research and development are located at the firm's headquarters. Therefore, strategic decisions affecting the branch plant are not made by local management, but rather by those answering to headquarters.

The limited insertion of branch plants into the local productive fabric, the constrained role of local managers in strategic decision-making and the drain on entrepreneurial resources restrict self-sustained development of the local economy. The mechanism as a whole inhibits the creation and growth of local firms and the diffusion of innovation, thus shackling the possibility of endogenous development.

Exogenous development policies, then, do not always attain self-sustained economic development because there is a "leakage" of the initial impulse, which reduces the diffusion capacity of inward investment. This leads to insufficient development in peripheral areas, not so much because a growth model which is foreign to the milieu is promoted, but rather because local development potential is not employed locally but exported to more developed and central regions.

The emergence of local initiatives in Europe

Exogenous development policy begins to lose ground from the beginning of the 1970s as a result of change in the performance of the economy, the preferences of governments in the adjustment of macroeconomic variables and the definition of new institutional frameworks. The need for substantial productive adjustment, both in more and less developed cities and regions, left a vacuum in industrial and regional policies in which local initiatives emerged to solve the problems arising with adjustment and restructuring in each city or region.

From the beginning of the 1970s, many regions and locations face serious problems in the labor market (high unemployment rates, low job creation, decreased income), although the nature and intensity vary from one area to another. The basic problem is the restructuring of productive systems. The situation is critical because it is imperative to adapt local agricultural or industrial productive systems which have lost markets and show low efficiency to the conditions of increasing competition in national and international markets.

Changes in demand, increased competition in the markets, transformations in product and process technologies and the reorganization of the large firm system have provided both threats and opportunities in the regional and urban system in advanced and less advanced economies. Some regions and cities face the inevitable decline of their economies while others discover new opportunities in the markets. In this way, the need to restructure local productive systems and adjust them to the new technological, commercial and institutional conditions has been created.

Local public managers were aware of the severity of productive restructuring, an international problem, and of its effects at the local level (widespread high unemployment rates and industry shut-downs). Since central administrations favored strategies aimed at controlling the great macroeconomic unbalances (inflation, public deficit, trade balance deficit) and largely abandoned regional and industrial policies, local managers increasingly promoted local initiatives and changes in local job markets. Thus local development policy emerged spontaneously. For the first time, local governments were designing and carrying out development policy and actively intervening in productive restructuring processes.

The exact quantity and characteristics of local development initiatives currently being implemented in European regions and cities is not known. However, pioneer studies directed by Bennett (1989) on the LEDA program of the Commission of European Communities and by Stöhr (1990) on local development experiences throughout Europe shed some light on the dimension of the phenomenon and on the characteristics of the initiatives. Most important is the fact that local development initiatives are widespread in Europe. They have emerged in territories whose productive systems are undergoing restructuring processes in very diverse productive sectors (such as agriculture, textiles, footwear, shipbuilding, manufacturing and services) and in cities and localities of all sizes (large metropolis, small and medium-sized cities and rural localities).

Bennett compares twenty-four experiences in the LEDA program throughout twelve member states. The following cases stand out: Sitia in Greece, with restructuring in the agrarian sector and promotion of the food industry and rural tourism; Tilburg in Holland, with a declining textile industry and expanding services; Hamburg in Germany, with adjustments in the naval sector and related industries as well as a stagnant service sector; Nottingham in England, with significant job loss in manufacturing, particularly in textiles and clothing; and Ravenna in Italy, with intense restructuring in the petrochemical industry.

Research directed by Stöhr studies forty-four experiences in rural areas, older industrial zones, medium-sized cities and metropolitan areas. Of particular interest are Dortmund in Germany, characterized by the shutdown of coal mining in the area and profound restructuring in the steel industry (Hennings and Kunzmann, 1990); Prato in Italy, with an innovative adjustment in textiles based on a peculiar district organization model (Camagni and Capello, 1990); Malmö in Sweden, faced with an acute crisis in the naval industry (Johannisson, 1990); and Swansea in Wales, suffering from rapid de-industrialization, particularly in manufacturing (Roberts *et al.*, 1990).

According to Valcárcel-Resalt (1992), in 1990 there were 258 local development experiences in Spain. Elsewhere (Vázquez-Barquero, 1993), I have studied and contrasted some of these initiatives in medium-sized cities. In some cases, the economy is specialized in manufacturing activities (Vitoria-Gasteiz). In others, these initiatives are taking place in cities with declining industrial sectors, such as textiles (Alcoy and Berga), or in those whose traditional industrial "filiere" (ship-building, fishing or the food industry) is undergoing intense restructuring processes (Vigo). In still other cases, these initiatives can be found in rural towns whose agricultural production is restructured as a result of the Spanish economic integration in the European Community (Estepa and Lebrija). Local development experiences are located in all kinds of areas – developed regions (Catalonia), less developed regions (Galicia and Andalucía), dynamic regions with intermediate development (Valencia) or in older industrial zones undergoing restructuring (Basque Country).

Local development policy takes on unique forms in each one of the European Union member states, as Pellegrin (1991) indicates. The way the state is organized (federal, regional or centralized), its spatial policy programs in central and local governments and the history of economic policy in each country are some of the factors that account for widely varying approaches in each country. The diversity of the dynamics of these policies in France as compared with those of Spain can serve to illustrate this phenomenon.

In France, the central administration promoted and managed local development policy through various cross-ministerial measures supporting the start-up and development of local initiatives. The Ministry of Labor stimulated the creation of the *Comités de bassin d'emploi*, made up of local politicians, unions and representatives of entrepreneurs and firms. These committees carried out training actions and fostered the development of productive activities with the support of local civil servants. At the same time, the Ministry of Agriculture promoted an active rural development policy through the *Associations du pays*, although with poor results.

Therefore, territorial organizations for the promotion of local development in France are closely linked to central administration. Except in the case of some private initiatives, such as the *Boutiques de Gestion* or reconverting societies created by large public enterprises, territorial organizations for the promotion of local development are a part of national networks with close ties to central administration. The Ministry of Industry has also provided support to new firms through the National Agency for the Creation of Firms, which is based on a network of local offices located in public or private organizations already present in the territory.

In Spain since the beginning of the 1980s town councils have promoted the creation and development of local initiatives under the auspices of the Constitution of 1978 which paved the way for the first democratic municipal governments. The transformation of INESCOP, a private quality control center created by the footwear firms in Elda, into a Technology Institute in 1978 can be considered a starting point of local economic policy in Spain. Other early innovative initiatives include the foundation of Industrialdeak, providing industrial land and services to firms in Oñate in the Basque Country in 1982, the establishment of the Department of Industrial Promotion, a development agency, in Lebrija in Andalucía in 1984, the creation in Vitoria, Basque Country, of the Municipal Agency for Economic Development and Employment, specialized in training and of Barcelona Activa, S.A., a firm incubator, both in 1986.

However, the differences between member states are less obvious than a first glance would suggest. In federal states, such as Germany, local authorities are self-governing, which allows them to launch their own local development initiatives. Still, the federal administration also has its functions and responsibilities in productive restructuring with regional and industrial measures (Bennett and Krebs, 1990). In centralized states, it would seem that local authorities would have less influence but, as the United Kingdom case shows, new kinds of action have been explored at the local level over recent decades which, to a certain extent, elude the control of the central administration.

Local initiatives in Latin America

An innovative aspect of local development policy is the spread of local initiatives in late-developed and developing countries throughout the 1990s. Although there are no systematic studies of the incidence of endogenous development policy, local initiatives in Latin America are increasingly made known through studies carried out by the Economic

Commission for Latin America and the Caribbean (ECLA)[2] and the Interamerican Development Bank (IDB).

Local initiatives throughout Latin America in the 1990s show a change in the approach to local development and an enrichment of earlier frameworks. Three illustrative cases will be presented here. The first presents the case of a city, Rafaela in Argentina, whose productive system follows the endogenous development pattern. The second involves a region currently undergoing a process of structural change, the "Gran ABC" in the state of São Paolo, Brazil where the location of external firms used to be the main factor in local development. And, finally, the case of a remote region with limited development potential, the Cuchumatanes Mountains area in western Guatemala, will be discussed.

Endogenous development and local policies in Rafaela

Local development policy emerged in Rafaela, Argentina at the beginning of the 1990s and, as Costamagna (1999) points out, represents a pioneer experience in Argentina and in Latin America. Deteriorated competitive capacity in the local firm system due to increased external competition caused by the Argentine economy opening up to international markets and the elimination of advantages in the exchange rate policy characterized the initial situation. Supported by a new generation of public and private managers, the municipal government searched for new opportunities for the local economy by encouraging local development initiatives.

Rafaela is a city of some 80,000 inhabitants in the province of Santa Fé, 500 kilometers from Buenos Aires. Located in one of the most dynamic economic hubs of South America, that linking Viña de Mar and Valparaiso in the Pacific with São Paolo and Porto Alegre in the Atlantic, the area specialized in dairy and refrigeration products and metal-mechanics activities (agricultural equipment and machinery and capital goods for the food industry) as well as the production of commercial, cultural and leisure-time services through an industrialization process initiated at the beginning of the twentieth century. Since the onset of industrial development, the area has shown considerable entrepreneurial dynamics and the ability to create cooperation among firms and institutions.

Since the late 1980s, Rafaela's productive system has faced increasing competition in the markets due to the gradual integration of Argentina into the international economy, the creation of MERCOSUR and, ultimately, the effect of globalization (Ferraro and Costamagna, 2000). Local firms could not provide an efficient response to changes in demand and the loss of market share due to the relative loss of human resources skill, the obsolescence of capital goods, delayed introduction of innovations and poor management and organization of the local productive system.

In 1991, the new municipal team in Rafaela not only determined to improve and modernize local public management, but also to take a leading role in the promotion of local economic development. Initially, the recently established Economic Planning Secretariat of the municipality analyzed the economic difficulties of the city and stimulated action on the part of local actors.

According to the Strategic Plan launched in 1996, local development policy in Rafaela aims "to empower the area as a regional productive center of international projection by upgrading human resources and technology, by projecting its cultural identity with solidarity and guaranteeing urban and environmental balance and an adequate standard of living of the population." Since 1991, the municipality and local actors came to understand that it was essential to promote the start-up and development of local firms, favor improvement in human resource skills and diffuse innovations. In order to attain these general goals, it was also deemed necessary to encourage an environment of cooperation among firms and institutions.

Since 1993, the town council and entrepreneurial institutions agreed that one of the key tools in local development policy in Rafaela would be an agency whose purpose would be to improve competitiveness in local firms. In 1996, local entrepreneurs and municipal authorities founded the Center for Entrepreneurial Development (Centro de Desarrollo Empresarial) and received funding from the Multilateral Investment Fund of the Inter-American Development Bank (IDB). The Center renders real services to local and regional firms, which lead them to improve productive quality, attain greater market share and increase the internationalization of small firms. The Center in Rafaela is part of a network of similar centers for entrepreneurial development sponsored by the IDB and the Industrial Union of Argentina, and is managed through a Foundation.

A second axis in local development policy is the promotion of research and technological development and their application to local productive activities. The importance of knowledge and learning to entrepreneurial development had long been acknowledged by the city of Rafaela and its public and private managers, as shown by the fact that the Agricultural Experimental Station of the National Institute of Agricultural Technology had been founded in 1926. In 1997, the Regional Center of Rafaela, under the auspices of the National Institute of Technology was founded. This Center integrates the Center for Technological Research in the Dairy Industry and the Center for Technological Research of Rafaela. Among the services available are laboratory analyses and tests, product development, technical consulting for local firms and the training of qualified workers.

Training is a recurring issue in all the institutions created in Rafaela over the 1990s. Initially, the town promoted the improvement of personnel skills in order to strengthen municipal management. The Center for

Entrepreneurial Development and the Regional Center in Rafaela consider formation strategic to obtaining entrepreneurial and technological development of Rafaela, as does the Institute for Qualification and Study for Local Development, a municipal entity founded in 1997 to accompany changes and transformations in the local community.

Finally, a critical feature of local economic policy in Rafaela is the city's institutional development (Costamagna, 1999). Over the 1990s, society and public and private organizations created a set of new institutions that have facilitated the administration of the city through agreements on economic, political and social aspects. Furthermore, trust and cooperation among firms and institutions have been strengthened and this has led to the expansion of local networks and subsequent improvement in firm competitiveness. In short, betterment of the institutional milieu has reduced transaction costs and encouraged economic and social development.

The restructuring of production and local development in the Gran ABC, Brazil

In December of 1990, the Inter-municipal Consortium of Gran ABC[3] was founded. This organism is the basis for joint action of the participating municipalities to promote regional and environmental development of the region (Leite, 2000). With an initial situation characterized by industrial crises, firm shut-downs and rising unemployment, the townships of the ABC region and, later, their social and institutional forces came to an agreement to undertake productive restructuring by promoting projects whose objectives included diversification of production and improvement in competitiveness.

Located in the southeast of the São Paolo metropolitan area, the Gran ABC region has a population of 2.2 million people, which has steadily grown over the last two decades (36.6 percent from 1980 to 1996). Considered one of the main axes of the Brazilian economic miracle, a highly specialized cluster (in car industry activities and in machinery) from the 1970s has been transformed into a diversified region with the presence of Polo Petroquímico of Capuava, a plastic industry group, a telecommunications sector and, more recently, an increase in service activities (65 percent of employment in 1998). Throughout the industrial development process, which began with the location of General Motors in 1930, until the late 1970s, society gradually acquired a high degree of social organization which has led it to create spaces for negotiation and social and economic agreements (Abramo, 1998).

In the 1980s, an acute industrial crisis affected the ABC region. Employment losses reached 35 percent between 1987 to 1996, particularly in large firms, and the unemployment rate rose above 20 percent in 1999 as a consequence of diminished competitiveness caused by economic opening and reduced protectionism. Greater pull of other locations in Brazil such as Minas Gerais, Río de Janeiro or the northern area of the state of São Paolo and a change in spatial strategy on the part of external firms located in the ABC region also contributed to this crisis. As Scott (2000) points out, the industrial crisis of Gran ABC was caused by the loss of competitive advantages in the region as a result of low quality human resources, limited innovative capacity, a lack of entrepreneurship and of flexibility within the local system.

In response to the need to restructure the industrial and productive system, the design and implementation of a local development policy was launched with the foundation in 1997 of the Regional Chamber of Gran ABC. This organism is based on an institutional agreement between the Inter-municipal Consortium of Gran ABC, the government of the state of São Paolo, large firms and trade associations of the region, associations of small firms and businessmen, unions, civic and university representatives. Local institutions share a particular view of local development, in which territory is considered a socially organized actor, capable of defining a strategy for economic and social development. The guidelines of this local development strategy are stated in the Founding Charter of the Regional Chamber. Some of its objectives are to promote productive restructuring processes, reduce employment loss and, eventually, create employment and improve the standard of living of the population.

Strategic actions for development of the region can be found in regional agreements drawn up in 1997 and 1998. First, the strategy encourages initiatives aimed at creating new firms and improving entrepreneurial and organizational capability in the region. The creation of a Guarantee Fund whose financial agent is the State Economic Bank contributes to better funding of small and micro firms. Other initiatives involve the revitalization of activities such as the furniture sector through the creation of a Design Center and aid to new activities.

In order to encourage the diffusion of innovations, a set of actions has been designed. These include such initiatives aimed at promoting technological modernization in small and medium-sized firms in order to increase their competitiveness and the launching of a Gran ABC Technological Pole through the creation of R&D centers jointly with universities in the region. An important feature of the project is its link to the region's productive fabric since R&D centers specialize in the automobile, petrochemical, lumber and environmental sectors.

Training is one of the priority actions of local development policy in the ABC region. The Plan of Professional Qualification provides for the installation of public vocational training schools, improved technical schools and, in general, worker formation in areas with a future in the region.

At the center of all of these action programs is the Economic Development Agency of the Gran ABC, founded in 1999 by the institutions of the public and private sector of the region and funded, at least in part, by the IDB. Some initial projects are the creation of a database of information on the region, the promotion of entrepreneurial initiatives and instrumentation of regional marketing programs.

Rural development in the Cuchumatanes

In the first quarter of 1994, Guatemala's Ministry of Agriculture, Cattle and Food (MAGA) launched the Project for the Rural Development of the Cuchumatanes Mountains area designed to last 7 years. From an initial context in which part of the peasant population located in peripheral zones of the country were submerged in poverty, the project aimed to generate sustainable development processes based on increased production and productive capacity of the local economy. Beginning as an initiative of the central state administration, the project was gradually decentralized and services were transferred to the local population who then led the development process of their own territory (Cifuentes, 2000).

The project affected 9,000 rural families located in the Cuchumatanes Mountains in the department of Huehuetenango[4] in western Guatemala bordering the Mexican State of Chiapas to the north and west. The main productive activities are agriculture and cattle farming. It is a multi-ethnic and multi-lingual region. The population had undergone profound serious internal conflict, particularly from 1980 to 1985, which destroyed unity and solidarity in the community and particularly reduced the cooperative and associative spirit that had emerged to some extent in the 1970s.

At the beginning of the 1990s, the level of development of the Cuchumatanes was extremely low since agricultural activities merely provided subsistence and used only traditional technologies. Families in the region farmed areas of less than 3.5 hectares in order to fulfill their basic needs. Productive activities showed very low returns. Net income per family in the rural areas was less than $1,200 a year. For this reason, the state administration, through agricultural extension programs and aid, hoped to improve poverty conditions in the population. But changes in external conditions (a peace truce, gradual integration of Guatemala into the Central American market and decentralization of state services) opened new opportunities to rural areas and, particularly, to the Cuchumatanes Mountains area.

The MAGA launched the Cuchumatanes Project in 1994. It received funding from the International Fund for Agricultural Development, the government of The Netherlands, the OPEP Development Fund and the World Food Program. Its objectives were to "promote and create a favorable environment for the creation of sustainable rural development processes which will contribute to generate a higher standard of living for the inhabitants of the Cuchumatanes Mountains through improved productive, entrepreneurial and management capacity for farmers and their organizations."

To attain these goals, project strategy has been designed and redesigned over and over during its 7 years of existence. A sectoral view was prominent and emphasis was placed on the peculiarity of the territory and productive diversity by identifying four production systems: the sheep-potatoes-grain system; the horticulture system; the traditional coffee system and the organic coffee system. The object is to improve the competitive advantages of each system over time by increasing product quality and producing goods for national and international markets, thus transforming a subsistence economy into a market economy.

The emergence and improvement of local entrepreneurial resources is key to the project and it was considered essential to promote self-management within the indigenous communities. Formerly inoperative cooperatives and associations were recovered and began to grow (Formal Organizations of Agricultural Producers). These entities also retrieved self-management experience and knowledge already existing in the local population. Moreover, more informally structured organizations or Interest Groups were encouraged, which brought people with common productive and commercial interests together.[5] In this way, local entrepreneurial capacity was stimulated and productive organization forms already existing in the area were reinforced.

One of the most important actions of the Cuchumatanes Project is the training of human resources. Not only does this action strengthen the capacities of local peasant leaders so that they can take on project and organization direction and management responsibilities. It also leads to the technical and professional qualification of those who provide technical services for each of the productive and commercial initiatives. Training is oriented toward radically improving the qualification of human resources and particular emphasis is therefore placed on the training of young people in the local communities so that they will specialize and go on to higher education.

In order to achieve the transformation of subsistence agrarian activities into market-oriented exploitations, the single most important factor is the introduction of innovations into productive processes. Thus, reproduction and feeding techniques have improved in ovine production, the technological package that led to the restructuring of natural coffee production into organic coffee was perfected and brought about increased coffee output and quality, and vegetable output and quality also improved. The adaptation and transfer of farming technology has made local products more competitive in national and international markets.

However, open markets are strategically central to the Cuchumatanes Project if the goals of achieving financial self-sufficiency, generating surplus, investing and promoting self-sustained economic development processes in the region are to be reached. To date, some cooperatives and associations have been relatively successful in the commercialization of organic coffee, ovine products and garlic, for example. But the project includes initiatives aiming to improve not only the marketing of local products and the purchase of raw materials and intermediate products, but also the profitability of these business endeavors. This is particularly true in the present stage in which the transfer of services to indigenous communities has to a large extent been completed.

Funding of project initiatives is instrumented through various means (Cifuentes and Menegazzo, 1998): loans to individual farmers or groups of peasants, using traditional guarantees; self-managed peasant banks which take in the savings of the farmers and use them to finance productive activities of their members; communal banks, aimed at funding initiatives launched by women and the concession of loans to members by cooperatives or associations whose activity is based on the difference existing between the interest rate paid by clients and the normal market rate.

Finally, the transformation of organizational instruments is also key to the Cuchumatanes Project. The decentralization of agricultural extension and social organization services was initiated in 1994 and gradually broadened and accelerated from 1998 on. It was brought about through agreements between the State and Formal Organizations of Agrarian Producers (OFPA), which regulate the transfer of services[6] to the OFPA, the work plans, the economic resources to be transferred and even the transfer of personal property and real estate. The OFPA, therefore, becomes a real Local Development Agency. In 1998 the Organizations Committee (Comité de Usuarios) was founded, integrating social organizations and representing them in the presence of public and private institutions. In July 1999, the Committee became the Association of Organizations of the Cuchumatanes, which made it the prime promoter of economic growth in the region and, therefore, the organization in charge of fostering endogenous development in the Cuchumatanes.

Local development strategy

The explosion of local initiatives in Europe during the 1980s and 1990s and in Latin America during the 1990s brings up several questions as to the reasons for their appearance and their objectives and strategies. Can they be considered a new generation of development policy?

An initial reflection on local development experiences would demonstrate that local communities have undergone a collective learning process with respect to adjustment and productive restructuring. In the face of such problems as unemployment, production decline and loss of markets, local managers have felt the need to improve local response to the challenges of increasing competition and changes in demand.

The diagnosis of the local economy and local response take on various forms in function of the specific characteristics of each territory. The specific conditions, productive specialization, available natural and human resources, presence of the local economy in national and international markets, the organization of the local productive system and the capacity for learning and response of the local community are some of the factors that make the difference.

In any case, the issue to be solved is how to integrate local economies into the international economy and how to make productive systems more competitive. The answer necessarily involves restructuring of the productive system and adjustment of each territory's institutional, cultural and social system to changes in the competitive environment.

In other words, the challenge facing cities and localities consists of restructuring their productive system in such a way that agricultural, industrial and service activities will improve their productivity and increase their competitiveness in local and external markets. Experiences in local development indicate that the path to be taken involves the design and execution of an entrepreneurial development strategy, implemented through actions geared toward the goals of productivity and competitiveness (see Figure 8.1).

Hence, there is general agreement that increased productivity and competitiveness are the two major goals of structural change in local economies. But these goals can be achieved in various ways, which can basically be grouped into two alternative strategies: the radical change strategy made up of a set of actions whose main goal is increased competitiveness (efficiency/effectiveness) of the local productive system no matter what the cost in terms of employment and environmental impact; and the step by step strategy that combines actions pursuing the goals of efficiency and equity over the short and long term.

The first strategy involves a technological leap, the production of new goods, alternative locations and, at any rate, a radical change in the center of gravity of the city or region's productive system with negative short-term consequences on employment, the systems of organization of production, the environment and local culture. The step-by-step strategy, in contrast, prefers to put the know-how and technological culture existing in the territory to use. It represents an advance in structural change by developing it from the productive fabric already in existence. It combines the introduction of innovations with maintaining jobs and it brings about transformations in such a way that they are accepted, adopted and led by the local society.

The second option in fact reconciles the objectives of efficiency and equity while also assigning priority to the social dimension. Nevertheless, since public aid counts on this strategy, there is the risk that the local economy may slide into a welfare economy model with the consequent danger to the continuance of the process of economic development.

This is, without a doubt, a simplification of the predicament that local communities encounter in the face of processes of restructuring and

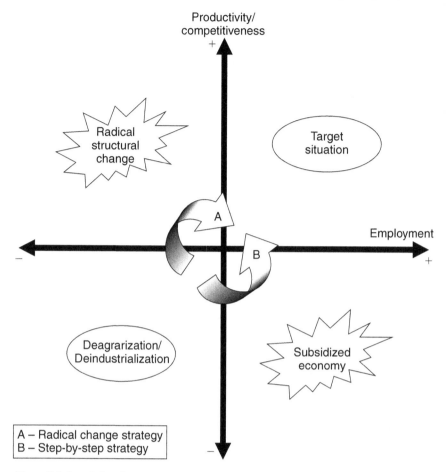

Figure 8.1 Local development strategy.

economic development since the conflict of interests within society is, of course, much more far-reaching. In reality, development aims to improve efficiency in the allocation of public resources, promote equality in the distribution of wealth and jobs and fulfill present and future needs of the population through the adequate use of natural and environmental resources, as will be discussed below.

Recent history shows that the first strategy encounters competitive barriers that are difficult to overcome in the short term. Moreover, radical structural change always incurs significant social and environmental costs that must be assumed. In urban and rural areas, the best practices would advise the adoption of step-by-step strategies, thus employing endogenous development potential and, subsequently, resources available within the territory.

Local initiatives have emerged as a result of local community learning dynamics as to transformation of local productive systems, their organizational capability and their responses to the challenges of technological change, globalization and increasing competition.

Local development action

Local response to global challenges is implemented through actions of a very diverse nature (Aghón *et al.*, 2001; Alburquerque, 1997; Vázquez-Barquero, 1993). Some target the building up of infrastructure, others attempt to compensate deficiencies and improve the non-tangible factors of development and still others aim to strengthen the organizational capability of the territory.

Building up of infrastructure for local development

Initiatives targeting the creation and improvement of public infrastructure and social capital are critical in processes of structural change because infrastructure is indispensable for the performance of the productive system. As Chisholm (1990) has indicated with reference to the case of Sheffield, investment in infrastructure and social capital endeavors to improve the attraction of the city and its surrounding area and make it an adequate place to live and work.

Local development measures include investments aimed at improving transportation and communications networks (such as the building of a bridge in Alcoy, Spain, or a freeway between Cocentaina and Alcoy), establishing suitable facilities for firm location (as with the industrial network in the Basque Country or the creation of industrial estates such as the "République" in Poitiers, France) and building social capital installations such as hospitals and schools.

In Latin America practically all the local development experiences involve improving accessibility, meeting the needs of social capital and making cities more attractive to live and produce in. The Villa de Salvador (Peru) initiative centers its strategy on the creation of an industrial park in order to provide industrial land, equipment and the services required by micro-firms and small and medium-sized firms. The town of Ilo (Peru) has proposed to overcome water supply deficits, through initiatives supported by the central administration, and develop infrastructure in the Industrial Park by re-investing proceeds from the sale of lots. Finally, the Local Economic Development Program in Alcaldía de Medellín in Colombia includes urban and metropolitan infrastructure projects.

As we have seen, these actions are also typical of traditional regional policy. In countries with a decentralized state their implementation is only possible through joint action of all competent administrations. In these initiatives, local actors play an important role by stimulating interest and action on the part of other administrations.

Fostering entrepreneurial capability

A differentiating feature of the new development policy can be found in those initiatives that aim to stimulate the creation and development of the non-tangible and qualitative aspects of local development. Examples of these initiatives are measures that influence factors such as start-up and development of firms, information within organizations and firms and the qualification of human resources, technological and innovative know-how and its diffusion and the local development culture.

Local initiatives aimed at encouraging the start-up and development of firms are the most common. In the European Union, the *Business Innovation Centers*, promoted by the Commission since 1984 are excellent examples. These initiatives vary depending on their promoters (local or external; public or private), on whether they appear spontaneously (the appearance of *boutiques* of firms in the late 1970s) or are regulated (law 44/86 in Italy to stimulate the emergence of young entrepreneurs in the Mezzogiorno), and on whether they target specific groups or not (women, young people, unemployed). As mentioned above when describing the cases of Rafaela, the Gran ABC and the Cuchumatanes, the creation and development of firms, particularly small and medium-sized firms and micro-firms, is one of the priorities of local initiatives in Latin America. In this way, the Agency for the Economic Development of the City of Córdoba in Argentina is oriented toward stimulating and promoting this goal. These initiatives strive to encourage new entrepreneurs to transform an idea into a feasible and competitive firm, prepare them for the risks ahead and inform and advise them as to available advantages.

Initiatives aimed at developing firms provide financial and real services. For example, private organizations in Lolland (Denmark) established the Lalandia Fund for the funding of small firms when the Nakskov shipyards, the most important firm in the area, closed down. The Investment Company of Limburg, in Belgium not only facilitates financial resources but also participates in programs targeting the formation of human resources in the area (LEDA, 1990).

The Textile Information Center in the Emilia Romagna (CITER), established in 1980, is a good example of how information services for small and medium-sized firms located in an advanced region foster productive restructuring and integration of the local system into the international economic system.

In Italy the promotion of exports in small local firms is implemented by firm consortia. These initiatives, whose goal is to create and expand external markets of associated firms, have rapidly expanded since the beginning of the 1980s with the support of central administrations.

In Latin America there are many experiences in fulfilling local firms' needs and demands for services. In 1992 the Municipal House of the Small Businessman (Casa Municipal del Pequeño Empresario) in the Town of Rancagua in Chile was founded to promote qualification in business management and render technical and financial assistance to micro-firms and small businesses. The Program for the Support of Small and Medium-sized Firms (Programa de Apoyo a la Pequeña y Mediana Empresa) in Antioquía, Colombia, aims to provide small textile and clothing industry entrepreneurs with knowledge of textile materials and design and provide technical consulting and export assistance through a strategic alliance with an Institute of Export and Fashion.

Finally, over the last decade in Latin America, as in Asia, various forms of micro-credit and financial support for micro-firms and small businesses have appeared. In Porto Alegre, for example, the prefecture, in collaboration with private economic and social agents, has founded the community credit institution PORTOSOL, a non-profit company whose two main principles are the combination of real guarantees and solidarity bonds, and provide services to small businessmen. Two examples of interest because of their excellent results in the funding of local entrepreneurial initiatives are the "Ventanilla de Créditos" (credit windows) for small peasant producers, a product of an agreement between the town of Concepción in Bolivia and the foundation of the Andean Development Fund, and the Fund for Micro-business Projects (Fondo de Proyectos para Micro-empresarios) in Ranquil, Chile.

Diffusion of technical innovation and knowledge

Another cornerstone of local development policy is the diffusion of innovation. The proliferation of technology and science parks throughout Europe, particularly since the mid-1980s, is a good illustration. The first parks established in the United Kingdom were those of Cambridge (1973) and Heriot-Watt in Edinburgh (1974) but they particularly spread during the 1980s (three in 1980; twenty in 1985; forty by the end of that decade). In Germany, the first technological park was constructed in 1984 and, from then on, there was rapid expansion throughout the country. In Italy, Bari was the site of the first park in 1984; in Spain, the first (1985) was in Zamudio, in the Basque Country.

When facing restructuring of the productive system in large metropolitan areas, some central administrations, such as the French and Japanese, have stressed the importance of diffusion of innovation. The creation of *technopôles* in France encouraged decentralization of activities through actions that attract innovative firms, principally in the French "sunbelt." In Japan, the policy of promoting technopolis endeavors to encourage structural change in underdeveloped regions by supporting high technology activities in peripheral locations and, also, providing firms with land, water and a good environment.

Technological Institutes, promoted by the government of the Region of Valencia, are the optimal instrument of new regional development policy in Spain. These centers provide services to local firms in the areas of quality control, technical assistance, diffusion of information and training and they also carry out R&D projects. Technological Institutes are specialized in a productive activity (footwear, ceramics, furniture, textiles and toys) and are located in towns whose productive system are also specialized in the same type of industries.

Actions aimed at improving the diffusion of innovations and knowledge are not yet as manifest in Latin America as they have been in Europe since the beginning of the 1980s. However, initiatives oriented toward the diffusion of innovations and knowledge are always a part of local development strategies, as seen when discussing the cases of Rafaela, the Gran ABC and the Cuchumatanes.

Finally, training policy plays a strategic role in the promotion of endogenous development because it attempts to respond to the needs arising from the rapid obsolescence of human resources on the one hand, and new demands of entrepreneurs and workers, on the other. Productive change must be accompanied by improvement in traditional training as well as the introduction of new trades demanded by the market (as in the cases of Vitoria and Tilburg).

When traditional productive activity becomes obsolete (agriculture, basic industry, manufacturing) and the production system is undergoing a restructuring process, as occurs in the mining and agricultural areas of Le Bruaysis (France) or in Sitia (Greece), then training becomes the core of the local development strategy. In these cases, the attitude of the population with respect to development and the economy must be changed through animation actions, such as those of Lebrija (Andalucía).

In Latin America, the qualification of human resources with respect to the needs and demands of local productive systems is one of the mainstays in local development. For example, in Medellín, Colombia, the corporation Paisajoven, with the support of the German agency GTZ, has established a system of vocational training based on the trades identified through research as most in demand by entrepreneurs. Also in Medellín, the Chamber of Commerce, jointly with other public and private entities, has founded a job observatory which evaluates and recommends adjustments in local employment programs.

The organization of local development

At the center of new development policy are actions aimed at improving the organization of development in the city or region in order to allow it to facilitate efficient response to the problems and challenges ahead.

Development of a locality or territory is organized through the decisions made by public and private agents. Frequently, as occurred in Hamburg, in Rafaela or Alcoy, in the early stages of the local development policy, local leaders stimulate the implementation of local initiatives, but they should count on explicit or tacit support from other local actors.

Increasing competition and uncertainty in the markets has led institutions and organizations to cooperate to reduce risk and take advantage of opportunities. Partnership and networking among firms and territorial organizations are the most common forms of cooperation. Partnership leads to transactions based on formal agreements among local public and private actors, a large number of whom prefer these arrangements. A good example is Hamburgische Gesellschaft für Wirtschaftstörderung, the Hamburg Society for Entrepreneurial Development, created in 1985, in which the municipal government, the Chamber of Commerce and various banks participate. Networking was less expanded at this time in spite of the fact that networks lead to informal relations among organizations and facilitate the making and implementation of decisions. A good example is the "network" of marine culture producers in Connemara, established by the regional development agency (Udaras na Gaeltachta), private fishing firms and cooperatives, the local university and a marketing firm.

In Latin America, endogenous development policy is also based on initiatives in which partnerships among public and private actors lead to its implementation. In Villa Salvador, Peru, the Autonomous Authority of the Cono Sur Industrial Park (Autoridad Autónoma del Parque Industrial del Cono Sur) was founded and brings together public and private agents working to develop the Industrial Park. In Jalisco, Mexico, local entrepreneurs, including executives of multinational firms and public actors, participate in the creation of local networks of suppliers.

Endogenous development policy

What are the characteristics of endogenous development policy? Are there differences between the policy of the 1960s and 1970s and local development policy as it is being implemented in Europe since the beginning of the 1980s and in Latin America over the last decade? Chisholm (1990) correctly summarizes the differences between the various models of regional/local development policy.

Traditional regional development policy was based on the concentrated growth model and aimed to improve territorial distribution of income through firm location incentives and investment in infrastructures. Both Keynesian and neoclassical policies conceived of regional development policy as a zero-sum game in that resources obtained by some regions would be at the expense of the others. In contrast, local development policy intended to overcome imbalances through the promotion of development in all territories with potential. Local economic policy is understood to be a non-zero-sum game capable of taking advantage of the development potential existing in the territory.

Adjustment of the productive system would be obtained through various mechanisms. From the point of view of traditional policies, the Keynesians argue that actions on demand would lead to the redistribution of investments and income, while neoclassical models maintained that market forces and mobility of the productive factors would induce adequate distribution of resources and the necessary, and possible, adjustments. In contrast, the dynamizing mechanism of local development strategies would be provided by the response of local actors to the challenges of increased competition which would unleash endogenous development processes.

Finally, the conceptualization itself of the various policies accentuates the differences. In the case of Keynesian policies, the idea is to induce the location of plants and firms in problem areas, while policies based on neoclassical thought attempt to eliminate obstacles that limit capital and labor flows from one territory to another. However, local development strategies and initiatives propose to stimulate the start-up and development of local firms and encourage the upgrading of specific resources to attract external firms.

9   Globalization and territorial dynamic

The appearance and evolution of local development policy is a sponta-neous response to the productive, technological and commercial changes that took place from the mid-1970s on. Regional and sectoral policies had become inadequate to accompany processes of productive restructuring leading public managers to launch initiatives that would facilitate produc-tive adjustment. This policy change was accompanied by institutional adaptation and new theories and approaches to economic development.

Local development policy undoubtedly represented a remarkable step forward since it allowed cities and regions to put development potential already existing in the territory to use in facilitating productive adjust-ment. Nevertheless, globalization significantly influences the dynamic of productive and spatial systems by generating new needs and demands to be met by the strategies of firms and territories.

This chapter seeks to show that the globalization process encourages spatial diversity and strategic behavior of economic agents and public and private organizations. After discussing the factors that have brought about the formulation and consolidation of local development policies, the spaces of globalization are identified. Then it is argued that the dynamic of regions and local productive systems is stimulated by globalization. The chapter will conclude by showing that globalization creates environments in which convergence between the territorial strategies of firms, in their search for competitive advantages, and the development strategies of local governments can take place, thus fostering processes of endogenous development.

Rationale for local development policy

The sweeping response of local communities in the European Union and recently, although to a lesser degree, Latin America, to the challenges of global competition leads one to believe that there are profound under-lying reasons accounting for the emergence of the new policy, its defini-tion and its permanence over the last two decades. A rationale for this phenomenon may be approached from three viewpoints: change in territorial circumstances, institutional change in management of the new policy and the application of new concepts and theories to policy definition.

Change in regional circumstance

The new generation of development policies comes to the aid of territorial and productive adjustment resulting from technological change and increasing competition in the markets. The redistribution policy of the 1950s and 1960s was instrumented within a stable environment in which indicators of per capita income and unemployment rates helped identify regions in trouble. These would then be targeted for intervention.

In the 1970s and 1980s, territorial circumstances changed. Firm shutdowns and increasing unemployment spread to cities and regions which had formerly been dynamic and developed territories during the upswing of the long economic cycle. Territorial dynamics (spatial and economic change) can no longer be accounted for by the concept of regional disparities, which reduced these dynamics to the relations between rich regions and poor regions or between the center and the periphery (Vázquez-Barquero, 1984). A new theoretical and analytic framework was clearly needed.

Change in demand caused a gap with respect to the supply of products, which meant reduced competitive capacity of both rich and poor regions and localities. The relative increase of production costs (labor, energy) altered firms' production functions and brought about such processes as de-industrialization, productive decentralization and increased competitive advantages in local industrial systems. Functional decentralization, increasing subcontracting and expansion of producer services also contributed to change in the productive systems of regions and cities.

These changes indicate that the development of regions and localities should be interpreted more with respect to qualitative than quantitative differences. The level reached in growth or unemployment rates, whether the dominant activity is industry or services, the size of the urban or regional population – these are no longer relevant factors. It is firm, city and regional competitiveness that is of importance now. And this means that the relevant variables in defining productive restructuring and regional growth are innovation, human resource qualification, technological and managerial capability of firms, the flexibility of entrepreneurial and institutional organizations and the integration of firms, cities and regions into competitive and innovative networks.

In this context, traditional regional and sectoral policies have demonstrated their inability to respond to the new circumstances. It was essential that development policy address the on-going processes and transformations by encouraging their dynamics and solving the dysfunctions caused by adjustments in the territorial model. To go against the grain by maintaining strategies such as the transfer of resources from rich regions to poor regions was not only inefficient, but also unfeasible since the dynamics of the process offset the policy.

Hence, development policy increasingly targets growth and structural change in cities and regions undergoing restructuring of their productive systems. Balance in redistribution of productive activity is reinforced by productive and functional decentralization and endogenous industrialization, which make leading industrial systems less polarized and more diffused, that is, production is less concentrated. In this way unemployed territorial resources can be used efficiently and reconstruction of the productive fabric of regional and urban economies can be achieved. Thus, the reduction of spatial differences in income and employment are achieved functionally, not because of program dictates.

Institutional change

Overcoming the circumstances requires new ways to regulate economic and social relations. In European Union countries, local actors are responding strategically to improve the position of cities and regions in the new international system. Simultaneously, change is taking place in state organizations, through decentralization of administrative offices and devolution of competence to regions and cities.

The impact of change in the accumulation model brought about unemployment, loss of performance in local economic systems and, consequently, the need to reform the productive structure of cities and regions. The challenge for local governments was, and is, critical because the economy is becoming progressively global, forcing them to face the need to respond locally to problems of adjustment and integration. Possible responses are limited and can be reduced to two basic strategies. Either a competitive strategy aimed at attracting external investment away from other competing cities is launched (zero-sum game), or a local development strategy designed to create the environment for local initiatives is developed to solve local problems (non-zero-sum game).

Thus, local initiatives have gradually emerged to accommodate the new circumstances and adjust the local productive system. In the 1980s, local and regional governments in European countries began to take on a key role in processes of structural change in response to the need to provide long-term solutions to the problems created locally by the restructuring of the international productive system.

The new role of local administrations is benefited by a change in strategy on the part of central administrations. Over the 1980s and 1990s, central governments come to accept neo-liberal positions and focus their activity on achieving macroeconomic goals (control of inflation and the public deficit) as they reduce the scope of regional and industrial policies.

As central administrations tend to relinquish their hold on the diffusion of innovation and the creation of employment, local and regional governments become increasingly involved in the regulation of productive adjustment and restructuring processes (Stöhr, 1990).

Local development strategy is also influenced by change in the institutional framework in which the productive system functions. Throughout Europe, local and regional administrations have gained or reinforced competences in cases such as the creation of the State of Autonomies in Spain, the recent granting of autonomy to Wales and Scotland in the United Kingdom, administrative decentralization in France and the implementation of the Constitution of 1948 in Italy. One could argue that decentralization and increasing local and regional authority are more motivated by organization and economic efficiency than by political factors, although with some reservations in the Spanish case.

In Latin America, the process of decentralization takes on various forms depending on whether the state is organized federally (Argentina, Brazil, Mexico, Venezuela) or centrally (Colombia, Chile, Ecuador, Peru). In federal countries, decentralization can have a variety of meanings. While in Argentina, it involves recuperating the federalism suppressed by state centralism, in Venezuela, as Boisier indicates, it is a matter of making a constitutional adjustment demanded by society for more than a century. In centralized countries, organization is also quite diverse. While in Chile the highest degree of territorial decentralization can be found but accompanied by low fiscal decentralization, Colombia not only manifests a process of political and territorial decentralization but also high fiscal decentralization (Madoery, 2001).

New concepts and theories

New development policy, adapted to the needs of local communities, has emerged spontaneously and has thus benefited from the creativity of those who first put it to work. The policy has gradually been elaborated through trial and error and its conceptualization has been reinforced with new theoretical contributions over the last 15 years.

The evolution of cities and regions is perceived in light of long-term economic dynamics. Economic growth is a result of increased productivity and competitiveness, accomplished through technological progress and improved resource quality, as we are reminded by the proposals of neo-classical thought on endogenous growth. But endogenous development theory goes beyond this point, in that it is able to provide instruments for action in uncertain and chance environments, as was seen in the first part of this book.

The territorial approach to analysis and policy is a critical feature of endogenous development theory. The importance of the territory in decisions on investment and location of firms is acknowledged, as accepted by the fields of International Trade and by Business Administration. The territorial approach to endogenous development can be understood in terms of flexible organization of production in both firms and territories, as the theories of industrial districts and innovative milieux argue. Moreover, one can also reason that innovation and technological diffusion are path dependent, as modern theories of innovation point out. Finally, institutions evolve thanks to collective learning as proposed by the theory of proximity.

Firms and organizations operate within an environment determined exogenously and evolved over time. The territory would be made up of a set of networks or, in other words, of a system of economic, social, political and legal relations. Moreover, firms and organizations belong to a milieu whose learning mechanisms and organization dynamics condition response to change in the environment, as the theory of innovative milieux holds.

Thus, endogenous development theory contributes to understanding the complex interactions between organization of production, technology, institution and city in the process of economic dynamics. Therefore, a great variety of spatial growth paths for cities and regions may be identified. Development policy aims to improve entrepreneurial and organizational capability and the quality of the productive factors, diffuse innovation throughout the local productive fabric and the territories and help to adapt institutions to make economic growth more efficient. In short, it undertakes to encourage local response to the challenges of increasing competition.

Diversity of the spaces of globalization

The most characteristic feature of present day globalization processes[1] is increased competition of firms and territories. New needs have emerged due to productive adjustment in response to the introduction of new product, process innovation and new modes of organization. To these one must add the needs arising over the last decade from the integration of firms and economies into increasingly expanded markets. That is, as Alburquerque (1998) states, the necessities arising from increased competition caused by accelerated globalization have been added to the need for productive efficiency.

As evolutionary theory holds, competition is a dynamic process, conditioned by the organization of markets and the competitive behavior of firms and industries, who define and implement strategies in order to surpass their competitors in the markets (Brenner, 1987; Metcalfe, 1998). It is precisely this competitive behavior that largely accounts for the introduction of innovations and for processes of growth and structural change in cities and regions. Firms do not compete in isolation but rather jointly with the productive and institutional environment.[2] Thus one can refer to competition among cities and regions.

It has been extensively argued throughout this book that globalization has accelerated change in productive and development processes in cities and regions thus giving rise to a new urban and regional system at a global scale or, if one prefers, to a new spatial division of labor at an international scale.

There is no question as to the fact that the introduction of innovations and productive and organizational changes reinforce the concentration of population as well as industrial and service activities. But the urban and regional system is increasingly polycentric and urban and regional hierarchies are declining as firm and city networks and relations intensify due to globalization.

This view does not entirely share the arguments of those who consider that globalization is a process led by those well equipped urban cities and regions in which knowledge, organization and productive capability are concentrated. The increase in services, particularly financial and producer services in general, is seen to have concentrated control in the global cities, establishing a new hierarchy in the urban system with New York, Tokyo and London at the top (Sassen, 1991).

This interpretation of internationalization and adjustment in productive and spatial systems is, at the least, an exaggeration of reality tinted by an ideological view of economic and spatial dynamics. The processes of internationalization of commodities, capital and production do not have the dimension that is assumed, as Ferrer (1996) and Budd (1998) argue, nor are they as important to the global cities themselves, as Gordon (1999) maintains when he points out that the influence of transformations in the international finance sector on London has been exaggerated.

In fact, one can argue that internationalization, or if you wish, globalization, has unfurled a wide variety of strategic possibilities to the entire city system (Gordon, 1999). In the case of European Union countries, for example, integration has transformed national city systems into European and global systems. Thus a limited number of cities hope to play a global role in high-level functions, although they must also compete with national cities with competitive advantages in specific services. But increased competition also provides opportunities to other medium-sized cities with innovative capability and endogenous development potential to specialize in specific functions in the new city system, as has been argued in Chapter 7.

The idea that the most important functions and activities of an urban system can be concentrated in just a few cities would not seem to be founded on technically rigorous arguments. In any case, this view lacks empirical evidence and does not acknowledge that the conversion of national urban systems into European or Latin American or global urban systems involves a change in interurban relations that transforms price and cost systems, as well as institutional and entrepreneurial relations on a global scale. On the other hand, the accumulation of functions in a city and the formation of a hierarchical system would imply greater agglomeration costs than in a more flexibly organized system.

Moreover, one should keep in mind that the productive system of the most dynamic cities and urban regions, which sustain the global economy, is in fact very diversified. The system consists of high-technology industrial activities such as micro-electronics, biotechnology, robotics or aerospace industry, as well as manufacturing activities characterized by standardized production in the 1950s and 1960s but restructured through innovations, such as the clothing and automobile industries, advanced service activities, such as marketing, design or technical assistance, and financial and leisure services.

It would not seem logical that diversification of production be accompanied by an accumulation of functions and activities in a limited number of global cities. In fact, both in terms of economic efficiency and location and agglomeration economies, a more flexible and less hierarchical international division of labor than that proposed by those who insist on the hierarchy of city systems on a global scale is in order.

The new spatial division of labor has led to new production and innovation spaces made up of multiple strategic networks from which the global economy is sustained (Veltz, 1996). The strengthening of local firm systems, the creation of subcontracting networks, externalization of production and the introduction of more flexible forms of organization in large firms has led to greater productivity and competitiveness of productive systems and, therefore, of innovative cities and urban regions (Scott, 1998). Moreover, new transportation and communications systems make firms and urban networks more efficient. Ultimately, network economies make urban systems more efficient which would seem to argue in favor of reduced hierarchies in new urban systems.

Globalization and increased competition, then, are shaping a new regional and urban system whose characteristics are gradually being defined. First, the organization of productive systems in cities and regions is becoming more flexible and relations among firms in each center have expanded even as the concentration of production tends to occur in more and more locations. Development is an ever more diffuse process because of increased urban density, the formation of firm clusters and the relative concentration of knowledge (Veltz, 1996). Furthermore, cities and regions tend increasingly to specialize and differentiate production as a consequence of growing competition in the markets. Therefore if urban and regional systems become more and more polycentric and differentiated on a global scale, development processes in countries will tend to accelerate.

The dynamics of new industrial and service spaces has led to a greater variety of locations in developed, late developed and developing economies. The location of industrial and service activities is not predetermined nor does it depend on the attachment to a predefined center or periphery. Rather, location is determined by the functions that each center is able to undertake and by the networks of international flow of commodities and capital (Castells, 1996), regardless of the territory in which the accumulation of capital takes place.

Finally, since globalization is an open-ended process, the dynamic of systems of cities and regions is a phenomenon that will continue to evolve and transform. The eventual design of these systems will depend on the competitive advantages of cities and regions, but the non-tangible factors of development, that is those that facilitate increasing returns, are gaining increasing importance and contribute to the expansion of urban and regional development.

As has been maintained throughout this book, economic development in cities and regions depends on the economies generated as a result of diffusion of innovation, flexibility of productive organization, institutional complexity and urban development. It is not a matter of internal economies of scale or urban economies as in the Fordist period. Present-day urban and regional development include external economies of scale, the reduction of transaction costs, economies of territorial diversity and specialization. When these processes behave synergically, whether spontaneously or induced through policies, self-sustained development processes are accelerated as a result of the effect of the H factor efficiency.

Isolation and integration within the global economy

Globalization is not alien to the dynamics of rural areas. On the contrary, globalization integrates some rural areas and excludes others, just as it does in urban areas. As Alburquerque (1998) indicates, the rural economic dynamic at present is rather peculiar and often critical[3] in a world in which a new international division of labor is taking place and, with it, a specialization of rural areas in productive activities and specific services. A good approach for analyzing the dynamics of rural areas would be from the point of view of integration.

The impact of globalization is not uniform since it also produces forces that tend to reinforce isolation mechanisms in the territory. As has been pointed out above, many firms and economies are only partially integrated or remain on the margin of the globalization processes and must therefore endure the effects of exclusion. However, development of these firms and economies is not necessarily restrained for this reason. On the contrary, when the economic, social and institutional conditions concur and the local community is able to rise to the challenge, endogenous development processes can be stimulated.[4]

Isolation is a multidimensional phenomenon caused by economic, spatial, social and cultural factors that restrict economic integration of a territory into a national and international economic system and the participation of their actors in decision-making on investment and location of firms (Atienza Úbeda, 1998). Undoubtedly, isolation refers to accessibility, but also to the lack of economic, social and institutional capability to respond strategically to the challenges of competition.

In Figure 9.1, a typology of territories is presented based on two variables, accessibility and learning and knowledge capability of territorial organizations and institutions. Remote regions are isolated territories with fragile productive systems. They are often territories with low population density and an aging population, where natural resources and historical and cultural heritage are progressively deteriorating and where the possibilities of following a path of endogenous development are very remote. The only feasible actions in the short term are subsidies and aid from public administrations aimed at stabilizing the population and preserving environmental resources and historical and cultural heritage.

The marginal zones of metropolitan areas are physically integrated into international markets but development is restricted by their inadequate

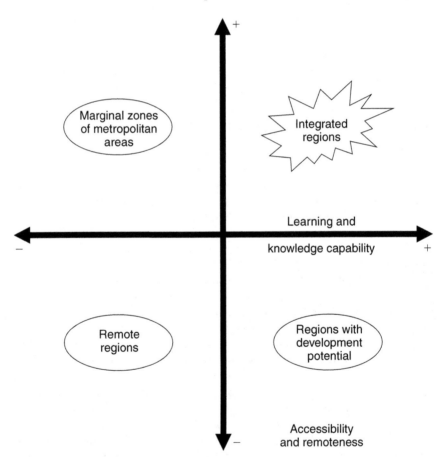

Figure 9.1 Integration within the global economy: types of territories.

learning and knowledge capability, accumulated in institutions and human resources. In these cases it is possible to channel local development policies into initiatives that combine investment in infrastructures and social capital, that is, training for social integration and to improve human resource skills. Support for improved entrepreneurial and organizational capability will aid businessmen in taking advantage of the opportunities arising from integration into national and international markets.

There are also those regions and cities that are physically remote but with development potential. When local communities wish to integrate their territories into the global economy, a space for endogenous development policy is created. Although they may be in need of an intense structural change, measures promoted by local actors are critical to finding a path of self-sustained development. A diagnosis of the area will indicate the weaknesses (difficulties of the main activity on the market, whether agricultural, industrial or raw materials; lack of entrepreneurial resources, insufficient skill level of human resources). Once strengths have also been identified (such as unused natural or human resources, savings from other activities, hidden externalities, local identity), it is possible to design a development program which will put the available competitive advantages to use and foster productive restructuring of the economy.

Finally, integrated areas are often regions with ample innovative capacity and highly developed productive, commercial and technological networks, where a high degree of institutional complexity and flexibility has been achieved and there is a significant number of entrepreneurial projects. Here development processes take on their own dynamics. Deficiencies related to the lack of certain infrastructures and services and the search for new opportunities or improved efficiency can generally be satisfied through private means without resorting to the support of a specialized agency.

In recent decades, accessibility of peripheral cities and regions has largely been overcome due to improved transportation and communications. However, even in the most advanced countries, there are territories of limited accessibility. This may be due either to insufficient or expensive transportation means and sluggish communication and information infrastructures, or to local infrastructure not adequately articulated to the main transportation and communication networks.

The central question lies, however, in what economic, social and institutional factors show serious weaknesses in competitive terms. These factors may include local entrepreneurship, the ease with which innovations are diffused and applied to the productive system or an institutional fabric that favors the functioning of the markets. When local productive systems in peripheral areas show a lack of organizational and learning capability (knowledge, introduction of innovation and strategic response of the local community), the competitiveness of territories is restricted and the presence of local firms in global markets is reduced.

Moreover, in many regions partially or totally excluded from processes of globalization, as occurs in the case of the Mezzogiorno in Italy (Rodríguez Pose, 1998), the institutional system is not sufficiently developed. When society lacks the institutions required by the market economy to function, productive activity will tend to suffer and will not develop with the necessary force within the local environment, thus constraining the generation of steady growth. When the institutional fabric is not sufficiently developed, even the best policies and practices fail to attain this objective.

The dynamics of local productive systems

The effect of globalization on local productive systems can vary considerably from one case to another. From the perspective of endogenous development, the impact will depend on how the productive system is organized, on the adequacy of local institutions to deal with productive and technological changes and on local capability to learn and innovate. Thus, the long-term dynamic of local economies will depend on the response of the actors to changes in the milieu.

Diversity of industrial spaces is acknowledged as fact by the various schools of thought. In some cases (Markusen, 2000) diversity is used to demonstrate the weaknesses of flexible production models, while other studies (Garofoli, 1994) argue that there are many local development models, but there are no general rules to account for their transformation. From the point of view of endogenous development, it would be of interest to analyze the diverse trajectories of local productive systems and point out the tendency to reinforce mechanisms that allow communities to participate in development processes. To identify some of the possible scenarios and organizational and productive adjustments that have been taking place for over a decade, the dynamic of some models of local productive systems can be analyzed.

If it is assumed, as it has been throughout this book, that organization (and relations) of local productive systems may conform to hierarchical models or may take the shape of networks, then one can describe a typology of industrial spaces if this criterion is contrasted with that of integration or non-integration of the firm system into the production filiere of the territory,[5] as Maillat and Grosjean (1999) suggest.

When local productive systems conform to a system of productive organization resulting from the use of local development potential and articulated through firm networks which stimulate horizontal relations of cooperation, two local development models can be identified:

- Local firm systems whose productive activities are integrated into the territory's value chain (A). The productive system is made up of a group of linked firms and regulation of the labor market and diffusion of technical knowledge are carried out within the district. The externalization of functions by the most dynamic firms and the relations among firms only confirm the existence of a local productive system firmly rooted in the territory. These are innovative milieux such as the Swiss Jura Arc (Maillat *et al.*, 1997).

- Local firm systems whose productive activities are integrated into the production "filieres" in other cities or regions (B). In this model the local productive system lacks the stages of the production filiere. Sometimes productive activities have been internationalized; sometimes some of the important stages of the value chain, such as research and development or strategic services to firms, are also located outside of the territory. The industrial district in Montebelluna in Italy is an example (Camagni and Rabellotti, 1997).

When local productive systems correspond to a model of production organization in which hierarchical relations among local and outside firms prevail, two more models can be identified:

- Productive systems formed around large firms that carry out all or the most important functions in the territory and whose activities are integrated in the local production filiere (C). The leading firm or firms buy from local and external suppliers and mainly sell in external markets. The labor market of the productive system and the diffusion of technical knowledge is controlled by the large firm and most investment decisions are made locally. Turin, headquarters of Fiat is a good example of this type of productive systems, as is Vigo, in Spain, where the Citroën plant is well integrated into the local production system and Pescanova, a local firm, leads transformations in the productive system (Vázquez-Barquero, 1993).
- Firms of an industrial space that belong to external production filieres and lack local links (D). The productive system is dominated by large firms that use the space in which they are located as a mere support for their economic and social relations. This would be the case of independent or subsidiary firms that produce for an external firm. Relations with local firms are minimal and both the labor market and diffusion of innovations and knowledge are controlled by the large firm. The Gran ABC in the state of São Paolo, Brazil, and the Research Triangle Park in the United States are two good examples.

The impact of globalization on the behavior of local firm systems varies considerably in these groups of productive systems.

In the case of local firm systems integrated in the territory (A),[6] the situations will vary depending on the productive system's capacity for response. Saxenian (1994) argues that globalization of production and markets fosters the creation of innovative firm systems and improves the position of productive systems based on firm networks. Therefore, endogenous development processes tend to continue and are compatible with the dynamics of globalization. On the other hand, Markusen considers that increased competition and the introduction of process and organization innovations can transform the internal organization of the productive system. In the case of Detroit, which at the beginning of the century was an industrial district comparable to Silicon Valley today, the formation of the automobile industry oligopoly and the flight of other productive sectors from the city have led to a more hierarchical productive system which has hindered diversification and caused serious problems in productive adjustment.

In the case of local systems of firms that are partially integrated into filieres from other regions (B), the evolution can also differ considerably. On the one hand, due to the weakness of their relations with local value chains (lack of research and development segments or producer service activities within the locality) the impact of globalization can generate dynamics very unlike endogenous development processes. Increased competition can lead to the disappearance of the district and the linking of remaining firms to segments of production filieres from other regions, as has occurred in the case of the footwear district of Val d'Uxo (Vázquez-Barquero and Sáez Cala, 1997). But the strong points of these systems (associated with the existence of specialized firms, with firm solid mechanisms of entrepreneurial and institutional interaction and local learning capability) can attract external firms searching for milieux with external economies which are not sufficiently exploited. In Montebelluna, productive restructuring has brought about decentralization of production to southeastern Asian countries and the arrival of external economic actors has externalized the area's center of decision-making.

In the case of productive systems led by external firms whose productive activity is integrated in the local production filiere (C), several scenarios may take place. In an analysis of the economic dynamic of Seattle, Markusen finds that the formation of technological poles around leading and innovative firms is a common strategic response to the challenges of competition in an increasingly globalized world. The specific characteristics of Boeing in Seattle have contributed to productive diversification in the region with the expansion of new technology sectors such as computer software, biotechnology or shipping activities giving rise to a unique kind of endogenous development.

Finally, when the productive systems are made up of firms with no local roots, integrated in external production filieres (D), that is, mere enclaves of external firms, their permanence in the region is unpredictable, depending on whether the conditions of cost/price and the value of the resources that led to their initial location in the area continue to exist. But, even in the case of substantial productive restructuring, it is not impossible for processes of endogenous development to take place, as occurs in the case of the Gran ABC discussed in Chapter 8.

Convergence of the strategies of large enterprise and those of the territory

Organizational and institutional change, then, seems to have made large enterprises a catalyst in economic growth, and cities and regions with growth potential become attractive locations for large enterprises. Do the territorial strategies of large enterprises and the economic strategies of cities and regions tend to converge? Does the result of these strategies favor endogenous development?

Globalization exerts a strong impact on large firms as well as on cities and regions (Veltz, 1993). The globalization process implies that large enterprises compete within global markets and also manage their branch plant network globally. However, generic advantages of a territory, such as low labor costs, no longer constitute a sufficient competitive advantage for a city or region. Firms prefer to locate their plants in places where the productive dynamic is immersed in processes of endogenous development. This allows them to take advantage of the territory's specific competitive advantages, which took shape as the accumulation process advanced.

In turn, the logic of globalization has made cities and regions compete among themselves on an international scale. They try to obtain competitive advantages by upgrading local resources and differentiating local productive activities. For this reason, cities and regions find it necessary to choose a path of endogenous development that will lead to a better competitive position, and at the same time that they launch strategies to attract innovative firms to their territory.

Large enterprise and local organizations coincide in the local space and therefore drive the same development process. The convergence of interests expands competitiveness of the large firm and of the territory which, in turn, foments a process of self-sustained development. Thus, competitiveness and the struggle for market share lead cities and regions to become partners of large enterprises.

A large firm selects its locations in response to the operating needs of the firm and the decision is conditioned by the attraction factors of the locality. The attributes of a location change as a result of the accumulation process and the continuous transformation of technology, production and organization. Cities and regions acquire new properties and qualities which appeal to large innovative organizations and, in this way, become a production and/or territorial milieu in which synergy and cooperation among public and private agents is possible (Fisher, 1994).

As Cotorruelo Menta (1996) suggests, the location of entrepreneurial activities and, therefore, the dynamics of local economic development, may be understood as the result of the interaction between strategies pursued by cities and regions to upgrade local resources and assets[7] and those of firms aimed at employing specific attributes of the territory to obtain competitive advantages. Thus, the same factors would be perceived in different ways by both strategies: from the point of view of the territory, they would be spatial competition factors and, from the firms' perspective, location factors.

From this perspective, the choice of a specific place for locating a multi-location firm production unit occurs when the spatial competition factors of a city/region sufficiently satisfy the firm's location factor demand or, at least, satisfy them better than any other alternative, according to the selection criteria of those responsible for the location decision. In other words, the choice of a place for the location of a branch plant will happen when the local attributes and factors of a city or region are known and evaluated by a firm, which then decides that these attributes will provide competitive advantages within the context of its present and/or future strategy.

The strategies of firms and those of cities and regions seem to share goals and objectives. Both claim that the attributes of the territory – production factors characteristics, the flexible organization of the productive system and its learning dynamic, the diffusion of innovations and knowledge, urban development and the flexibility of the institutional environment for entrepreneurial development – will allow firms locating there to enjoy competitive advantages.

At present, market competition compels plants to locate in territories with specific, not just generic, resources and assets.[8] Among specific resources that favor competition, one should point out infrastructure with strategic value (nowadays, multi-modal transportation and telecommunications), skilled and specialized human resources, technological and entrepreneurial knowledge cumulated over time within the territory and the sense of identity and image of the city or region.

Local development policy contributes, in particular, to the surge and development of these types of specific factors through investment in infrastructure, which improves the attractiveness of the cities and regions, training initiatives for upgrading human resources, activities aimed at the diffusion of entrepreneurial culture or through initiatives which foster the diffusion of technical innovation and knowledge within the productive and social fabric.

The common space shared by large enterprise and the territory also affects the firm's productive system and the local production structure (Perrin, 1990). Made up of suppliers, auxiliary firms and related firms that form a local system of competitive firms capable of generating agglomeration economies, "clusters" organize and structure the territory and confer potential competitive advantages on those firms located there.

New modes of organization assign growing priority to the externalization of functions through subcontracting to firms located near the production unit of the large enterprise. Subcontracting allows large firms to reduce production and transaction costs, benefit from supplier specialization and improve competitiveness. For this reason, places whose productive systems are organized as industrial districts attract inward investment.

Through initiatives that promote the "software" of development (entrepreneurship, diffusion of innovation, training) and strengthen firm networking, local development policies improve competitiveness of local productive systems and, thus, coincide with the strategies of large firms (OECD, 1996b and 1997).

Finally, large enterprises fit more easily into territories where open competition prevails, where there is an entrepreneurial culture and where the regulation of the economy facilitates market performance. Local development policy helps the market function, that is, it influences the way firms are created, organized, managed and how they compete on an international scale (Maillat, 1998; OECD, 1996c and 1997). Competition and cooperation among firms become facilitators of local economic development when a territory is characterized by an advanced system of relations between firms and organizations and by a learning dynamic.

Strategic convergence of large firms and cities/regions would necessarily lead to a strengthening of local development processes. Perroux's concept of local development comes to mind. External innovative firms would lead the dynamics of the productive fabric, they would generate the diffusion of innovation and promote cooperation among firms. Linkage and exchange among firms would facilitate the formation of economies of scale that are external to the firms, but internal to the local productive system.

In fact, a convergence of two complementary processes takes place. On the one hand, the large external firm would act as a catalyst in the development process. Attracted by the existence of local resources and assets, which have come about due to the accumulation of know-how and skills, these firms exert an invigorating effect on the territory by promoting organizational capability and learning dynamic within the local system. In turn, local development strategy would activate endogenous development potential that exists in the city or region.

Large firms and the places of endogenous development

The foregoing discussion shows that there is a high degree of potential compatibility and synergy between territorial strategies of large firms and development strategies of cities and regions. This leads to the proposal that large innovative firms can play a significant role in endogenous development policy.

However, this conclusion should be qualified somewhat in response to certain questions about the processes that stimulate the integration of branch plants into local productive systems. What kind of firms and economic activities are we talking about? Are we referring to all kinds of cities and regions or only to those with specific resources? Do less developed regions also have specific resources that can enable them to attract inward investment?

First of all, it should be pointed out that the discussion has been put forth in terms of territorialization[9] of economic development (Storper, 1997), a concept including only one part of the localization processes of firms. Therefore, one can refer to productive activities that are territorialized and others that are not, as well as to cities and regions that have specific resources that are attractive to global firms and others that are not. As Storper points out, few industries are truly territorialized, that is, whose efficiency depends on specific resources found in specific places. Perhaps the most characteristic activities of this type are those that produce differentiated goods, those in which high quality goods with technological innovation content are produced and those that produce specialized services (such as those that satisfy unique distinct tastes).

However, perhaps the most significant fact in recent decades is that globalization and increased competition in the markets have led to more territorialization of firm productive processes. Activities in which standardized goods could be produced anywhere with routine production methods (clothing, footwear or automobiles) in the 1950s and 1960s, are now involved in processes of differentiation of production and of technological innovation which oblige them to move toward the territorialization of production. Growing competition leads firms to make changes in their organization system and seek plant locations in places where specific resources (material and immaterial) are available.

On the other hand, only certain territories, such as dynamic metropolitan areas, technological and industrial districts and some rural areas with a potential for endogenous development, possess the specific resources and assets that attract inward investment. Cities and regions in industrial decline and regions with fragile productive systems and severe environmental degradation are not usually attractive spaces for innovative firms, unless intense local development policy moves to modify these characteristics.

The most dynamic metropolitan areas and technological districts form innovative milieux with highly skilled human resources and innovative firms. Firm networks allow them to obtain economies of scale and reduced transaction costs. These types of resources attract branch plants specialized in the production of quality goods and services.

Endogenous industrialization areas whose production system is organized as an industrial district may be attractive for industrial activities that produce differentiated goods. The networks of specialized firms guarantee efficient subcontracting of production tasks and service activities, which will lead them to improve competitiveness and their positioning within the markets.

Rural areas with potential for endogenous development, that have natural and skilled human resources and an institutional system which stimulates innovative firm activity, are attractive regions for industrial firms that require a milieu with a high quality natural environment and for those that produce consumer services that satisfy global tastes. But this is not so for regions that are remote or isolated and lacking in qualified human resources and quality natural resources.

Critics of large enterprise often maintain that the specific resources and attributes that attract the most innovative firms are not present in less developed regions. This criticism does not always reflect reality, given that restructuring and structural change in recent decades has permitted the discovery of development potential, even in less favored and peripheral regions, allowing them to launch strategies of endogenous development compatible with those of large innovative firms.

Over the last few decades, migratory flows have been reduced and improved training and education have brought about the concentration of skilled human resources in less developed cities and regions. Structural change associated with industrial restructuring and the increased importance of the service sector along with the consideration of the natural environment as a factor of spatial competition for territories, have contributed to the revalorization of regions that were formerly irrelevant to firms. Improved transportation and communication infrastructure along with decreasing transportation costs have improved accessibility to and from regions and cities formerly considered distant and peripheral. Finally, the growing use of new technologies is rapidly bringing about a reassessment of resources in less developed cities and regions.

Thus, integration of innovative firms within the local productive system depends on the type of productive activity, the way the branch plant is articulated within its enterprise[10] and on the organizational model of the city/region production system. Depending on the technical, productive and institutional relations that are established between the operating unit and the local milieu, different levels of synergy and various forms of cooperation between the enterprise and the city/region can emerge which will lead to specific dynamics for local development.

Diversity and endogenous development

Throughout the 1990s the globalization process increased its pace which exerted a considerable impact on the dynamics of urban and regional economies. Greater competition generated processes of economic integration which, in turn, caused the shutdown of firms and unemployment. However, these processes also led to the creation of new enterprises, improvement of the most competitive firms and new alliances and agreements.

Due to productive restructuring in local economies, an increase in productive and territorial diversity took place. Therefore, globalization fostered diversity of economic spaces, including rural and more undeveloped areas, and stimulated the dynamics of the various models of local productive systems.

Increased competition among firms and territories has led cities and urban regions to strengthen their competitive advantages through improved local resources, differentiation and specialization of their productive systems and specialization, all of which has contributed to greater urban diversity and has made urban systems less hierarchical. In this way a new scenario emerges characterized by new needs and demands from firms and the local society for new responses in terms of local development policy.

10 The new generation of endogenous development policies

In the last two chapters it has been shown that the concept and application of development policy has been undergoing radical change since the mid-1970s. In fact, a new approach emerged in the 1980s which held that development potential available in the territory should be put to use through local initiatives in order to achieve growth in cities and regions.

There is agreement that the endogenous development approach has meant a significant advance in regional and industrial policy, both conceptually and functionally. Recently, some authors (Helmsing, 1998; Maillat, 1997) have pointed out that a new generation of local development policies has begun to emerge in both developed and developing countries as a result of the effects of globalization on the dynamics of productive and spatial systems and of changes in firm and territorial strategies.

This chapter focuses on the present-day situation and perspectives of endogenous development policy. After commenting on the strengths and weaknesses of local development policy, the chapter argues that local initiatives arising over the last decades show that changes are, in effect, taking place. Since globalization also affects the way development processes are conceived and implemented, development policies of cities and regions should be approached as a response to new needs and demands on the part of firms and local actors for public services. The changes are, to a great measure, significant since local development policy tools are increasingly oriented toward facilitating the generation of externalities, interactive learning on the part of firms and organizations and adaptation of the institutional environment.

The evaluation of local development policy

Spontaneously appearing as local communities respond to the challenges of productive adjustment, the local development policy is characterized by its strategic view of economic development, providing local actors with the capacity to stimulate productive restructuring and, subsequently, improve the employment rate and welfare of local communities.

What are the most positive aspects of local development policy? First of all, it should be stressed that local development policy stimulates productive adjustment processes. When development policy from outside has become less feasible, adjustment of local productive systems to new competitive conditions necessarily turns to local initiatives. Therefore, by assuming leadership in processes of structural change, local and regional governments participate in the solution to the problems that restructuring of the international productive system causes in the economies of localities and territories.

The new approach promotes those initiatives that aim to develop specific cities and regions, not the spatial distribution of productive activity and income among the territories of a country. It works to improve the quality of infrastructures and production factors, to diffuse innovation within the productive fabric, stimulate the start-up and development of firms and organize development through intermediary agencies.

Second, change from the Fordist capital accumulation model to that of flexible production makes the new regional policy more effective than traditional policy, as Ettlinger points out. When the Fordist model prevails, redistributing actions and measures are usually inefficient because the performance of the production system is founded on the disparity of the spatial division of labor. Logically, local development is impossible (Lasuén, 1973) and coercion on the part of the state can be inefficient because center–periphery dynamics are still in place.

Nevertheless, in today's scenario, regional development policy is more effective when the productive system can be adjusted to the model of flexible accumulation. This is due to the fact that flexible production has a different spatial rationale because ties among firms are all located in a given territory. This fact also explains why local development policy can create an environment favorable to the emergence and development of local firms, even when endogenous development does not always adjust to flexible production models.

Furthermore, local development policy is efficient, in the sense that it exploits development potential arising from adjustments in the productive system from the mid-1970s on. Diminished inter-regional factor flows have meant that the human and financial resources can be kept in the cities and regions. On the other hand, new activities in the area of services (tourism, civil assistance and health, for example) and environment, along with the introduction of new technologies led to the use of resources that were of less interest in the preceding phase of the long economic cycle. Moreover, improved transportation and communications means and infrastructure as well as lower transportation costs have made more remote or peripheral territories increasingly accessible and attractive. Finally, the increased use of new technologies has rapidly led to a revalorization of resources existing in territories in less developed regions.

These arguments provide the answer to the question posed by Polèse

(1994): Why is it that the market does not guarantee the use of local resources? Local development policy attempts to enhance the performance of market mechanisms. With local initiatives, it is hoped the obstacles to economic growth will be overcome. By influencing endogenous development factors, local development policy encourages economic agents to use local resources competitively.

Local development policies, on the other hand, encourage local societies to participate in development. Historically, local entrepreneurs have played a leading role in development processes when private investments were the main factor in productive change and adjustment. Today, local development policies extend leadership and actions to other groups in the local society. In particular, public agents who represent local society in democratic systems assume, for the first time, the responsibility of actively participating in the design and implementation of local economic development strategies.

Moreover, local opinion leaders are often committed to the design of endogenous development strategy and endogenous development strategy is actually founded on the active response of local society to challenges arising from increasing competition. The new strategy, then, requires a new mindset on the part of society. Development strategies based on direct subsidy must give way to new active formulae directed toward competitive development.

What are the shortcomings of the second generation of regional policies? The question of coordination among the various actors stands out. Local development policy is designed and instrumented by public and private actors who resort to many different strategies. Experiences in local development show that coordination of these actors and their strategies is frequently one of the weak points of the new regional policy. For policy to be efficient, a concurrence between top-down measures that promote structural change, and bottom-up actions that promote territorial development is desirable, as Boekema suggests. Local initiatives must be coordinated with sectoral and regional policies of central and regional administrations if the limitations of each type of policy are to be neutralized.

When sectoral and regional policies are implemented alone, not only is development potential squandered, but the dynamics and adjustment of local economies are also endangered when priority is given to territorial redistribution over productive adjustment. If emphasis were to be placed on local initiatives alone, local productive system ties with national and international systems would not always be taken into account and the role of globalization in the adjustment of the productive system would be unknown.

However, coordinating the actions of public and private actors is always a challenge. For this reason, a strategic view from the local perspective is significant to the economic development of a region or a city because it demonstrates the need for joint action on the part of the actors. Hence, as we have indicated above, the organization of development through partnerships and networks tends to become one of the central axis of local development policy.

Local development strategy, then, stresses the role of local initiatives in development processes. However, it also proposes that a synergy take place between local initiatives of each territory and the actions of the other administrations and organizations that promote structural change. But, as Boisier (1997) maintains, it is only possible to coordinate local initiatives with the sectoral and regional policies of other administrations and organizations when there is a collective project backed by the civil society and social and political actors.

The lack of critical masses in territorial and management units, on the other hand, is an important constraint in many local initiatives because it reduces efficiency in the use of the instruments. Each one of the instruments (such as business innovation centers, technological institutes or training centers) require that local demand for services be sufficient to guarantee that the center will be able to operate with low unit costs. However, administrative borders often make it necessary for cities and regions to join together to coordinate action over a larger space thus obtaining economies of scale which lead to improved efficiency of intermediate organizations. Regulation in countries does not always facilitate proposed solutions to reach the necessary dimension. In this case, the agents may resort to the formation of institutional partnerships and networks to attain the territorial dimension required by development agencies to be efficient and effective.

Finally, another important shortcoming of local development policy is that it lacks a well defined legal and institutional framework. When local autonomy is not institutionalized nor provided with the necessary budgetary resources, or when decentralization and devolution of competencies to local communities has not yet become operative or extended to the entire national territory, local governments find their capacity for local action restricted. Then local development policy, unable to reach all the territories, will remain in the more dynamic and entrepreneurial towns and regions. For this reason, the search for funding of local initiatives is always a complex task. Private banks are not particularly interested in participating in projects to promote local development and in initiatives to start up and develop firms. On the other hand, public financing is severely restricted for a lack of local development policy framework. For this reason, local actors can be forced to use financial resources designed for other purposes, which can cause problems in the management of the initiatives.

In brief, local development policy has overcome the experimental stage. It is of great use in productive restructuring processes and contributes to regional and local development. An acceptable body of doctrine has undoubtedly been consolidated, but the change in scenario as a result of globalization's rapid advance calls for a revision of the strategy, at the least, if not a whole new generation of policies.

Local development in times of globalization

The transformations caused by increasing competition and globalization go beyond changes in territorial and productive processes and also affect the way development processes are conceived and promoted. New ways of dealing with productive adjustment by reinforcing endogenous development processes have been discussed above. The specific nature of recent local development initiatives would seem to indicate that a new generation of development policies is emerging (see Figure 10.1).

The polycentric view of development

Globalization has created a new scenario for regions and cities that directly compete with each other to maintain and attract investment. In this context, territories wishing to increase the welfare of their inhabitants and improve their position over their rivals must provide an efficient strategic response. If they do not do so, their competitive position will worsen over the long term, which would lead to a situation in which their level of well-being could be diminished, at least in relative terms.

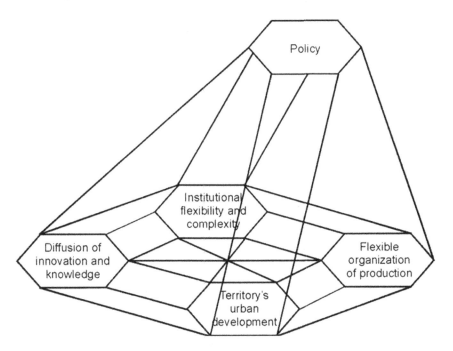

Figure 10.1 New generation of local development policies.

The new generation of policies meets this challenge with a view that considers development a widespread, diffuse process depending on the growth trajectories of cities and regions. Although this approach is far from traditional positions inspired by models of concentrated growth, it does point out that regional development requires the location of productive activity in a limited number of urban settlements to which investment and resources flow. These are spaces with sufficient dimension to compete (large cities, city networks, counties or entire regions); the adequacy of their size will depend on the type of actions necessary to foster development of the territory.

As in the case of local development policy, the new generation of policies decidedly takes a territorial approach to development in that it considers the use of each territory's development potential strategic to the growth of regions and cities. Moreover, these policies hold that regional and urban development is rooted in the territory and that economic dynamics depend on the conditions of the milieu in which firms emerge and develop and knowledge is diffused, and on the response of local actors to changes in the milieu.

Systemic view of development

In sharp contrast to earlier generations of development policy, new approaches to the development of cities and regions are more sensitive to initiatives encouraging the formation of networks. As Bramanti and Maggioni (1997) maintain, globalization has stimulated both new modes of organization for productive activity and new entrepreneurial strategies. Informal relations among firms have increased, as have direct contacts between firms and firm technicians and managers, subcontracting of activities, cooperation agreements and strategic alliances. New internal organizational plans of enterprises allow firm networks to be employed more efficiently and territorial strategies to be instrumented to achieve improved competitiveness and market share. Thus, globalization has stimulated increased flows and relations among firms and actors of the various environments and it has linked success in the markets to efficiency of productive and institutional grids. This is why the new generation of policies must necessarily be sensitive to local milieux by proposing measures rooted in local contexts and aimed at solving problems in the entire local productive system and networks, rather than in individual firms.

This implies a fundamental change in development strategy. The first generation of development policies targeted the creation of infrastructures and the location of external firms through incentives. The second generation emphasized initiatives encouraging the upgrading of nontangible development resources through instruments such as Firm Incubators, Business and Innovation Centers, Technological Institutes or Training Centers. The new generation of development policies gives preference to those initiatives that favor the creation and development of networks among firms, organizations and institutions located within the same territory or in other strategically complementary territories.

This orientation of the new generation of policies is based on the idea that globalization is inducing the development of networks of firms, organizations and cities. Therefore, in order to improve the performance of an economy, it is necessary to influence the system of actors, supporting not only firms but also organizations and institutions. If the final goal is to foster learning capacity and local response, actions should affect the entire local milieu.

Sustainable development with multiple goals

As in the case of local development policy, new development strategy aims to improve efficiency in the allocation of public resources, bring about a fair distribution of wealth and employment and satisfy both present and future needs of the population by adequately putting natural and environmental resources to use.

The objectives of efficiency, equity and ecology are expressing the conflicting interests in each and every one of the territories. This is why local development strategies must reach a balance and, in any case, establish priorities among objectives and actions. When economic objectives are given priority, for example, equity and ecology should act as constraints for the final objective sought (see Figure 10.2).

Insofar as it establishes competitive development of cities and regions as a top-priority objective, the new development strategy is somewhat distanced from the first two generations of development policies. It clearly differs from traditional development policies whose main objective was to

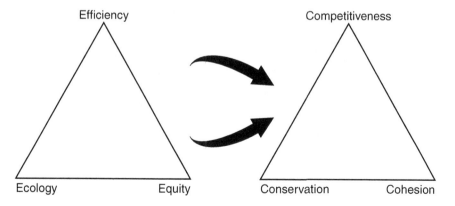

Figure 10.2 Development, a process of multiple goals.

reduce regional disparity existing in the territory; it was deemed impossible in a global economy for local and regional administrations to adopt a development strategy based on spatial equity within the whole system.

Furthermore, the new strategies expand the proposals of the second generation of policies, whose strategic objective was to encourage entrepreneurial capacity within the territory and improve firm productivity and competitiveness. The initiatives proposed by the new generation aim to improve the milieu in which the productive systems are inserted, thus converting territories into spaces for living and producing in present and future generations, according to the Brundtland report (WCED, 1987).

This new generation of development policies reinforces the ecological dimension by assigning greater importance to the non-tangible dimensions of development. Not only do new strategies increasingly take into account the need to reduce environmental deterioration, but, as Durán (2000) points out, environmental protection becomes a source of opportunity leading to the creation of firms and jobs. These initiatives stimulate organic agriculture whose products are increasingly in demand in higher income markets. They promote urban and rural tourism, which attracts travelers and tourists and leads to the protection of the historical, cultural and environmental heritage. They generate research and production activities in the area of renewable energy sources and create service activities and technical assistance for environmental protection. In sum, the new generation of policies proposes to attain multiple objectives by simultaneously promoting sustainable economic and social development.

Sectoral development and public policy

The new generation of development policies goes a step farther in local development strategies by combining both horizontal initiatives with sectoral action. Horizontal initiatives directed at all kinds of firms and activities in a locality promote the start-up and development of firms, the diffusion of innovation and information and the upgrading of human capital. Strategic activities fostering the growth of cities and regions are also encouraged by the new generation of policies.

This approach goes beyond the view of integrated development. Here, the identification of competitive activities leads to the design of initiatives in various productive sectors, such as tourism and industrial activities, which, in turn, makes regions and cities more competitive. New strategies also attempt to combine local initiatives with actions that emanate from the main policies of public administrations.

Cooperation of local and external agents

Like the preceding generation of policies, the emerging group encourages participation of the local society and economic, social and political actors in development processes. But important differences exist between the new generation of policies and the two previous generations with regard to the proposals in the area of organization and management of development strategy.

As has been stressed above, development is rooted in the territory's productive, cultural and institutional context, which explains why the dynamics and consolidation of growth depend on the support of the civic society and those actors who make decisions as to public and private investment. Development, then, involves designing and implementing initiatives with the support of all kinds of actors. When policy is instrumented through strategic planning, agreement among the actors must even be reached as to procedure.

Experiences in local development policy show that management and implementation of development initiatives is most effectively carried out through intermediary organizations whose executive boards include representatives from entrepreneurial organizations, unions, educational and research centers and territorial public administrations. Thus, intermediary organizations are still essential to promoting endogenous development processes, but their efficiency is conditioned by the institutional context where change comes about gradually and slowly.

Globalization requires a greater presence of external firms rooted in the area who show interest in endogenizing some of their functions. While in traditional policy the strategic development actor was the central administration and in local development policy it was the local community, in the new generation of policies external firms must also be taken into account since, in certain conditions, they can become a catalyzing element in local development processes.

Finally, multiple actors with varying objectives and strategies have gradually adapted development policy to the new institutional environment. These policies have been negotiated among all the actors whose interests converge in cities and spaces of accumulation. Globalization has conditioned the strategies of countries, cities and firms, thus favoring the territorialization of development processes.

As Helmsing (1998) has suggested, however, these initiatives cannot be merely local since they are necessarily aimed at improving the position of urban and regional economies within the global system of cities and regions. Their scope must go beyond the limits of the local and national economy and must become increasingly more international. This is why strategic alliances and efficient forms of cooperation among public and private firms and organizations must be encouraged.

New ways for service delivering

Globalization and increasing market competition is giving rise to new needs and demands on the part of firms and productive systems. The problems of firms are not limited to overcoming insufficiencies in specific and isolated productive factors, such as the qualification of human resources, gathering sufficient information to acquire new machinery or gaining entrance to a new market. In fact, increased market competition requires that the use of skilled human resources be combined with the introduction of innovation in capital goods in order to improve the local firms' positioning in international markets. That is why local development policy tries to flexibly integrate the various types of tools and better adjust all of them to demand. Changes in the demand for services by firms and local productive systems require a change of direction on the part of inter-mediate organizations who are, no doubt, rushing to provide the new products and services. Even the way services are delivered is changing.

Policy tools aimed at improving the productive factors are being aban-doned in favor of those improving firm learning processes and their own response to whatever challenges they are facing. These new instruments attempt to teach firms to create and develop their own entrepreneurial cooperation networks, expand and modify their commercial logistics and learn to innovate within the firm itself. This means development agencies and intermediate organizations take on a more active role, as their prod-ucts and services become better adapted to firm needs and demands.

New tools for local development

However, the new scenario is causing change in local development initi-atives. Those that aim to improve factors associated with the non-tangible content of development, such as human resource training, diffusion of innovation or multiplying entrepreneurial capability in the territory, still play an important role. However, the new generation of policies increas-ingly stresses the development of those factors – knowledge, qualification, the creation of innovations and, particularly, the creation of networks of firms and organizations – that make the territory a more competitive and attractive place to invest and contribute to sustainable development and the adaptation of institutions to changes.

Innovation and knowledge centers for global competition

Increased competition and globalization necessarily lead to the inter-nationalization of innovations. For this reason firms not only need and demand traditional services offered by technological centers, such as quality control, technical certification, resistance tests or employee train-ing, but also require services which facilitate the formation of firm net-works and the learning process.

Moreover, local development policies combine very diverse instruments depending on the specific weaknesses and needs of local firms and locali-ties. The SMEPOL project,[1] for example, identified four main barriers to the diffusion of innovation and knowledge: lack of firm funding to invest in new products and processes, lack of accessibility to strategic information, absence of interaction between firms and suppliers of intermediate goods and services and lack of skilled human resources (STEP Group, 1999).

The specific tools through which local development policy is implemented aim to meet precise firm demands and overcome precise barriers. All of the technology policy tools evaluated within the SMEPOL project are similar in that they propose to change innovative capability of firms by improving the introduction of innovation and knowledge and facilitating the diffusion of innovation within the productive fabric and the territory. But each one of these instruments was designed to make available services which would meet specific needs, and even underlying needs, of local firms. That is, they are "ad hoc" tools, a common characteristic of all those used to implement endogenous development policies.

As has been argued throughout this book, the acceleration of globalization over the last decade has increased competition in the markets and therefore new services aimed at improving the quality of their goods and products are demanded by firms. Productivity and competitiveness of firms and, ultimately, their internal and external economies increasingly depend on the quality of productive factors and processes, service activities (commercial, marketing, etc.) and the diffusion of innovations in the territory (Bramanti and Maggioni, 1997). In fact, diffusion of knowledge and innovation throughout firm networks is an interactive process that encourages each enterprise to develop the most adequate learning forms and generate new knowledge (Malecki, 1991), the foundation of firm competitiveness.

Therefore, recent innovation centers attempt to influence the learning process within and among firms and extend their sphere of action to other actors within the territorial innovation system. One initiative is to upgrade human resources in firms and transfer the tacit knowledge necessary to stimulate innovation. Networks and cooperation between research centers and firms are also encouraged in order to implant mechanisms of creation and diffusion of innovation. Creative interaction and learning among institutions and firms are thus generated.

The simultaneous existence of various modes of development, productive systems and territories as well as diverse needs and demands accounts, then, for the diversity of local development tools. A typology can be formulated based on two criteria. One is the target of the instrument, whether a firm (in which case the goal will be to increase the firm's productivity) or a firm system (where the objective is to increase externalities through interaction and improvement of knowledge). The second is the reactive and proactive nature of services rendered. These may target the upgrading of factor quality demanded by firms by providing public or private services or they may aim to help firms learn to innovate and produce services in their relations with other firms and institutions by encouraging interactive learning.

If these criteria are applied to present-day tools for local development, the following types of technological policy centers can be identified: technological transfer units in the universities, which provide services to firms to upgrade the quality of their resources; business and innovation centers, such as those promoted by the European Commission, whose objective is to help firms learn how to innovate; technology institutes, such as those of the Valencian Region in Spain or Rafaela in Argentina, which attempt to improve the externalities of local productive systems with initiatives targeting the upgrading of productive factors; and, finally, the new generation of centers for global competition such as the Limburg Innovation Center (knowledge-intensive industry clustering) (see Figure 10.3).

The SMEPOL report found that most instruments for development and innovation are of the first type while there are few in the last cat-

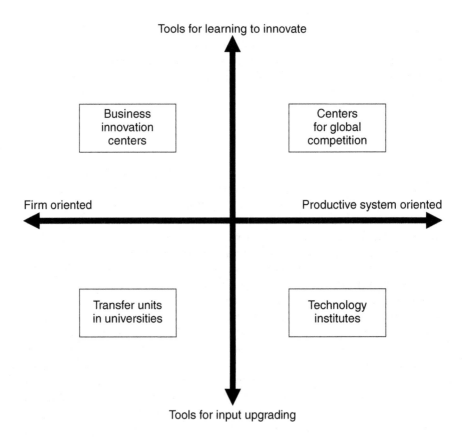

Figure 10.3 Policy tools for innovation.

egory. However, local development policies now tend to be increasingly interactive and oriented toward improvement in territorial externalities. Thus, it is foreseeable that in coming years the fourth type, that is the centers for global competition, will become more prevalent at the same time as instruments from the preceding generation are gradually adapted to meet the firms' and territories' new needs and demands for services.

The organization of production and development of firms

Globalization originates new needs and demands for services to facilitate the development of firms, productive systems and local economies. The new technologies have brought new products and ways of carrying out economic transactions, all of which require new services to firms. Increasing competition also creates new needs on the part of firms who then require different forms of productive organization. It is therefore necessary to foster the creation and enabling of firm networks that will lead to more competitive productive systems and local economies.

The instruments that provide services to local firms, such as centers for firm start-up, are undergoing change. Firms need to upgrade their real time access to information on commercial opportunities, capital goods or entrepreneurial cooperation. They find it necessary to develop electronic commerce, they need digital certification services and, in general, they need to adapt their logistics to competitively meet demand for their goods and services.

The restructuring of local productive systems, on the other hand, can be promoted through initiatives that stimulate the formation of clusters of firms as occurs in Eindhoven, Holland. The adjustment of the two large firms that give impulse to development in the region, Philips Electronics and DAF Trucks, caused serious problems in the local job market. In response to this situation, public and private actors cooperated in an action program which aimed to reinforce the position of small and medium-sized firms in the region through the formation of clusters. Although this program received funding from the European Union, it is the private sector that is carrying out the cluster formation projects through leading firms in each sector (Berg *et al.*, 1999).

Perhaps the most innovative contribution that has taken place over the last decade was in Italy when Law 317/91 was passed. This legislation considered the possibility of bringing about productive adjustment and economic development by supporting firm clusters and industrial districts. It assigns a decisive role to regions, and indirectly, to local communities. It gives competencies to them to support both the diffusion of innovations and the access of firms to strategic services for the development of firm clusters. The measure also recognizes their capability to intervene in "external economies" and the control of processes of change in industrial districts. Some regions such as Lombardy later presented their own set of norms for its application (Garofoli, 1995).

The Italian law 317/91 undoubtedly represents an innovation in public support of productive restructuring processes. For the first time, clusters, local productive systems and industrial districts are considered possible targets of industrial policy which in the past had targeted individual firms or productive sectors. Moreover, the law acknowledges that there is interaction between firms (firm systems) and the territory within the economic dynamic and it stresses the role of local development policy ("bottom-up approach") for productive restructuring processes. However, as Garofoli (2001) points out, the implementation of this kind of initiative can encounter difficulties in identifying the productive systems to be targeted.

Finally, in Galicia, Spain, the regional government encourages cooperation among local firms and reinforcement of production chains to improve competitive advantage through the Plan for the Support of Business Clusters (Plan de Potenciación de Clusters Empresariales). For this reason, strategic plans for the naval, wood and furniture, automobile and ornamental rock industries have been designed to identify joint actions by local firms. The creation of the Innovation and Service Centers (Centros de Innovación y Servicios), specialized in each one of the clusters, facilitates coordination of the initiatives (González Gurriarán, 2001).

Sustainable urban development

Globalization and decentralization are accelerating the urbanization process to the extent that by 2025 the urban population is expected to make up two-thirds of the world population. The cities of the twenty-first century are, more than ever, the space for development since they provide and concentrate a large part of the specific factors. But if cities are to play a strategic role in development processes and agglomeration economies are to be used by firms, not only must investments in infrastructures and social capital be made. It is also necessary to promote sustainable urban development processes.

Initiatives aimed at obtaining urban sustainability should consider such important questions as the complexity of the urban system, the physical and environmental character of cities and the need to combine short and long-term measures (Camagni *et al.*, 1996). Urban policy initiatives will be all the more effective when they explicitly act on the economic, social and physical systems that structure the city. The effectiveness of environmental measures depends on the combination of policies responding to immediate needs (efficient and flexible metropolitan mobility) and those of a more structural nature (location of productive activity, housing and transportation infrastructure).

From the perspective of endogenous development, it is important to define the scope of the city since globalization and increased international competition leads to the gradual functional integration of urban and regional metropolitan levels and the emergence of horizontal networks of cities (Barrios, 2000). Urban and metropolitan systems are increasingly complex. Thus if economic and social progress and the surge of hidden agglomeration economies are to be guaranteed, it is necessary to integrate and bind the metropolitan region and the city network with policies that target the connection of the intra-metropolitan and city network (through transportation and communications infrastructure) the rendering of regional services (training, culture, knowledge, leisure) and the environmental quality.

To do this, local administrations must cooperate in the organization of the metropolitan and regional territory's actors, if possible through a metropolitan and regional strategic agreement. The success of innovative projects to improve competitive position requires the formation of networks of actors, as shown in the case of Bilbao Metropoli-30 in which public organizations, firms and other institutions cooperate to promote the revitalization of the region of Bilbao (Berg *et al.*, 1999).

Economic development requires a framework of social and environmental sustainability. As discussed earlier, globalization generates poverty and social exclusion in cities of developed and less developed countries by causing metropolitan fragmentation as a result of real estate dynamics and urban lifestyles. Some refer to this phenomenon as the two-speed city (Cariola and Labacana, 2000; Camagni *et al.*, 1996). In today's urban societies, the losers who make up the city of the "excluded" and the winners who belong to the "included" are clearly separated, thus causing a gap that restricts the use of development potential existing in the territory.

To neutralize the negative effects of social exclusion, cities have launched urban development initiatives such as neighborhood restructuring in Caracas (Baldó and Villanueva, 1996; Villanueva, 1998). A good example is the Catuche project of 1993, an initiative which relied on the Jesuit Fathers of the Pastora to provide this marginal neighborhood with the basic services and social capital needed to improve the environment and living conditions of the population. Some of the most important actions of this initiative are the environmental clean-up of the Catuche River, improved relations among neighbors, the building or reconstruction of public services and new housing and the promotion of micro-firms to carry out the construction jobs. The project was managed through the Consortium of the Quebrada de Catuche, made up of members from the community of Catuche, representatives from the promoters and professional participants. Funding came from the Caracas Town Hall (Alcaldía), from the national government and non-governmental organizations.

For economic development to take place the initiatives necessary to maintain the environment and control environmental problems in cities and urban regions must be launched, since one of the major causes of pollution is that more than 60 percent of world productive activity is concentrated in cities (European Environmental Agency, 1995). A variety of situations affect the relation between development and environment. In the beginning stages of development, economic growth with improvement of infrastructures and social capital contribute positively to environmental quality. In other situations, environmental quality creates a propitious milieu to live and work and is therefore a decisive factor in attracting investment and continued urban development. But, conflicting interests sometimes arise between environment and economic growth which forces cities to establish compromise initiatives based on the best interests of the city's inhabitants.

Without exception, the economic development of urban regions is always sustainable development. Therefore, local development strategies increasingly include initiatives aimed at achieving improved environmental quality such as reduction of environmental contamination and sewage treatment. The conservation of the historical heritage and the promotion of a better conserved environment with the creation of open spaces, conservation of parks and restoration of historical town centers. In Urbania, a small city of 6500 inhabitants in the province of Pesaro in the region of the Marches, for example, some local initiatives include the restoration of various sites such as the Ducal Palace, which houses the Civic Museum, the museum of art and the library, the Parco Ducale on the outskirts of the city, a historical leisure area of the Dukes of Urbino, and the theatre.

Finally, the best practices (OECD, 1994) recommend that initiatives such as a polycentric organization of cities and urban regions, revitalization of urban centers, the policy of urban containment, which has been applied in the United Kingdom for more than 20 years, integrated planning of transportation and construction of infrastructures for new technologies and communication be implemented to achieve sustainable development of cities and urban regions. The ultimate goal, in fact, is to make cities more attractive. To do this, cities must be "marketed" and sustainable urban development policies must be implemented to change the perception of the city that inhabitants, visitors and people living in other cities have.

Negotiated planning

The globalization process creates increased competition in the markets for firms and local productive systems which creates new needs and demands in the institutions that regulate development processes. Since competition is a dynamic process that depends on the actors' strategies, the content and form that local development strategy will take is altered by the evolution of economic, social, technological and institutional conditions. The adaptation of local development policies to a new institutional milieu becomes a set of actions to be negotiated by the economic, social and political actors of the city or region.

The demand for new forms of organization and management of territorial policy has brought about a new approach to economic planning based on negotiation and consensus among actors with interests in a territory which, from the 1990s on, has gradually become institutionalized, although not without tension between central and local or regional administrations. Thus, negotiated territorial pacts, a form of negotiated planning, have appeared and the idea of the need to establish planning agreements between external firms and local administrations is becoming widely accepted.

A territorial pact is basically an agreement between public and private actors on diverse initiatives to promote local development in a region. It is therefore an instrument that facilitates, through public funding, the coordinated implementation of these actions by the various specialized actors. Territorial pacts are, in fact, the manifestation of association of actors in a territory and can be designed and promoted by local public administrations, chambers of commerce as well as representatives of entrepreneurs, workers and the local society.

The first territorial pacts emerged in southern Italy to fill the vacuum created by the suppression of the policy for the Mezzogiorno in 1991 and were later extended to the rest of Italy, the European Union and Latin America (Mele, 1999). As has been argued above, the fact that local institutions make their own economic policy decisions through consortiums, pacts, joint management of services, agreements with other institutions and organizations, is associated with the increasing awareness of the fact that decreased presence of the central administrations leads to greater management efficiency and increased social solidarity as well as institutional change.

But institutional transformations attempt to adapt to changes in the economic, political and social system and respond to the demands of economic and social actors. As has been argued in the previous chapter, when the strategies of large firms and territories converge, endogenous development processes are reinforced. This conclusion would lead us to restore some of the most sophisticated elements of growth pole theory which exogenous development policies of the 1960s and 1970s were unable to implement.

The first step would be to reconsider national and regional government incentive policies. Specific regulation that would guarantee the involvement of inward investment in local endogenous development (Latella, 1997) should be incorporated into policy. Incentives for firms could be negotiated within the context of a local development plan in which priority goals and actions, including the investment projects of external firms and of the public administrations, would be defined.

Incentives would be negotiated case by case, as Florio (1996) suggests, based on an agreement between the large firm and the central, regional and/or local government. Also stipulated in this agreement would be public and private commitments made for reaching the goals of the local development plan. The agreement should indicate the kind and amount of incentives as well as the specific responsibilities of local government and the large firm.

The local government would agree to carry out the actions specified in the local development plan. Depending on the needs and requirements of each territory, these actions would place more or less emphasis on investment in infrastructures, communications and transportation, social overhead capital, environment, initiatives contributing to improve the quality of non-tangible factors of development, expansion of networking and the local organizational capability or the creation of an institutional climate favorable to the start-up and development of local firms.

The external firm, for its part, would commit to meeting the specific goals, contributing to job creation through direct investment and stimulating the creation and development of local firms through subcontracting, and the demand for locally produced goods and services. Other aspects, such as the integration of the branch plant within the local system, the large firm's contribution to upgrading worker skills and the diffusion of innovation, the degree of autonomy of the subsidiary plant in the management of local activities and collaboration with local institutions, would also be set out in the planning agreement.

The planning agreement, then, would include the strategic goals of both the large enterprise and the city/region, coordinate actions of common interest to the firm and the territory, and specify control and follow-up mechanisms for the agreements reached. Actually, what the agreement would do is formalize the convergence between the large enterprise's territorial strategy and the economic strategy of the city/region.

Interaction and synergy for endogenous development

In this chapter it has been argued that productive, spatial and organizational effects of globalization have defined a new scenario that requires change in development policies. There are clear indications that a new generation of development policies, targeting improvement of organization and institutional grids, has begun to emerge.

Cities and regions must respond effectively to the challenges of globalization and therefore require instruments to help develop their competitive advantages. This can be achieved through a combination of initiatives and actions that stimulate endogenous development potential and attract outside resources or, in other words, through the synergic action of endogenous and exogenous development.

The challenges of globalization and experiences accumulated in endogenous development policy suggest that the role of urban and regional administrations in development policy should be reconsidered, and elements of growth poles and incentive policies should be recovered and revitalized. At the center of the new policy approach is the creation of a fund for local development where firms and organizations that contribute with their investments to the development of a territory could find financial support.

The third generation of development policies demands strategic action in a world in which competition is increasingly intense. Both initiatives and actions should be defined and implemented within a general development strategy for a city or region. If efficiency and effectiveness are main goals, agents making decisions as to public and private investment should reach agreements on objectives and priority actions and coordinate the progress of their initiatives. This requires an institutional system that favors consensus as to the design and implementation of urban and regional development plans.

One of the foremost characteristics of the new generation of endogenous development policies is the joint action on all the determinant factors of endogenous development in order to achieve a combined effect to place the city or region in a better competitive position. Diffusion of knowledge, efficient productive organization, sustainable development and institutional flexibility should be stimulated simultaneously in order to make feasible the interaction among all of the factors. It is in this way that the conditions for economic and social progress are created.

Notes

2 Endogenous development: an approach for action

1 In local economies, one can identify, for example, a given productive structure, labor market, entrepreneurial capability and technological know-how, natural resources and infrastructures, an institutional and social system, tradition and culture around which economic growth and structural change are articulated.

2 Giuliano Bianchi (1998) points out that when one refers to local production systems (to industrial districts), one is referring to spatial systems of small firms that are historic territorial formations and not abstract constructions with no reference to specific times and spaces. He suggests that the production, spatial and social models be referred to as an interpretative framework for analyses.

3 In the Spanish case, for instance, local products are, in general, those of mature technology such as textiles and clothing, footwear, foods, ceramics, furniture, tool machinery or plastics (Vázquez-Barquero, 1988).

4 This definition includes contributions from such different sources, from a methodological point of view, as those of Coffey and Polèse (1984 and 1985) and those of Walter Stöhr (1981 and 1985).

5 This implies that technological change is endogenous to the firm and the evolution of technology can be accounted for by firm's need to find strategic solutions in order to maintain its profit rate and market share.

3 On the theoretical roots of endogenous development

1 When we speak of "local development" we are referring to processes of endogenous development and when "local economic development" is used, the economic dimension of development will be the focus in the discussion.

2 Endogenous growth theory solves some of the most disputed questions of the neoclassical growth model, such as decreasing returns. It interprets growth under more realistic assumptions, expands the endogenous variables of the model by introducing, for example, technological progress into the production function. Some authors argue that growth occurs in conditions of imperfect competition.

3 Rosenstein-Rodan quoted Allyn Young when pointing out that increasing returns flow toward firms, not only due to an increase in their size but also as a result of growth in the industry and in the whole industrial system (Scitovski, 1954). The generation of external economies occurs because growth allows firms to rise above indivisibility, which encourages specialization and better use of resources.

4 But it has also been somewhat well received into neoclassical thought through

the works of Jorgenson (1961, 1966 and 1967) and Kelley, Williamson and Cheetham (1972). Jorgenson (1967, p. 290) distinguishes two tendencies in transitional or dualistic growth models. A classical tendency (Lewis and Fei-Ranis) holds that the industrial sector has all the labor necessary at the level of real wages (in agricultural goods). A neoclassical tendency (Jorgenson, Kelley and others), maintains that it is not possible to have sufficient labor in the industrial sector without sacrificing agricultural production.

5 The neoclassical version of the transitional (dualistic) growth model (Jorgenson, 1961 and 1967) maintains that growth in the modern sector (and in production in general), if economically feasible, is determined by the size of the population and initial dimension of fixed capital. Economic growth would ultimately depend on the factors of production and technological change.

6 Jorgenson maintains that self-sustained growth depends on the feasibility of the modern sector and the existence of increasing surplus in the agrarian sector.

7 Endogenous development theory is also interested in identifying factors that unleash processes of industrial development. On occasion, these are due to the reaction of the local community to a situation of need caused by the loss of economic viability in agrarian activity or by a natural disaster. The cause can also be due to chance, or imitation mechanisms from successful experiences. But, always, a necessary factor is the existence of demand, local and/or external, sufficient to absorb the supply of local products.

8 There is no unified dependence theory. Two tendencies can be identified, the post-Keynesian tendency (Furtado, Sunkel) and the neo-Marxist tendency (Frank, Amin, Cardoso and Santos). Their basic differences reside in the method of analysis of the accumulation process and the categories they use in the analysis (Vázquez-Barquero, 1982). Two versions within the neo-Marxist current can be identified, a moderate version (Cardoso), which defends the possibility of dependent development, and a radical version (Amin, Frank and, to some extent, Santos), who claim this is not feasible and, therefore, constitutes development of underdevelopment.

9 Dependence, according to Santos (1970b), corresponds to a situation in which the development of some countries is determined by that of others to which the former is subjected. Thus peripheral economies can only grow as a reflection of the expansion of advanced economies.

10 They therefore reasoned that the only way to break the vicious circles of growth was socialist development.

11 They argued that when a large and differentiated domestic market exists and national investment is significant, dependent industrialization is viable.

12 The objective of local economies, according to Friedmann and Douglas (1978), is the satisfaction of the basic needs of local communities through self-centered development and the promotion of their own skills. Among their proposals, the creation of agropolitan districts, the devolution of competence to local communities, agrarian reform and commitment on the part of the central government to guarantee inter-regional equity through the transfer of resources.

4 Networking and the organization of development

1 Camagni (1991) defines the concept of network as a closed set of selected and explicit links of a firm with preferential partners, in the ambit of complementary assets and market relations, which has been established with the main objective of reducing static and dynamic uncertainties.

2 Hakansson and Johanson (1993) consider that an industrial network is formed

by actors (the firms located in a territory), resources (human, natural, infrastructure), economic activities (of a productive, commercial, technical, financial or service nature) and their relations (interdependence and exchanges).

3 Since the mid-1970s, research on local firm systems has grown considerably, particularly in industrialized countries and in late developed countries, as has been pointed out earlier and can be seen from the bibliography of this book. Since the mid-1990s, studies have begun to appear on how local firm systems work in newly industrialized countries and developing countries. See van Dijk and Rabellotti, 1997; Rabellotti and Schmitz, 1999; Schmitz, 1995; and Nadvi, 1997.

4 Fuà (1983) contends that industrial districts have emerged and developed in areas where a specific social and cultural system (work ethics, social mobility, entrepreneurship), is firmly inserted in the territory.

5 The most common departments of Fordist firms are management and coordination, finance, R&D, production, marketing, sales, purchasing and other smaller areas such as traffic, engineering, legal, personnel and public relations (Chandler, 1990).

6 Chandler indicates four ways for industrial firms to grow: horizontal integration through the acquisition and merger of firms, vertical integration, geographic expansion and the production of new products related to existing technology or markets.

7 The new organizational modes have come about as a result of the natural evolution of firms (with patrimonial, financial and contractual growth), which has brought about two important divisions: institutional (separation of ownership from the control of the firm) and organizational (separation of operating decisions from strategic decisions). In this way the firm is able to maintain economic power and control (Williamson, 1981).

8 Bueno Campos (1992) maintains that "in the large firms one observes that activities such as strategic planning, marketing, design, R&D and strategic decisions were reserved for headquarters. Purchasing and manufacturing, with 'just-in-time' techniques, are displaced toward suppliers, sales and distribution and even portfolio management are also contracted to third firms through, for example, franchises." The firm's economic power is maintained through contracting.

9 Amin and Tomaney (1997: 98–99) point out that innovative firm subsidiaries possess certain characteristics that make them likely to promote endogenous development in underdeveloped regions and they list the attributes that justify a revision of the role of inward investment as a stimulus for self-sustained local economic development.

5 Innovation and development

1 Rosegger (1996) defines technology as human knowledge embedded in production; that is, it is the application of traditional and/or scientific knowledge with the purpose of systematically producing goods and services. Traditional technologies are related to the know-how that is a product of experience and has been systematized due to reflections based on perception and experimentation through production and has been transmitted from generation to generation. On the other hand, advanced technologies are those techniques, based on more formalized knowledge usually called "scientific knowledge," and employed to produce, transport and distribute goods and services.

2 Schumpeter defines innovation as the introduction of a new good, a new production method, the opening of a new market, the use of a new supply source or the creation of a new industrial organization.

3 As we have pointed out above, the view of innovation as an endogenous component of economic growth has recently been incorporated into neoclassical thought through endogenous growth models and also constitutes a part of the theory of endogenous development.

4 Technical knowledge consists of the stock of techniques and know-how that individuals and organizations have acquired through learning and activities aimed at discovering how things work, creating new goods and inventing production methods. Information is the flow of knowledge, normally codified and transmitted through some communication media.

5 It is difficult to establish the dividing line between public and private goods when talking about technological knowledge. However, patents and other instruments designed to protect property rights help define the playing field.

6 Rosegger (1996) proposes the following model of the stages of technological change: Basic research leads to discoveries which are added to scientific knowledge. Applied investigation produces inventions that are added to the stock of technical ideas (ideas not yet tried out), some of which will be developed. Only if the development is successful will they become innovation and only when innovation is diffused will it have an effect on the economy as a whole.

7 The concept of routine is analogous to that of the gene and firms would be analogous to live organisms in biology.

8 A classical example used in the literature is the traditional typing keyboard (QWERTY), whose innovation goes back to the end of the nineteenth century and is associated with an arrangement of the letters in such a way that the most experienced typists would not be "jammed." In spite of the fact that mechanical and electronic typewriters could overcome these difficulties, the traditional keyboard is still in use.

9 Freeman and Soete (1997) classify the strategies as offensive, defensive, imitative, dependent, traditional or opportunist.

10 Epidemiological models consider that diffusion is a social phenomenon that leads to the transmission of innovation by contact. Rosegger (1996) indicates that this theory has significant conceptual limitations. First is the fact that this approach presupposes that there is always a fixed population of potential adopters. Other limitations are the idea that decisions to adopt innovation are not based on rational criteria (except that the decision to adopt innovation is made because competitors did so) and the fact that the diffusion curve does not indicate time as a dimension in innovative processes.

11 The GREMI (Groupe de Recherche Européen sur les Milieux Innovateurs) was founded in 1984 by Philippe Aydalot and, since then, has brought together some twenty research groups from Europe and the United States that have done research into the development of productive systems and technological innovation (Bramanti and Ratti, 1997).

12 As Bramanti and Ratti (1997) point out, learning mechanisms require the integration of productive processes and innovation in space and time. The milieu acts as an organized market in which information on prices and quantities of the firms' goods is exchanged as well as other relevant information: codes, language, routines, worldviews and strategies.

13 The transmission of knowledge is coded and tacit (Rosegger, 1996). Coded knowledge appears in various forms – instructions for use, plans and designs, product specifications or in technical articles and books. Tacit knowledge is the result of learning from persons and firms and is essential in interpreting coded knowledge.

14 As Freeman and Soete (1997) point out, there is a tendency to focus the analysis of innovation on inventions and radical innovation. However, this is an

excessively restrictive view, which conceals a significant part of the innovative capacity of firms.

15 Pavitt (1984) identified four large groups of manufacturing activities with different behaviors as to innovation: supply-dominated sectors (agriculture, textiles, clothing, leather, printing and publishing, wood products and simple metal products), specialized sectors (mechanical and instrumental engineering), sectors intensive in scale economies (transportation, durable electrical goods, metal products, food, glass and cement products) and science-based sectors (electronics, biotechnology, pharmaceutical industry).

16 The institutional context refers to the existence of a legal and administrative system that favors entrepreneurial activity and creates a social and cultural environment inclined toward innovation. It also refers to labor and social attitudes open to technological progress, and a patent system that regulates industrial property rights without obstructing the diffusion and adoption of innovation.

17 Linear innovation models maintain that scientific advancements occur and are transmitted sequentially: they emerge in scientific institutions and are progressively transferred to the economic sector. In contrast, interactive models consider that innovations arise as a result of firm relations with the market through contacts within the network of local and/or regional actors.

6 Institutions for development

1 Among the activities which bring about transaction costs, Eggertsson (1990, p. 15), following Coase (1937), lists the following: the search for information on prices and quality of commodities and productive factors, the search for potential buyers and sellers, the making of contracts, assessment of contractual partners in order to control the fulfillment of contract terms, the enforcement of contracts and the protection of property rights.

2 Dasgupta (1988), on the other hand, points out that, for economists, economic transactions are based on trust and the reputation of individuals and organizations. "For trust to be developed between individuals they must have repeated encounters, and they must have some memory of previous experiences. Moreover, for honesty to have potential as a concept there must be some cost involved in honest behavior. And finally, trust is linked with reputation and reputation has to be acquired."

3 Local industrialization is in fact a process where birth, development and maturity is based on a combination of causes that go from necessity to the availability of natural resources, and/or good location. It is a process that in the case of late developed countries of southern Europe has appeared spontaneously and often by chance. In any case the existence or creation of a market for the local products is a necessary condition for maintaining the development process.

4 Simon has pointed out that in environments of uncertainty and incomplete knowledge, it is not possible to maintain the hypothesis of global maximization of the neoclassical model, but the economic agents can make rational decisions. Based on the concept of "bounded rationality," it is possible to argue that the agents can choose from a set of limited possibilities.

5 Williamson (1993) believes that "bounded rationality is a cognitive assumption to which economic agents are 'intentedly rational, but only limitedly so...' Opportunism is a self-interest-seeking assumption."

6 The new forms of governance would emerge as a "trial-and-error search process" aimed at the solution of problems that occur in environments of change characterized by diversity and complexity of institutions. The selection

of institutions and mechanisms of governance is carried out according to an evolutionary model as a function of the solutions that lead to solving problems and reducing turbulence in the environment (Campbell and Lindberg, 1991; Jessop, 1995).

7 See Chapter 9 for a brief reference to the process of decentralization in Europe and Latin America.

8 This is a rather ambiguous concept referring to the presence of multiple actors in the territory who relate through interactions within the network of institutions. Structures of domination or coalition are formed among these actors.

9 See Chapter 3 for a definition of pecuniary and technological externalities.

10 Organizational proximity can be interpreted as a network whose functioning generates the pecuniary or technological externalities that Antonelli (1995) calls dynamic externalities. Those could benefit all the members of the network.

11 In Europe there are very diverse forms of organizations that have been successful in the promotion and support of local initiatives, such as Local Enterprise Agencies in the United Kingdom, *Boutiques de Gestion* in France, Local Development Funds in Sweden, Technological Centers in Germany, Technological Institutes in Spain and Financial Agencies in Italy.

7 Cities, a place for development

1 It is not until the twentieth century that the phenomenon of urbanization becomes generalized. At the beginning of the century, France and Japan were rural countries (60 percent and 80 percent, respectively, of the population was rural) a fact that would be associated with the diffusion of the Fordist production model in Europe and Asia.

2 Earlier, Schumpeter had established that technological and organizational change were the basic factors of economic development, and Lampard had proposed that change is a factor of the urbanization process. Lasuén (1973) points out that the type of entrepreneurial organization (multi-location and multi-product) conditions the diffusion of innovation and, therefore, influences growth and urbanization.

3 Among the factors that account for tertiarization, are the appearance of new tasks associated with the adoption of product and process innovations, increased productivity in the manufacturing sector causing labor displacement toward other activities, and the effect of firm reorganization leading to the externalization of service activities that were formerly performed within the firms.

4 One of the elements that characterize globalization is the increased specialization of cities in certain producer services. This usually implies the concentration of specific services in a limited number of cities. A good example, as Sassen (1998) points out, is the financial sector and that of related activities.

5 Borja and Castells (1997) contend that there are many spatial models because the history, culture and institutions of each city or region determine economic and technological processes.

6 This thesis is based on the central place theory, which claims that cities and central places form a hierarchic system. Forces exist, such as transportation and communication systems, polarized organization of productive activity and agglomeration economies, that lead to the concentration of important functions in large cities to the detriment of regional and smaller cities. This argument is reinforced when the theory of central places is combined with growth pole theory (Lasuén, 1974), because it allows us to account for the processes of development and urbanization by associating economic development with the evolution of the hierarchic structure of city systems.

7 It is not only, as Nijkamp and Salomon (1989) point out, that these processes depend on the characteristics of the diffusion model, local resistance to change and/or the initial conditions of each area/city. The explanation must also be found in the fact that late developed countries overlay polarized industrialization and diffuse industrialization models, which implies differentiated behavior by economic agents with regard to decisions to innovate.

8 Although it is difficult to evaluate the direct influence of new transportation and communication systems on urban development, there is no doubt, as Törnqvist (1986) indicates, that new opportunities for areas and cities, firms and agents, are made available, thus favoring both geographic concentration and decentralization of productive activity.

9 As was pointed out in earlier chapters, perhaps one of the most significant events of recent decades is the development of networks which take advantage of local synergies and strengthen cooperation among firms (Kamann, 1988). The development of firm networks has significant territorial effects, as Kamann and Nijkamp (1988) make clear. The creation of products and technology gives rise to new networks that benefit the area in which they have emerged, in detriment to localities whose products have been substituted. Moreover, the concentration or diffusion of the various functions of the network (management, sales, production, research) are decisive in the organization of the territory.

10 The polycentric urban model describes networking as a way to organize the urban framework (Cappellin, 1990). Networks are made up of nodes or local units among which are established interactive and exchange relationships based on complementation and specialization of functions within the centers, or relations of cooperation among similar centers. Synergetic or complementary networks lead to the formation of externalities within the internal network, which do not necessarily depend on relations among continuous nodes.

11 The works of DATAR (Reclus, 1989) represent significant progress in the attempt to define the European urban system by means of supply indicators, which show the endogenous development potential with which each territory (or city) initiates competition at a continental level in the setting of the Single Market.

12 The highest level of city management is made up of public local institutions, firms, economic and social organizations (entrepreneurial and labor associations) and the leaders of opinion whose decisions condition public and private investment in the city.

13 According to the strategic planning approach, citizens and firms located in an urban place are the owners of the city. As in organizations, they expect that city management will lead to the fulfillment of their needs and expectations in terms of patrimony and profits.

8 Local development policy

1 Friedmann and Weaver (1979) doubt as to whether the theory refers to centers that were already undergoing a major phase of growth or to cities that merely showed a certain potential instead of actual performance. Furthermore, it was difficult to measure the impact of the policy since it was never clear what indicator was appropriate – whether job creation within the formal and/or informal economy, population, income with or without a measure of its distribution.

2 The ECLA, along with the German agency GTZ, are developing the Project "Local Economic Development and Decentralization in Latin America" whose objective is to identify to what extent local development processes are gaining

ground as decentralization processes take place (Aghon *et al.*, 2001). IDB, on its part, attempts to analyze the results of local development processes through case studies in order to evaluate the feasibility of funding for local development in Latin America.

3 Made up of the municipalities of Santo André, São Bernardo de Campo, São Caetano do Sul, Diadema, Mauá, Ribeirão Pires and Río Grande da Serra.

4 The area includes the townships of Chiantla, Todos Santos Cuchumatán, San Juan Ixcoy, San Pedro Soloma, San Rafael La Independencia, San Miguel Acatan, San Sebastian and Santa Eulalia.

5 The communal banks that bring peasant women together represent a specific type of Interest Group.

6 Decentralization has taken place in agricultural technical assistance services, the adaptation and transfer of agricultural technology, technical management assistance, accounting and marketing.

9 Globalization and territorial dynamic

1 Although globalization may be a controversial concept, it cannot be denied that the increase in economic, political and institutional relations at the international level since the end of the 1980s has generated forces that tend to come together in a geographically more diversified global system.

2 This question is currently the object of a great amount of discussion as Maillat and Grosjean (1999) remind us. Some authors such as O'Brien (1992) maintain that, due to advances in telecommunications, one location is as good as another. Therefore, it is not important where firms and economic decision-makers locate. All economies and firms would be integrated in a global system dominated by a few large firms. Veltz (1996), more sensitive to territory, maintains that globalization tends to promote the concentration of knowledge and productive capacity in a reduced group of well-equipped areas which allows firms to use quality resources and obtain economies of scale. The intersection of multiple networks gives rise to poles that configure the so-called "archipelago" economy.

3 Alburquerque points out that the situation in the rural world can become very difficult as a consequence of the crisis in traditional agriculture, depopulation, the lack of basic infrastructure and environmental deterioration.

4 Boisier (1998) points out that areas not sufficiently integrated or on the margin of the globalization process can generate their own development process. He quotes Tania Bacelar de Araujo who writes that "policies of backward regions are perfectly compatible with the globalization process."

5 The first criterion would reflect the type of interactions among firms located in a place, while the second would indicate whether the activities of firms located in a territory are a part of its value chain (Porter, 1990) or, on the contrary, are external to the city or region's production filiere (Maillat and Grosjean, 1999).

6 In Chapter 7, when discussing local productive systems and models of excellence, it was indicated that the creation and diffusion of incremental and radical innovations reinforces processes of endogenous development.

7 Resources are understood as the factors constituting the territories' potential for development that have not yet been employed, while assets would be factors already put to use (Colletis and Pecqueur, 1995).

8 The value of generic factors of a territory is expressed in market prices and, therefore, these factors are included in the firms' investment decisions. However, specific factors would be those resources linked to a territory as a result of an accumulation process of know-how and which are often non-quantifiable and not always reflected in price (Colletis and Pecqueur, 1995).

9 "Territorialized economic development ... consists ... in economic activity that is dependent on territorially specific resources. These 'resources' can range from asset specificities available only from a certain place or, more importantly, assets that are available only in the context of certain inter-organizational or firm-market relationships that necessarily involve geographic proximity, or where relations of proximity are markedly more efficient than other ways of generating these asset specifications." (Storper, 1997: 170).

10 The integration of a subsidiary plant into the local productive system depends on its position within the organization of the enterprise, on the legal and financial relations that link the local unit to the enterprise and on the modes of management, decision-making and control procedures of the enterprise. However, it is also conditioned by the system of procedures, symbols, conventions and the manner of coordination that characterize the territory (Dupuy and Gilly, 1997).

10 The new generation of endogenous development policies

1 The "SME Policy and Regional Dimension of Innovation (SMEPOL)" Project analyzed and evaluated forty local development instruments in eleven European regions. The project is funded through the TSER program of the European Commission and was carried out by research teams from the following institutions: the STEP group from Norway, the University of Economy and Business in Vienna, the University of Southern Denmark, the University of Pavia, Italy, the Institute of Economic Research in Maastricht, Netherlands, the Autonomous University of Madrid and the University of Middlesex in the United Kingdom.

References

Abramo, L. (1998) *Mercado de trabajo, flexibilización y nuevas formas de regulación*, Santiago de Chile: ILPES/CEPAL, mimeo.

Aghon, G., Alburquerque, F. and Cortés, P. (2001) *Desarrollo Económico Local y Descentralización en América Latina: Un Analisis Comparativo*, Santiago de Chile: CEPAL/GTZ.

Alburquerque, F. (1997) "El proceso de construcción social del territorio para el desarrollo económico local" in *Serie Ensayos, LC/IP/R.180* ILPES-CEPAL.

—— (1998) "Cambio tecnológico, globalización y desarrollo económico local," unpublished paper, International Seminar on Globalization and Local Economic Development, Santiago de Compostela: Sociedade para o Desenvolvimento Comarcal de Galicia, 19–21 November.

—— (2001) *Evaluación y reflexiones sobre las iniciativas de desarrollo económico local en America Latina*, Madrid: Consejo de Investigaciones Científicas, mimeo.

Alfonso Gil, J. (1997) "Instituciones económicas: contornos de la triada básica" in *Economistas* 73: 128–136.

—— (1999) "The dynamics of socioeconomic change: an approach," Madrid: Departamento de Estructura Económica y Economía del Desarrollo, Universidad Autónoma de Madrid, mimeo.

Amin, A. (1989) "Flexible specialization and small firms in Italy: myths and realities" in *Antipode* 21, 1: 13–34.

—— (1993) "The globalization of the economy. An erosion of regional networks?" in G. Grabher (ed.) *The Embedded Firm: On the Socioeconomics of Industrial Networks*, London: Routledge.

Amin, A. and Robins, K. (1990) "The re-emergence of regional economies? The mythical geography of flexible accumulation" in *Environment and Planning D, Society and Space* 8: 7–34.

—— (1991) "These are not Marshallian times" in R. Camagni (ed.) *Innovation Networks*, London: Belhaven Press.

Amin, A. and Thrift, N. (1993) "Globalization, institutional thickness and local prospect" in *Revue d'Économie Regional et Urbain* 3: 405–427.

Amin, A. and Tomaney, J. (1997) "El potencial de desarrollo regional de las inversiones externas en las regiones menos favorecidas da la Comunidad Europea" in A. Vázquez-Barquero, G. Garofoli and G.P. Gilly (eds) *Gran empresa y desarrollo económico*, Madrid: Síntesis.

Amin, S. (1970) *L'accumulation à l'échelle mondiale*, Paris: Anthropos.

—— (1973) *Le développement inégal. Essai sur les formations sociales du capitalisme périphérique*, Paris: Minuit.

Antonelli, C. (1995) "Economies des réseaux: variété et complementarieté" in A. Rallet and A. Torre (eds) *Economie industrielle et economie spatiale*, Paris: Economica.

Aoki, M. (1990) "Toward an economic model of the Japanese firm" in *Journal of Economic Literature* 28, 1: 1–27.

Arocena, J. (1986) *Le développement par l'initiative locale. Le cas français*, Paris: L'Harmattan.

—— (1995) *El desarrollo local: un desafío contemporáneo*, Caracas: Nueva Sociedad.

Arrow, K.J. (1962) "The economic implications of learning by doing" in *Review of Economic Studies* 29: 155–173.

—— (1974) *The Limits of Organization*, New York: Norton.

Asheim, B.T. and Isaksen, A. (1997) "Location, agglomeration and innovation: Towards regional innovation systems in Norway" in *European Planning Studies* 5: 299–330.

—— (1998) "Theoretical background for evaluating selected innovation policy instruments," Unpublished document, Brussels: SMEPOL Project meeting, 2–3 March.

Atienza Úbeda, M. (1998) "Aproximación al estudio de la integración y el desarrollo de las regiones históricamente aisladas," unpublished thesis, Departamento de Estructura Económica, Universidad Autónoma de Madrid.

Axelrod, R. (1984) *The Evolution of Cooperation*, New York: Basic Books.

Aydalot, P. (1985) *Economie régionale et urbaine*, Paris: Economica.

—— (1986) *Milieux innovateurs en Europe*, Paris: Economica.

Aydalot, P. and Keeble, D. (eds) (1988) *High Technology, Industry and Innovative Environments*, New York and London: Routledge.

Baldó, J. and Villanueva, F. (1996) "Plan de reestructuración de los barrios de la estructura urbana" in H. Garnica (ed.) *Los Barrios no tienen quien les escriba*, Diario El Universal, 9 December: 1–4.

Barrios, S. (2000) "Areas Metropolitanas: qué ha cambiado? La experiencia de la Caracas metropolitana" in *Cuadernos del Cendes* 43: 51–84.

Barro, J.R. and Sala-i-Martin, X. (1995) *Economic Growth*, New York: McGraw Hill.

Becattini, G. (1979) "Dal settore industriale al distretto industriale: alcune considerazione sull'unita di indagine dell'economia industriale" in *Rivista di Economia e Politica Industriale* 1: 7–21.

—— (1987) "L'unità di indagine" in G. Becattini (ed.) *Mercato e forze locali: il distretto industriale*, Bologna: Il Mulino.

—— (1997) "Totalità e cambiamento: il paradigma dei distretti industriali" in *Sviluppo Locale* 4, 6: 5–24.

Bellandi, M. (1986) "El distrito industrial en Alfred Marshall" in *Estudios Territoriales* 20: 31–44.

—— (2001) "Local development and embedded large firms" in *Entrepreneurship and Regional Development*, 13: 189–210.

Bellet, M., Colletis, G. and Lung, Y. (eds) (1993) "Economie de proximité" in *Revue d'Economie Regional et Urbaine*, monographic issue, 3.

Bellet, M., Kirat, T. and Largeron-Leteno, C. (eds) (1998) *Proximités: approches multiformes*, Paris: Editions Hermès.

Benko, G. and Lipietz, A. (1992) *Les régions qui gagnent*, Paris: PUF.

Bennett, R. (1989) "Local economy and employment and development strategies: analysis for LEDA areas" in *LEDA Report*, Brussels: European Commission.

Bennett, R. and Krebs, G. (1990) "Towards a partnership model of local economic development initiatives in Britain and Germany" in R.J. Bennet, G. Krebs and Zimmerman (eds) *Local Economic Development in Britain and Germany*, London: Anglo-German Foundation.

Berg, L. van den, Braun, E. and Meer, J. van den (1999) "Competitividad y cohesión metropolitana" in *Papeles de economía española* 80: 248–265.

Bernabé Maestre, J.M. (1983) *Industrialización difusa en la provincia de Alicante*, Valencia: Facultad de Geografía, Universidad de Valencia, mimeo.

Berry, B.J.L. (1972) "Hierarchical diffusion: the basis of development filtering and spread in a system of growth centers" in N.H. Hansen (ed.) *Growth Centers in Regional Economic Development*, New York: Free Press.

Best, M. (1990) *The New Competition: Institutions of Industrial Restructuring*, Cambridge, Mass.: Harvard University Press.

Bianchi, G. (1998) "Requiem for the Third Italy? Rise and fall of a too successful concept" in *Entrepreneurship and Regional Development* 10: 93–116.

Birch, D.L. (1979) "The job creation process" in *Program on Neighborhood and Regional Change*, Cambridge, Mass.: MIT Press.

Blakely, E.J. (1989) *Planning Local Economic Development: Theory and Practice*, London: Sage.

Boisier, S. (1997) "El vuelo de una cometa. Una metáfora para una teoría de desarrollo territorial" in *Serie Ensayos, 97/37*, Santiago de Chile: Economic Commission for Latin America.

—— (1998) *Desarrollo descentrado y descentralizado en América Latina*, Santiago de Chile: Economic Commission for Latin America, mimeo.

Borja, J. and Castells, M. (1997) *Local y global. La gestión de las ciudades en la era de la información*, Madrid: Taurus.

Bramanti, A. and Senn, L. (1993) "Entrepreneurs, firm, 'milieu': three different specifications of networking activities" in D. Maillat, M. Quevit and L. Senn (eds) *Réseaux d'innovation et milieux innovateurs: un pari pour le développment régional*, Neuchâtel: Gremi-Edes.

Bramanti, A. and Maggioni, M.A. (1997) "The dynamics of milieux: the network analysis approach" in R. Ratti, A. Bramanti and R. Gordon (eds) *The Dynamics of Innovative Regions*, Aldershot: Ashgate.

Bramanti, A. and Ratti, R. (1997) "The multi-faced dimensions of local development" in R. Ratti, A. Bramanti and R. Gordon (eds) *The Dynamics of Innovative Regions*, Aldershot: Ashgate.

Brenner, R. (1987) *Rivalry: in Business, Science, Among Nations*, Cambridge: Cambridge University Press.

Brown, B. and Butler, J. (1993) "Networks and entrepreneurial development: the shadow of borders" in *Entrepreneurship and Regional Development* 5: 101–116.

Brusco, S. (1982) "The Emilian model: productive decentralization and social integration" in *Cambridge Journal of Economics* 6: 167–184.

Bueno Campos, E. (1992) "Organización flexible y gestión del cambio" in *Documentos IADE, 28*, Madrid: Universidad Autónoma de Madrid.

Budd, L. (1998) "Territorial competition and globalisation: Scylla and Charybdis of European Cities" in *Urban Studies* 35: 663–685.

Camagni, R. (1991) "Local 'milieu,' uncertainty and innovation networks: towards a new dynamic theory of economic space" in R. Camagni (ed.) *Innovation Networks: Spatial Perspectives*, London: Belhaven Press.

—— (1992) "Organisation économique et réseaux des villes" in P.H. Derycke (ed.) *Espace et dynamiques territoriales*, Paris: Economica.

—— (1993) *Principi di economia urbana e territoriale*, Rome: La Nuova Italia Scientifica.

—— (1994) *Processi di utilizzazione e difesa di suoli nelle fasce periurbane*, Milan: Fundazione Cariplo.

—— (1998) *The City as a Milieu: Applying the GREMI Approach to Urban Evolution*, Milan: Politecnico di Milano, mimeo.

Camagni, R. and Capello, R. (1990) "Towards a definition of the maneuvering space of local development initiatives: Italian success stories of local development" in W.B. Stöhr (ed.) *Global Challenge and Local Response*, London: Mansell.

Camagni, R. and Rabellotti, R. (1997) "Footwear production system in Italy" in R. Ratti, A. Bramanti and R. Gordon (eds) *The Dynamics of Innovation Regions*, Aldershot: Ashgate.

Camagni, R. *et al.* (1996) "Cities in Europe: globalisation, sustainability and cohesion" in *European Spatial Planning*, Rome: Presidenza del Consiglio dei Ministri.

Campbell, J.L. and Lindberg, L.N. (1991) "The evolution of governance regimes" in J.L. Campbell, J.R. Hollingsworth and L.N. Lindberg (eds) *Governance of the American Economy*, Cambridge: Cambridge University Press.

Cappellin, R. (1990) "Networks nelle città e networks tra città" in F. Curti and L. Diappi (eds) *Gerarchie e reti di città: tendenze e politiche*, Milan: Franco Angeli.

Cardoso, F.H. (1971) "Teoria de la dependencia o análisis de situaciones concretas de dependencia?" in *Revista Latinoamericana de Ciencia Política*, 1, 3: 402–414.

—— (1972) "Dependency and development in Latin America" in *New Left Review*, 74: 83–95.

Cariola, C. and Labacana, M. (2000) "Transformaciones en el trabajo, diferenciación social y fragmentación de la metropoli" in *Cuadernos del Cendes* 43: 85–119.

Castells, M. (1989) *The Informational City*, Oxford: Basil Blackwell.

—— (1996) *The Information Age: Economy, Society and Culture. Volume I: The Rise of the Network Society*, Cambridge, Mass.: Blackwell Publishers.

Chandler, A. (1982) "The M-form, industrial groups American style" in *European Economic Review* 19: 3–23.

—— (1990) *Scale and Scope. The Dynamics of Industrial Capitalism*, Cambridge, Mass.: Harvard University Press.

Chesnais, F. (1994) *La mondialisation du capital*, Paris: Syros.

Chisholm, M. (1990) *Regions in Recession and Resurgence*, London: Unwin Hyman.

Cifuentes, I. (2000) *Proyecto Cuchumatanes. Transferencia de servicios técnicos a las organizaciones de productores*, Huehuetenango, Guatemala: Ministerio de Agricultura, Ganadería y Alimentación.

Cifuentes, I. and Menegazzo, G. (1998) "El gestor de crédito campesino, un ensayo de descentralización de los servicios gubernamentales de crédito," Unpublished paper, International Seminar on Community Management of Natural Resources, Washington, D.C., May.

Coase, R.H. (1937) "The nature of the firm" in *Economica* 4: 386–405.

—— (1960) "The problem of the social cost" in *Journal of Law and Economics* 3, 1: 1–44.

—— (1984) "The new institutional economics" in *Journal of Legal Studies* 140, 1: 22–231.

Coffey, W.J. and Polèse, M. (1984) "The concept of local development: a stages model of endogenous regional growth" in *Papers of the Regional Sciences Association* 55: 1–12.

—— (1985) "Local development: conceptual basis and policy implications" in *Regional Studies* 19: 85–93.

Colletis G. and Pecqueur, B. (1995) "Dinámica territorial y factores de la competencia espacial" in A. Vázquez-Barquero and G. Garofoli (eds) *Desarrollo económico local en Europa*, Madrid: Colegio de Economistas de Madrid.

Colletis, G., Gilly J.P. *et al.* (1999) "Construction territoriales et dynamiques economiques" in *Sciences de la Société* 48: 25–46.

Costa Campi, M.T. (1988) "Descentramiento productivo y difusión industrial. El modelo de especialización flexible" in *Papeles de economía española* 35: 251–276.

—— (1992) "Cambios en la organización industrial: cooperación local y competividad internacional" in *Economía industrial* 286: 19–35.

Costa Campi, M.T. *et al.* (1993) *EXCEL. Cooperación entre empresa y sistemas productivos locales*, Madrid: Instituto de la Pequeña y Mediana Empresa Industrial.

Costamagna, P. (1999) *Iniciativa de desarrollo económico local. La articulación y las interacciones entre instituciones. El caso de Rafaela*, Santiago de Chile: CEPAL/GTZ Project, mimeo.

Cotorruelo Menta, R. (1996) *Competitividad de las empresas y de los territorios*, Madrid: Inmark, mimeo.

—— (1997) "Gestión estratégica y marketing de ciudades," Working document, Madrid: Inmark.

Courlet, C. and Soulage, B. (1995) "Dinámicas industriales y territorio" in A. Vázquez-Barquero and G. Garofoli (eds) *Desarrollo Económico Local en Europa*, Madrid: Colegio de Economistas de Madrid.

Crevoisier, O. and Camagni, R. (eds) (2000) *Les Milieux Urbains: Innovation, Systemes de Production et Encrage*, Neuchâtel: IRER/EDES.

Crevoisier, O., Maillat, D. and Vasserot, J. (1990) *L'apport du milieu dans le processus d'innovation: le cas de l'Arc Jurassien*, Neuchâtel: IRER-Université de Neuchâtel, mimeo.

Dabat, A. (2000) *Globalización: capitalismo informático-global y nueva configuración espacial del mundo*, Mexico: Universidad Nacional Autónoma de Mexico, mimeo.

D'Arcy, E. and Guissani, B. (1996) "Local economic development: changing the parameters?" in *Entrepreneurship and Regional Development* 8: 159–178.

Dasgupta, P. (1988) "Trust as a Commodity" in D. Gambetta (ed.) *Trust, Making and Breaking Cooperative Relations*, Oxford: Basil Blackwell.

Davelaar, E.J. (1991) *Regional Economic Analysis of Innovation and Incubation*, Aldershot: Avebury.

Dickens, P. (1992) *Global Shift*, New York: Guilford.

Dieperink, H. and Nijkamp, P. (1988) "Innovative behavior. Agglomeration economies and R and D infrastructure" in *Empec* 13: 35–77.

Dijk, M.P. van and Rabellotti, R. (eds) (1997) *Entreprise Clusters and Networks in Developing Countries*, London: Fran Cass.

Dixit, A. and Stiglitz, J. (1977) "Monopolistic competition and optimum product diversity" in *American Economic Review* 67, 3: 297–308.

Dosi, G. (1984) *Technical Change and Industrial Transformation*, London: Macmillan.

—— (1988) "Sources, procedures and microeconomic effects of innovation" in *Journal of Economic Literature* 36: 1126–1171.

Dosi, G., Teece, D. and Winter, S. (1992) "Toward a theory of corporate change: preliminary remarks" in G. Dosi, *et al.* (eds) *Technology and Enterprise in an Historical Perspective*, Oxford: Clarendon.

Dunning, J. (1993) *Multinational Enterprises and the Global Economy*, Reading: Addison Wesley.

Dupuy, J.C. and Gilly, J.P. (1997) "Las estrategias territoriales de los grupos industriales" in A. Vázquez-Barquero, G. Garofoli and G.P. Gilly (eds) *Gran empresa y desarrollo económico*, Madrid: Síntesis.

Durán, G. (2000) *La ecologización de las políticas de desarrollo local*, Madrid: Universidad Autónoma de Madrid, mimeo.

Eggertsson, T. (1990) *Economic Behaviour and Institutions*, Cambridge: Cambridge University Press.

Ettlinger, N. (1992) "Modes of corporate organization and the geography of development" in *Papers in Regional Science* 71, 2: 107–126.

European Commission (1994) *Coopération pour l'aménagement du territoire Européen. Europe 2000+*, Brussels, mimeo.

European Environmental Agency (1995) *Europe's Environment: the Dobris Assessment*, Copenhagen.

Fei, J. and Ranis, G. (1961) "A theory of economic development" in *The American Economic Review* 51, 3: 533–565.

—— (1974) *Development of Labor Surplus Economy: Theory and Policy*, Homewood, Illinois: Richard D. Irving.

Ferraro, C. and Costamagna, P. (2000) *Entorno institucional y desarrollo productivo local. La importancia del ambiente y las instituciones para el desarrollo empresarial. El caso de Rafaela*, Buenos Aires: CEPAL, LC/BUE/R.246.

Ferrer, A. (1996) *Historia de la globalización*, Buenos Aires: Fondo de Cultura Económica.

Fisher, A. (1994) *Industrie et espace géographique*, Paris: Masson.

Florio, M. (1996) "Large Firms, Entrepreneurship and Regional Development Policy" in *Entrepreneurship and Regional Development* 8: 263–295.

Frank, A.G. (1966) "The development of underdevelopment" in *Monthly Review* 17: 17–31.

—— (1967) *Capitalism and Underdevelopment in Latin America: Historical Studies of Chile and Brazil*, New York: Monthly Review Press.

Freeman, C. (1987) "The challenge of new technologies" in *Interdependence and Cooperation in Tomorrow's World*, Paris: OECD.

—— (1988) "Diffusion: the spread of new technology to firms, sectors and nations" in A. Heertje (ed.) *Innovation, Technology and Finance*, London: Frances Pinter.

Freeman, C. and Soete, L. (1997) *The Economics of Industrial Innovation*, Cambridge, Mass.: MIT Press.

Freeman, C., Clark, C. and Soete, L. (1982) *Unemployment and Technical Innovation: A Study of Long Waves and Economic Development*, London: Frances Pinter.

Friedmann, J. and Douglas, M.J. (1978) "Agropolitan development: toward a new strategy for regional planning in Asia" in F. Lo and K. Salih (eds) *Growth Pole Strategy and Regional Planning Development Policy*, Oxford: Pergamon.

Friedmann, J. and Weaver, C. (1979) *Territory and Function*, London: Edward Arnold.

Fuà, G. (1983) "L'industrializzazione nel nord est e nel centro" in G. Fuà and C. Zachia (eds) *Industrializzazione senza fratture*, Bologna: Il Mulino.

—— (1988) "Small-scale industry in rural areas: the Italian experience" in K.J. Arrow (ed.) *The Balance Between Industry and Agriculture in Economic Development*, London: Macmillan.

Fukuyama, F. (1992) *The End of History and the Last Man*, London: Hamilton.

Furtado, C. (1964) *Development and Underdevelopment*, Berkeley, CA: University of California Press.

—— (1970) *Economic Development in Latin America*, Cambridge: Cambridge University Press.

Garofoli, G. (1983) "Le aree sistema in Italia" in *Politica ed Economia* 11: 7–34.

—— (1992) *Endogenous Development and Southern Europe*, Aldershot: Avebury.

—— (1994) "Economic development, organization of production and territory" in G. Garofoli and A. Vázquez-Barquero (eds) *Organization of Production and Territory: Local Models of Development*, Pavia: Gianni Iuculano.

—— (1995) *Industrializzazione diffusa in Lombardia*, Pavia: Gianni Iuculano.

—— (1999) "Lo sviluppo locale: Modelli teorici e comparazioni internazionali" in *Meridiana* 34–35: 71–96.

—— (2001) "Livelli di governo e politiche di sviluppo locale" in G. Becattini, M. Bellandi, G. Dei Ottati and F. Sforzi (eds) *Il caledoscopio dello sviluppo locale*, Torino: Rosenberg & Sellier.

Gilly J.P. and Pecqueur, B. (1998) "Regolazione dei territori e dinamiche istituzionali di prossimità" in *L'Industria* 3: 501–525.

Gilly, J.P. and Torre, A. (2000) "Introduction générale" in J.P. Gilly and A. Torre (eds) *Dynamiques de Proximité*, Paris: L'Harmattan.

Glaeser, E. (1997) *Learning in Cities*, Harvard University, mimeo.

—— (1998) "Are cities dying?" in *Journal of Economic Perspectives* 12, 2: 139–160.

González Gurriarán, J. (2001) *Los clusters en Galicia como instrumento de integración y cooperación para la mejora competitiva*, Universidad de Vigo, mimeo.

Gordon, I. (1999) "Internationalisation and Urban Competition" in *Urban Studies* 36: 1001–1016.

Gordon, R. (1991) "Innovation, industrial networks and high-technology regions" in R. Camagni (ed.) *Innovation Networks: Spatial Perspectives*, London: Belhaven Press.

Gore, C. (1984) *Regions in Question. Space, Development Theory and Regional Policy*, London: Methuen.

Grabher, G. (1993) "Rediscovering the social in the economics of interfirm relations" in G. Grabher (ed.) *The Embedded Firm. On the Socioeconomics of Industrial Networks*, London: Routledge.

Granovetter, M. (1973) "The strength and weak ties" in *American Journal of Sociology* 78, 3: 1360–1380.

—— (1985) "Economic action and social structure: the problem of embeddedness" in *American Journal of Sociology* 91, 3: 481–510.

—— (1992) "Problems of explanation in economic sociology" in N. Nohria and R.G. Eccles (eds) *Network and Organization, Structure, Form and Action*, Boston: Harvard Business School Press.

Hakansson, H. (ed.) (1987) *Industrial Technological Development: a Network Approach*, London: Croom Helm.

Hakansson, H. and Johanson, J. (1993) "The network as a governance structure. Interfirm cooperation beyond markets and hierarchies" in G. Grabher (ed.) *The Embedded Firm. On the Socioeconomics of Industrial Networks*, London: Routledge.

Hall, P. (1991) "Moving information. A tale of four technologies" in J. Brotchie, M. Batty, P. Hall and P. Newton (eds) *Cities of the 21st Century*, Harlow: Longman Cheshire.

—— (1993) "Forces reshaping urban Europe" in *Urban Studies* 30, 6: 883–898.

Handy, C. (1990) *The Age of Unreason*, New York: Harvard Business School Press.

Harrison, B. (1994) *Lean and Mean: The Changing Landscape of Corporate Power in the Age of Flexibility*, New York: Basic Books.

Helmsing, A.H.J. (1998) *Theories of Regional Industrial Development and Second and Third Generation?*, The Hague: Institute of Social Studies, mimeo.

Hennings, G. and Kunzmann, K.R. (1990) "Priority to local economic development: industrial restructuring and local development responses in the Ruhr areas. The case of Dortmund" in W.B. Stöhr (ed.) *Global Challenge and Local Response*, London: Mansell.

Hirschman, A.O. (1958) *The Strategy of Economic Dynamic*, New Haven: Yale University Press.

Hirst, P. and Thompson, G. (1996) *Globalization in Question*, Cambridge: Polity Press.

Hirst, P. and Zeitlin, J. (eds) (1989a) *Reversing Industrial Decline? Industrial Structure and Policy in Britain and Her Competitors*, Oxford: Berg.

—— (1989b) "Flexible manufacturing and the competitive failure of UK manufacturing" in *Political Quarterly* 60, 2: 164–178.

Hodgson, M.G. (1988) *Economics and Institutions*, Cambridge: Polity Press.

Hoover, E.M. and Vernon, R. (1959) *Anatomy of a Metropolis*, Cambridge: Cambridge University Press.

Jessop, B. (1995) "The regulation approach, governance and post-Fordism: alternative perspectives on economic and political change" in *Economy and Society* 24, 3: 307–333.

Johannisson, B. (1987) "Anarchists and organizers-entrepreneurs in a network perspective" in *International Studies of Management and Organization* 17: 49–63.

—— (1990) "The nordic perspective: self-reliant local development in four Scandinavian countries" in W.B. Stöhr (ed.) *Global Challenge and Local Response*, London: Mansell.

—— (1995) "Paradigms and entrepreneurial networks – some methodological challenges" in *Entrepreneurship and Regional Development* 7: 215–231.

Johannisson, B. and Nilsson, A. (1989) "Community entrepreneur: networking for local development" in *Entrepreneurship and Regional Development* 1: 3–20.

Johannisson, B., Alexanderson, O., Nowicki, K. and Senneseths, K. (1994) "Beyond anarchy and organization: entrepreneurs in contextual networks" in *Entrepreneurship and Regional Development* 6: 329–356.

Jorgenson, D.W. (1961) "The development of a dual economy" in *Economic Journal* 71: 309–334.

—— (1966) "Testing alternative theories of the development of a dual economy" in I. Adelman and E. Thorbeck (eds) *Theory and Design of Economic Development*, Johns Hopkins Press.

—— (1967) "Surplus agricultural labour and development of a dual economy" in *Oxford Economic Papers* 19, 3: 288–312.

Kamann, D.J.F. (1988) "Spatial Differentiation in the Impact of Technology on Society," Unpublished doctoral thesis, Groningen: Faculty of Economics, University of Groningen.

Kamann, D.J.F. and Nijkamp, P. (1988) "Technogenesis: incubation and diffusion" in *Series Research Memoranda*, Amsterdam: Department of Economics, Free University of Amsterdam.

Kaufman, L.J. and Jacobs, H.M. (1987) "A public planning perspective on strategic planning" in *Journal of the American Planning Association* 53: 23–33.

Kaufmann, A. and Tödtling, F. (1999) "Innovation support for SMEs in upper

Austria" *SMEPOL report* no. 1. Vienna: Institute for Urban and Regional Studies. Vienna University of Economics and Business Administration.

Keeble, D. (1990) "New firms and regional economic development: experience and impact in the 1980s" in *Cambridge Regional Review* 1.

Keeble, D. and Weber, E. (1986) "Introduction" in D. Keeble and E. Weber *New Firms and Regional Development in Europe*, London: Croom Helm.

Kelley, A.C., Williamson, J.G. and Cheetham, R.J. (1972) *Dualistic Economic Development, Theory and History*, Chicago: University of Chicago Press.

Kooiman, J. (1993) "Finding, speculation and recommendations" in J. Kooiman (ed.) *Modern Governance. New Government. Society Interactions*, London: Sage.

Krugman, P. (1990) *Geography and Trade*, Leuven and Cambridge, Mass.: Leuven University Press and MIT Press.

—— (1995) *Development, Geography, and Economic Theory*, Cambridge, Mass.: MIT Press.

Lasuén, J.R. (1969) "On growth poles" in *Urban Studies* 6: 137–161.

—— (1973) "Urbanization and development. The temporal interaction between geographical and sectoral clusters" in *Urban Studies* 10: 163–188.

—— (1974) "A generalization of the growth pole notion" in R.S. Thomas (ed.) *Proceedings of the Commission on Regional Aspects of Development of the IGU, 1*, Canada.

—— (1976) *Ensayos sobre economia regional y urbana*, Barcelona: Ariel.

Latella, F. (1997) "Hacia un cambio del papel de la gran empresa en el desarrollo de las regiones atrasadas?" in A. Vázquez-Barquero, G. Garofoli and G.P. Gilly (eds) *Gran empresa y desarrollo económico*, Madrid: Síntesis.

LEDA (1990) "Orientations for local employment development in urban areas: Good practice in policy instruments" in *LEDA Report, DG V*, Brussels: European Community Commission.

Leite, M.P. (2000) *Desenvolvimento econômico local e descentralização na América Latina: a experiência da Câmara Regional do Grande ABC no Brasil*, Santiago de Chile: CEPAL/GTZ Project.

Leone, R.A. and Struyk, R. (1976) "The incubator hypothesis: evidence from five SMSAs" in *Urban Studies* 13: 325–331.

Lewis, A. (1954) "Economic development with unlimited supplies of labour" in *The Manchester School of Economic and Social Studies* 22: 139–191.

—— (1955) *The Theory of Economic Growth*, London: George Allen & Unwin.

—— (1958) "Unlimited labour. Further notes" in *The Manchester School of Economic and Social Studies* 26: 1–32.

Lucas, R.E. (1988) "On the mechanics of economic development" in *Journal of Monetary Economics* 22 1: 129–144.

Lundvall, B.A. (ed.) (1992) *National Systems of Innovation*, London: Frances Pinter.

—— (1993a) "Explaining interfirm cooperation and innovation" in G. Grabher (ed.) *The Embedded Firm. On the Socioeconomics of Industrial Networks*, London: Routledge.

—— (1993b) "User-producer relationship, national systems of innovation and internationalization" in D. Foray and C. Freeman (eds) *Technology and the Wealth of Nations*, London: Frances Pinter.

Madoery, O. (2001) *Gobierno y política local en Argentina*, Rosario: Consejo de Investigaciones, Universidad Nacional de Rosario, mimeo.

Maillat, D. (1990) "SMEs, innovation and territorial development" in R. Cappellin and P. Nijkamp (eds) *The Spatial Context of Technological Development*, Aldershot: Avebury.

—— (1995) "Territorial dynamic, innovative milieus and regional policy" in *Entrepreneurship and Regional Development* 7: 157–165.

—— (1997) "Innovative milieux and new generation of regional policies" in D. McCafferty and J.A. Walsh (eds) *Competitiveness Innovation and Regional Development in Ireland*, Dublin: Regional Studies Association (Irish Branch).

—— (1998) "Interaction between urban systems and localized productive systems" in *European Planning Studies* 6: 117–129.

Maillat, D. and Grosjean, N. (1999) "Globalization and territorial production systems" in M.M. Fischer, L. Suarez-Villa and M. Steiner (eds) *Innovation, Networks and Localities*, Berlin: Springer-Verlag.

Maillat, D., Nemeti, F. and Pfister, M. (1995) "Distrito tecnológico e innovación: el caso del Jura suizo" in A. Vázquez-Barquero and G. Garofoli (eds) *Desarrollo económico local en Europa*, Madrid: Colegio de Economistas de Madrid.

Maillat, D., Lechot, G., Lecoq, B. and Pfister, M. (1997) "Comparative analysis of the structural development of milieux: The watch industry in the Swiss and French Jura Arc" in R. Ratti, A. Bramanti and R. Gordon (eds) *The Dynamics of Innovation Regions*, Aldershot: Ashgate.

Malecki, E.J. (1991) *Technology and Economic Development: the Dynamics of Local, Regional and National Change*, London: Longman.

Malecki, E.J. and Tootle, D. (1996) "The role of networks in small firms competitiveness" in *International Journal of Technology Management* 11: 43–57.

Markusen, A. (2000) "Des lieux-aimants dans un espace mouvant: une typologie des districts industriels" in G. Benko and A. Lipietz (eds) *La richesse des régions*, Paris: PUF.

Marshall, A. (1890) *Principles of Economics*, London: Macmillan.

—— (1919) *Industry and Trade*, London: Macmillan.

Martín, C. (2000) *The Spanish Economy in the New Europe*, London: Macmillan.

Massey, D. (1984) *Spatial Divisions of Labour. Social Structures and Geography of Production*, London: Macmillan.

Maskell, P. Eskelinen, H., Hannibalsson, I., Malmberg, A. and Vatne, E. (1998) *Competitiveness, Localised Learning and Regional Development*, London and New York: Routledge.

Meijer, M. (1993) "Growth and decline of European cities: changing positions of cities in Europe" in *Urban Studies* 30, 6: 981–990.

Mele, G. (1999) *L'attuazione degli strumenti della programmazione negoziata*, Rome: Confindustria, mimeo.

Metcalfe, J.S. (1998) *Evolutionary Economics and Creative Destruction*, London: Routledge.

Monsted, M. (1995) "Processes and structures of networks: reflections on methodology" in *Entrepreneurship and Regional Development* 7: 193–213.

Morgan, K. (1997) "The learning region: institutions, innovation and regional renewal" in *Regional Studies* 31: 479–503.

Nadvi, K. (1997) "The cutting edge: collective efficiency and international competitiveness in Pakistan," IDS Discussion Paper, 360, Brighton: Institute of Development Studies.

Nelson, R. (1995) "Recent evolutionary theorizing about economic change" in *Journal of Economic Literature* 33: 48–90.

—— (1999) "How new is new growth theory?" in *Challenge* 40, 5: 29–58.

Nelson, R. and Winter, S. (1974) "Neoclassic versus evolutionary theories of economic growth" in *Economic Journal* 84: 886–905.

—— (1977) "In search of a useful theory of innovation" *Research Policy* 6: 36–76.

—— (1982) *An Evolutionary Theory of Economic Change*, Cambridge, Mass.: Harvard University Press.

Nijkamp, P. and Salomon, I. (1989) "Future spatial impact of telecommunications" in *Transportation Planning and Technology* 13: 275–287.

North, D.C. (1981) *Structure and Change in Economic History*, New York: Norton.

—— (1986) "The new institutional economics" in *Journal of Institutional and Theoretical Economics* 142, 2: 230–237.

—— (1990) *Institutions, Institutional Change and Economic Performance*, New York: Cambridge University Press.

—— (1991) "Institutions" in *Journal of Economic Perspectives* 5, 1: 97–112.

—— (1994) "Economic performance through time" in *The American Economic Review* 83, 3: 359–368.

O'Brien, R. (1992) *Global Financial Integration: the End of Geography*, London: Royal Institute of International Affairs.

OECD (1987) *ILE Programme*, Paris: OECD.

—— (1992) *Technology and the Economy. The Key Relationship*, Paris: OECD.

—— (1993) "A new perspective on adjustment and reform," Background document, Conference on Local Development and Structural Change, Paris: Cooperative Action Program on Local Initiatives for Employment Creation, OECD.

—— (1994) *Urban Travel and Sustainable Development*, Paris: Environment Directorate.

—— (1996a) *Globalization and Linkages to 2020. Challenges and Opportunities for OECD Countries*, Paris: OECD.

—— (1996b) *Ireland. Local Partnership and Social Innovation*, Paris: OECD.

—— (1996c) *Networks of Enterprises and Local Development. Local Economic and Employment Development Programme*, Paris: OECD.

—— (1997) *Italy's National Hatchery. The Experience of SPI*, Paris: OECD.

—— (1999) *The Future of the Global Economy. Towards a Long Boom?*, Paris: OECD.

Ohmae, K. (1990) *The Borderless World. Power and Strategy in the Global Marketplace*, London: HarperCollins.

—— (1995) *The End of the Nation State*, New York: The Free Press.

Oman, C. (1994) *Globalization and Regionalization, The Challenge for Developing Countries* Paris: OECD.

Ottati, G. Dei (1994) "Trust, interlinking transactions and credit in the industrial districts" in *Cambridge Journal of Economics* 18: 529–546.

Pavitt, K. (1984) "Patterns of technical change: towards a taxonomy and a theory" in *Research Policy* 13: 343–373.

Pecquer, B. and Silva, M.R. (1992) "Territory and economic development: The example of diffuse industrialization" in G. Garofoli (ed.) *Endogenous Development and Southern Europe*, Aldershot: Avebury.

Pedersen, P.O. (1970) "Innovation diffusion within and between national urban systems" in *Geographical Analysis* 51: 252–268.

Pellegrin, J.P. (1991) *Le rôle des organismes intermédiaires dans le développement territorial*, Paris: OECD, Programme ILE, mimeo.

Pérez, C. (1986) "Las nuevas tecnologías, una visión de conjunto" in C. Osminami (ed.) *La tercera revolución industrial*, Mexico: Grupo Editor Latinoamericano.

Perrat, J. (2000) "Dynamiques des firmes et politiques de dévelopment régional et local" in J.P. Gilly and A. Torre (eds) *Dynamiques de Proximité*, Paris: L'Harmattan.

Perrin, J.C. (1990) "Organization industrielle: la composante territoriale" in *Notes de Recherche du CER, 112*, Aix-en-Provence.

——— (1991) "Réseaux d'innovation, milieux innovateurs, développement territorial" in *Révue d'Économie Régionale et Urbaine* 3/4: 343–374.

Perroux, F. (1955) "Note sur la notion de pôle de croissance" in *Économie appliquée* 7: 307–320.

Piore, M. and Sabel, C.F. (1984) *The Second Industrial Divide*, New York: Basic Books.

Polèse, M. (1994) *Économie urbaine et régionale. Logique spatiale des mutations économiques*, Paris: Economica.

Porter, M. (1990) *The Competitive Advantage of Nations*, New York: Free Press.

Precedo Ledo, A. (1996) *Ciudad y desarrollo urbano*, Madrid: Síntesis.

Pyke, F., Becattini, G. and Sengenberger, W. (eds) (1990) *Industrial Districts and Inter-firm Cooperation in Italy*, Geneve: International Institute for Labour Studies.

Quevit, M. (1991) "Innovative environments and local/international linkages in enterprise strategy: a framework for analysis" in R. Camagni (ed.) *Innovation Networks: Spatial Perspectives*, London: Belhaven Press.

Quigley, J.M. (1998) "Urban diversity and economic growth" in *Journal of Economic Perspectives* 12, 2: 127–138.

Rabellotti, R. and Schmitz, H. (1999) "The internal heterogeneity of industrial districts in Italy, Brazil and Mexico" in *Regional Studies* 33, 2: 97–108.

Rallet, A. and Torre, A. (1995) *Économie industrielle et économie spatiale*, Paris: Economica.

Rebelo, S. (1991) "Long-run policy analysis and long-run growth" in *Journal of Political Economy* June, 99: 500–521.

Reclus (1989) *Les villes européennes, Rapport pour la DATAR*, Paris: La Documentation Française.

Reis, J. (1987) "Os espaços da industrializaçâo. Notas sobre a regulaçâo macroeconomica e o nivel local" in *Rivista Critica de Ciencias Sociais* 22: 13–31.

Richardson, H. (1984) "The regional policy in a slow-growth economy" in G. Demko (ed.) *Regional development. Problems and policies in Eastern and Western Europe*, London: Croom Helm.

Roberts, P., Collis, C. and Noon, D. (1990) "Local economic development in England and Wales: successful adaptation of old industrial areas in Sedgefield, Nottingham and Swansea" in W.B. Stöhr (ed.) *Global Challenge and Local Response*, London: Mansell.

Rodríguez Pose, A. (1998) *Dynamics of Regional Growth in Europe*, Oxford: Clarendon Press.

Rodwin, L. (1963) "Choosing regions for development" in C.J. Friedrich and S.E. Harris (eds) *Public Policy: Yearbook of the Harvard University Graduate School of Public Administration*, Cambridge, Mass.: Harvard University Press.

Romer, M.P. (1986) "Increasing returns and long run growth" in *Journal of Political Economy* 94: 1002–1037.

——— (1990) "Endogenous technological change" in *Journal of Political Economy* 98: 71–102.

Rosegger, G. (1996) *The Economics of Production and Innovation*, Oxford: Butterworth-Heinemann.

Rosenberg, N. (1976) *Perspectives on Technology*, Cambridge: Cambridge University Press.

—— (1982) *Inside the Black Box: Technology and Economics,* Cambridge: Cambridge University Press.

Rosenstein-Rodan, P.N. (1943) "Problems of industrialization of Eastern and South-Eastern Europe" in *Economic Journal* 53: 202–211.

—— (1961) "Notes on the theory of the big push" in H. Ellis (ed.) *Economic Development for Latin America,* London: Macmillan.

Rostow, W. (1960) *The Stages of Economic Growth: a Non-communist Manifesto,* Cambridge: Cambridge University Press.

Sabel, C.F. (1989) "Flexible specialization and the reemergence of regional economies" in P. Hirst and J. Zeitlin (eds) *Reversing Industrial Decline? Industrial Structure and Policy in Britain and Her Competitors,* Oxford: Berg.

Sachs, I (1980) *Strategies de l'écodéveloppement,* Paris: Les Éditions Ouvrières.

Sáez Cala, A. (1999) "El proceso de innovación de las PYMEs valencianas," Working document for the SMEPOL Project, Madrid: Facultad de Ciencias Económicas de la Universidad Autónoma de Madrid.

Sala-i-Martin, X. (1994) *Apuntes de crecimiento económico,* Barcelona: Antoni Bosch.

—— (2000) *Apuntes de crecimiento económico,* 2nd edition, Barcelona: Antoni Bosch.

Santos, T. dos (1968) "El nuevo carácter de la dependencia" in *Cuadernos de Estudios Socioeconómicos 10,* Santiago: CESO – Universidad de Chile.

—— (1970a) "The structure of dependence" in *American Economic Review* 60, 2: 231–236.

—— (1970b) "Dependencia económica y alternativas de cambio en América Latina" in *Revista Mexicana de Sociología* 32, 2: 417–463.

Sassen, S. (1991) *The Global City: New York, London, Tokyo,* Princeton, NJ: Princeton University Press.

—— (1998) "Ciudades en la economía global: enfoques teóricos y metodológicos" in *Revista Eure* 71: 5–25.

Saxenian, A. (1994) *Regional Advance, Culture and Competition in Silicon Valley and Route 128,* Cambridge, Mass.: Harvard University Press.

Schmitz, H. (1995) "Collective efficiency: growth path for small-scale industry" in *Journal of Development Studies* 31: 529–566.

Schmookler, J. (1966) *Invention and Economic Growth,* Cambridge, Mass.: Harvard University Press.

Schumpeter, J.A. (1934) *The Theory of Economic Development,* Cambridge, Mass.: Harvard University Press.

—— (1943) *Capitalism, Socialism and Democracy,* New York: Harper and Row.

Scitovski, T. (1954) "Two concepts of external economies" in *Journal of Political Economy* LXII, 2: 143–151.

Scott, A. (1988) *New Industrial Spaces,* London: Pion.

—— (1998) *Regions and the World Economy,* Oxford: Oxford University Press.

—— (2000) "Revitalização industrial nos municípios do ABC, São Paolo. Análise, diagnóstico e recomendações para uma nova política e um novo regionalismo" BID, mimeo.

Sénat (1994) "Aménagement du territoire" in *Les rapports du Sénat* I and II, 343, Paris.

Silva, M.R. (1987) "O desenvovimento industrial do Val do Ave," Oporto: CCRN, Ministry of Planning.

Silverberg, G., Dosi, G. and Orsenigo, L. (1988) "Innovation, diversity and diffusion: a self organizing model" in *Economic Journal* 98: 1032–1054.

Smith, D.A. and Timberlake, M. (1995) "Cities in global matrices: toward mapping the world system" in P.L. Knox, and P.J. Taylor (eds) *World Cities in a World System*, Cambridge: Cambridge University Press.

Solow, R. (1956) "A contribution to the theory of economic growth" in *Quarterly Journal of Economics* 78: 65–94.

STEP Group (1999) "SME Policy and the Regional Dimension of Innovation," Unpublished final report, TSER Program mimeo, Brussels: European Union Commission.

Stöhr, W.B. (1981) "Development from below: the bottom-up and periphery inward development paradigm" in W.B. Stöhr and D.R. Taylor (eds) *Development from Above or Below?*, Chichester: J. Wiley and Sons.

—— (1985) "Selective selfreliance and endogenous regional development" in Nohlen and Schultze (eds) *Ungleiche Entwicklung and Regionalpolitik in Südeurope*, Bochum: Studienverlag Dr. N. Brockmeyer.

—— (ed.) (1990) *Global Challenge and Local Response*, London: Mansell.

Stöhr, W.B. and Taylor, D.R.F. (eds) (1981) *Development from Above or Below?*, Chichester: J. Wiley and Sons.

Stöhr, W.B. and Tödling, F. (1979) "Spatial equality – some antithesis to current regional development doctrine" in H. Folmer and J. Oosterhoven (eds) *Spatial Inequalities and Regional Development*, Leiden: Nijhoff.

Storper, M. (1997) *The Regional World*, New York: The Guilford Press.

Streeck, W. (1991) "On the institutional conditions of diversified quality production" in E. Matzner and W. Streeck (eds) *Beyond Keynesianism*, Aldershot: Elgar.

—— (1992) *Social Institutions and Economic Performance: Studies of Industrial Relations in Advanced Capitalist Economies*, London: Sage.

Sunkel, O. (1969) "National development policy and external dependence in Latin America" in *The Journal of Development Studies* October: 23–48.

—— (1973) "Transnational capitalism and national disintegration in Latin America" in *Social and Economic Studies* 22, 1: 132–176.

Swan, T.W. (1956) "Economic growth and capital accumulation" in *Economic Record* 32: 334–361.

Törnqvist, G. (1986) *System of Cities in Changing Technical Environment*, mimeo, Department of Social and Economic Geography, Lund: University of Lund.

Ugarteche, O. (1997) *El falso dilema. América Latina en la economía global*, Caracas: Nueva Sociedad.

Valcárcel-Resalt, G. (1992) "Balance y perspectivas del desarrollo en España" in C. del Canto (ed.) *Desarrollo rural. Ejemplos europeos*, Madrid: IRYDA, Ministerio de Agricultura y Pesca.

Valdés, B. (1999) *Economic Growth. Theory, Empirics and Policy*, Cheltenham: Edward Elgar.

Vázquez-Barquero, A. (1982) "Crecimiento dualista versus crecimiento dependiente. Las limitaciones de la teoría del desarrollo económico" in *Investigaciones económicas* 17: 107–125.

—— (1983) *Industrialization in Rural Areas. The Spanish Case*, Report, OECD meeting, Senigallia, July 7–10, CT/RUR/113/06, OECD.

—— (1984) "La política regional en tiempos de crisis" in *Estudios territoriales* 15–16: 21–37.

—— (1988) *Desarrollo local. Una estrategia de creación de empleo*, Madrid: Pirámide.

—— (1992) "Local development and flexibility in accumulation and regulation of capital" in *Entrepreneurship and Regional Development* 4: 381–395.

—— (1993) *Política económica local*, Madrid: Pirámide.

—— (1999) "Inward Investment and Endogenous Development. The convergence of the strategies of large firms and territories?" in *Entrepreneurship and Regional Development*, 11: 79–63.

—— (2000) "The productive dynamics and urban development: the response of Vitoria to the challenge of globalization" in O. Crevoisier and R. Camagni (eds) *Les Milieux Urbains: Innovation, Systemes de Production et Encrage*, Neuchâtel: IRER/EDES.

Vázquez-Barquero, A. and Sáez Cala, A. (1997) "The dynamics of local firm systems" in R. Ratti, A. Bramanti and R. Gordon (eds) *The Dynamics of Innovative Regions*, Aldershot: Ashgate.

Veltz, P. (1993) "Logiques d'entreprise et territoires: les nouvelles règles du jeu" in M. Savy and P. Veltz (eds) *Les nouveaux espaces de l'entreprise*, Paris: l'Aube/Datar.

—— (1996) *Mondialisation, villes et territoires: l'économie d'archipel*, Paris: PUF.

Vence Deza, X. (1995) *Economía de la innovación y del cambio tecnológico*, Madrid: Siglo XXI.

Veseth, R. (1998) *Selling Globalization: the Myth of the Global Economy*, Boulder: Lynne Rienner.

Villanueva, M. (1998) "Proyecto Quebrada de Catuche. Programa de habilitación física de barrios (PROHABITAT)" Unpublished paper, Seminar on "Programas Sociales, Pobreza y Participación Ciudadana in Caracas," Cartagena: Banco Interamericano de Desarrollo.

Wade (1996) "Globalization and its limits: reports of the death of the national economy are greatly exaggerated" in S. Berger and R. Dore (eds) *National Diversity and Global Capitalism*, Ithaca, NY: Cornell University Press.

Waterman, P. (1998) *Globalization, Social Movement and the New Internationalism*, London: Massell/Castells.

Welfens, J.P., Addison, T.J., Audretsch, B.D., Gries, T. and Grupp, H. (1999) *Globalization, Economic Growth and Innovation Dynamics*, Heidelberg: Springer.

Williamson, O.E. (1975) *Markets and Hierarchies: Analysis and Antitrust Implications*, New York: The Free Press.

—— (1981) "The modern corporation: origins, evolution, attributes" in *Journal of Economic Literature* 19: 1537–1568.

—— (1985) *The Economic Institutions of Capitalism: Firms, Markets, Relational Contracting*, New York: The Free Press.

—— (1993) "Calculativeness, trust and economic organization" in *Journal of Law and Economics* XXXVI: 453–486.

—— (2000) "The new institutional economics. Taking stock, looking ahead" in *Journal of Economic Literature* XXXVIII: 595–613.

WCED (World Commission on Environment and Development) (1987) *Our Common Future*, Oxford: Oxford University Press.

Zeitlin, J. (1989) "Local industrial strategies: introduction" in *Economy and Society* 18, 4: 367–373.

Index

Page numbers in *italics* refer to figures or tables

Printed in the United States
by Baker & Taylor Publisher Services